T5-BQA-477

From Canonical Criticism to Ecumenical Exegesis?

Studies in Reformed Theology

Editor-in-chief

Eddy Van der Borght (*Vrije Universiteit Amsterdam*)

Editorial Board

Abraham van de Beek (*Vrije Universiteit Amsterdam*)
Martien Brinkman (*Vrije Universiteit Amsterdam*)
Dirk van Keulen (*Theological University, Kampen*)
Daniel Migliore (*Princeton Theological Seminary*)
Richard Mouw (*Fuller Theological Seminary, Pasadena*)
Emanuel Gerrit Singgih (*Duta Wacana Christian University, Yogjakarta*)
Pieter Vos (*Protestant Theological University, Amsterdam*)
Conrad Wethmar (*University of Pretoria*)

VOLUME 30

The titles published in this series are listed at *brill.com/srt*

From Canonical Criticism to Ecumenical Exegesis?

A Study in Biblical Hermeneutics

By

Peter-Ben Smit

BRILL

LEIDEN | BOSTON

Cover illustration: The Aachen Mosaic from the roof of the Octagon Chapel. © Helen Gaasbeek, MTh.

Library of Congress Cataloging-in-Publication Data

Smit, Peter-Ben, 1979-
 From canonical criticism to ecumenical exegesis? : a study in biblical hermeneutics / by Peter-Ben Smit.
    pages cm. -- (Studies in reformed theology, ISSN 1571-4799 ; VOLUME 30)
  Includes bibliographical references and index.
   ISBN 978-90-04-30100-9 (pbk. : alk. paper) -- ISBN 978-90-04-30101-6 (e-book)
 1. Bible--Canonical criticism. 2. Bible--Hermeneutics. I. Title.

 BS521.8.S65 2015
 220.601--dc23

2015020196

BS
521.8
.S65
2015

ISSN 1571-4799
ISBN 978-90-04-30100-9 (paperback)
ISBN 978-90-04-30101-6 (e-book)

Copyright 2015 by Koninklijke Brill NV, Leiden, The Netherlands.
Koninklijke Brill NV incorporates the imprints Brill, Brill Hes & De Graaf, Brill Nijhoff, Brill Rodopi and
Hotei Publishing.
All rights reserved. No part of this publication may be reproduced, translated, stored in a retrieval system,
or transmitted in any form or by any means, electronic, mechanical, photocopying, recording or otherwise,
without prior written permission from the publisher.
Authorization to photocopy items for internal or personal use is granted by Koninklijke Brill NV provided
that the appropriate fees are paid directly to The Copyright Clearance Center, 222 Rosewood Drive,
Suite 910, Danvers, MA 01923, USA.
Fees are subject to change.

This book is printed on acid-free paper.

Contents

Preface   VII

1   Introduction   1
1.1   Research Question, Method and Structure   6
1.2   What is Canonical Criticism? A Note on Terminology   10
1.3   The Emergence of the Canonical Approach   13
1.3.1   *The State of the Canonical Debate and the Current Study*   15
1.4   Selection of Authors   17

2   Canonical Exegesis of the New Testament Gospels: Five Cases   19
2.1   Brevard S. Childs   19
2.1.1   *The Canonical Approach of Brevard S. Childs*   20
2.1.2   *Presentation of a Representative Exegesis*   26
2.1.3   *Analysis*   36
2.1.4   *Conclusions*   39
2.2   James A. Sanders   40
2.2.1   *The Canonical Approach of James A. Sanders*   42
2.2.2   *Presentation of a Representative Exegesis*   46
2.2.3   *Analysis*   50
2.2.4   *Conclusions*   52
2.3   Peter Stuhlmacher   53
2.3.1   *The Canonical Approach of Stuhlmacher*   55
2.3.2   *Presentation of a Representative Exegesis*   62
2.3.3   *Analysis*   67
2.5.4   *Conclusions*   71
2.5   Joseph Ratzinger/Pope Benedict XVI   72
2.5.1   *The Canonical Approach of Joseph Ratzinger*   73
2.5.2   *Presentation of a Representative Exegesis*   75
2.5.3   *Analysis*   83
2.5.4   *Conclusions*   85
2.6   The "Amsterdam School of Exegesis"   86
2.6.1   *The Canonical Approach of the "Amsterdam School of Exegesis"*   89
2.6.2   *Presentation of a Representative Exegesis*   93
2.6.3   *Analysis*   99
2.6.4   *Conclusions*   102

3 Canonical Exegesis Considered: Heuristic Potential and
   Potential Pitfalls   103
   3.1   Scripture and Community: The World in Front of the Text   103
         3.1.1 *The Interrelationship between Text and Community*   104
         3.1.2 *Scripture as the Book of the Church*   105
         3.1.3 *Is Every Critic a Theologian?*   108
         3.1.4 *Points of Convergence with Contemporary Hermeneutical
                Thought*   111
   3.2   Justice to the Texts?   113
         3.2.1 *Canonical Exegesis and the "Final Form" of the Text*   114
         3.2.2 *The Canonical Dimension of the Texts Themselves*   115
         3.2.3 *Listening to the Claims of Texts*   120
         3.2.4 *Interpretation through Tradition*   121
         3.2.5 *Interpretation and Praxis*   122
   3.3   The World "Behind the Text?"   122
         3.3.1 *History, Witness, and Revelation*   122
         3.3.2 *The Canonical Process and the World behind the Text*   126
         3.3.3 *Concluding Observations: Canonical Approaches and
                History*   127
   3.4   Potential Pitfalls   127

4 Canonical Criticism: On the Road Towards Ecumenical
   Hermeneutics?   139
   4.1   Introduction   139
   4.2   Contemporary Ecumenical Hermeneutics and Canonical Criticism:
         An Inventarisation and Comparison   142
         4.2.1 *Introduction*   142
         4.2.2 *Hermeneutics in the Ecumenical Movement until 1963*   143
         4.2.3 *Hermeneutics at the World Conference on Faith and Order in
                Montreal (1963)*   150
         4.2.4 *From "Montreal" to a Treasure in Earthen Vessels (1998)*   153
         4.2.5 *Hermeneutics in the Church. Towards a Common
                Vision (2013)*   165
   4.3   Ecumenical and Canonical Hermeneutics: Compatibilities and
         Challenges   167

5 General Conclusions and Outlook: Perspectives for Canonically
   Inspired Exegesis   173

   Bibliography   183
   Index   204

Preface

The publication of this volume marks an important stage of a long journey with the topic of canonical interpretation, starting at the University of Amsterdam in the late 1990s, continued at the Universities of Sheffield and Bern, deepened at General Theological Seminary, and finally concluded at VU University Amsterdam, Utrecht University, and the Old Catholic Seminary at the latter university, which are the three academic institutions that I currently have the privilege of serving. A stay at the University of Pretoria as associated researcher of the Faculty of Theology (Prof. Kobus Kok) greatly furthered the completion of this manuscript. Various seminars of the European Association of Biblical Studies (notably its "Canonical Approaches to the Bible" – group), the Society for Biblical Literature, and the Societas Oecumenica gave me room to work out the ideas contained in this volume. This study also constitutes the outcome of my interaction with the holy Scriptures of Christianity in both an academic and an ecclesial context. The latter is of importance: the ecclesial context, in the Old Catholic Churches of the Netherlands and Switzerland and in the Episcopal Church (USA), invites academic reflection on the nature and functioning of holy texts, while the academic study of religious texts invites reflection on the use and role of these texts in the communities that consider them as sacred. This partial biographical disclosure is of significance, because it says something about the attitude with which this study has been written. This attitude was and is nurtured both by my academic settings and by the ecclesial context in which I live. Such settings and contexts also come with inspiration from teachers, both in terms of content and in terms of academic attitude, Karel Deurloo, Loveday Alexander, Ulrich Luz, Urs von Arx, and J. Robert Wright, and from colleagues. Fortunately, these colleagues are many and include the people and clergy of the Diocese of Haarlem, in particular of the parish of Amsterdam, and its bishop Dirk J. Schoon, my colleagues in the field of New Testament studies at VU University Amsterdam, notably Martinus C. de Boer, Bert-Jan Lietaert Peerbolte, Arie Zwiep, and Jan Krans, as well as the leadership of the Faculty of Theology of this university, dean Wim Janse and professors Joke van Saane and Eddy Van der Borght, who encourage my exploration of the role of diversity and dialogue in teaching theology. My colleagues at Utrecht University's Department of Philosophy and Religious Studies, especially the head of department, professor Martha Frederiks, and the faculty of the Old Catholic Seminary: dean Mattijs Ploeger, and the lecturers Joris Vercammen, Wietse van der Velde, Remco Robinson, and Jan Hallebeek. I am also grateful for those who accompany me in this life, grateful in particular for Helen.

Peter-Ben Smit
Amsterdam/Utrecht, 2015

CHAPTER 1

Introduction

This study explores the potential of so-called canonical approaches to the study of the New Testament, using the exegesis of the canonical gospels as a case study. As the title of the study indicates, it will also explore the interface between canonical criticism and ecumenical hermeneutics as two disciplines that are preoccupied with the interrelationships between text, community, and interpretative traditions. In doing so, it specifically seeks to tease out the heuristic potential of these approaches, especially when they are brought into dialogue with one another, rather than to act as a "defense" or reconceptualization of canonical approaches to exegesis. This is, in part, because the interrelationship between text, "reading helps" such as a rule of faith, and reader as is of primary interest here can be seen as constitutive of any kind of exegesis and therefore needs no defense. Given that the interest of this study is heuristic, any attempt to launch into apologetics will be avoided – or at least, such is the author's attempt.

The starting point of the study, however, is the analysis of five different canonical approaches to Scripture, in particular to the New Testament, and specifically to the Gospels. Both theory and exegetical practice are analyzed; this is achieved by concentrating on scholars who offered both significant theoretical input to the debate on canonical criticism and who produced a substantial body of exegetical work. Furthermore, the selection of scholars discussed here has been made in such a way that those who have been selected can be considered as especially representative of the early and formative period of canonical criticism (even if, in the case of Ratzinger, the main work on canonical criticsm appeared relatively late). The analysis undertaken in this study is achieved by addressing the following question: "what are the advantages and disadvantages of the "canonical approach" as expressed in scholarly discussion, and how are they reflected in the actual use of this method in the exegesis of the four New Testament gospels by five prominent representatives?" Based on the answers found, further hermeneutical considerations are offered which, indeed, move in the direction of ecumenical hermeneutics and exegesis, and explore the potential of a dialogue between canonical and ecumenical hermeneutics.

By way of introduction, a few remarks about the relevance of the topic of canonical approaches to Scripture and the surrounding debate will be offered, before turning to the methodology and structure of this study.

© KONINKLIJKE BRILL NV, LEIDEN, 2015 | DOI 10.1163/9789004301016_002

What has become known broadly as canonical criticism or canonical exegesis,[1] has become a topic of intense scholarly debate during the past ca. forty years,[2] with much at stake, both for those who are interested in fostering the relationship between church, theology, and Scripture, and therefore, also for those who wish to see a much looser connection between these three things.[3] While the debate has primarily concerned academics for a long time,

---

1   On this terminology, see below, 1.2.

2   See e.g. the emphasis that Max Seckler ("Über die Problematik des biblischen Kanons und die Bedeutung seiner Wiederentdeckung," *ThQ* 180 [2000], 30–53, 30–31) places on the year 1970; in that year, Ernst Käsemann edited *Das Neue Testament als Kanon* (Göttingen: Vandenhoeck & Ruprecht, 1970), under the impression that "die Zeit für eine repräsentative Dokumentation der Kanondebatte und für eine zusammenfassende Sichtung und Würdigung des auf diesem Feld in der jüngeren Vergangenheit Erreichten" had come (Seckler, *o.c.*, 30), or, as he put it in his introduction: "Über die Entstehung und Geschichte des neutestamentlichen Kanons sind wir vortrefflich informiert. Seine theologische Relevanz ist dagegen heftiger denn je zuvor umstritten." (Ernst Käsemann, "Einführung," in: idem [ed.], *o.c.*, 9–12) Somewhat in line with this, and like Käsemann's volume (399–410) entailing a program for the role of the canon in theology – in the case of Käsemann: a program that heavily emphasized the interpretative principle "was Christum treibet" –, also another book appeared in 1970: Brevard S. Childs' *Biblical Theology in Crisis* (Philadelphia: Westminster Press, 1970), a book that is now widely regarded "als wirksamste Inaugurationsschrift für jene neue Ära der Kanondebatte…., zu deren bekanntestem, aber auch umstrittestem Vertreter Childs alsbald geworden ist." (Seckler, *o.c.*, 30).

3   See Seckler, "Problematik," 31: the newer discussion about the canon considers the canon as a theme of central theological importance, rather than a subtopic of the *Einleitungswissenschaft*. See e.g. Thomas Söding, "Der Kanon des alten und neuen Testaments. Zur Frage nach seinem theologischen Anspruch," in: Jean-Marie Auwers/Henk Jan de Jonge (ed.), *The Biblical Canons* (Louvain: Peeters, 2003), xlvii-lxviii, xlvii: "Der theologische Anspruch des Kanons ist enorm. Die Wahrheit des Evangeliums steht auf dem Plan, die Normativität des Ursprungs, die Unüberholbarkeit eines Anfangs, der alles Kommende zu bestimmen beansprucht, und die Notwendigkeit fortwährender Erinnerung an ein vergangenes Geschehen und Zeugnis. Beim Kanon geht es um das Kriterium der Unterscheidung zwischen "wahr" und "falsch" in Sachen des Glaubens, der Hoffnung und der Liebe." On the stakes in general, see also: Thomas Söding, *Einheit der Heiligen Schrift. Zur Theologie des biblischen Kanons* (Freiburg: Herder, 2005), 18–55. – Note also the remark by Ricoeur: "The opponent from outside will remember the old opposition between reason and authority from the age of the Enlightenment, and the opponent from within will invoke the conflict mentioned within this very scripture between the spirit and the law, between the liberty of the Holy Spirit and the authority of the Church." (Paul Ricoeur, "The Canon between the Text and the Community," in: Peter Pokorný/Jan Roskovec (ed.), *Philosophical Hermeneutics and Biblical Exegesis* [Tübingen: Mohr Siebeck, 2002], 7–27, 7–8; the text was [poorly] translated from the French original by Peter Stephens.)

Joseph Ratzinger/Benedict XVI[4] placed emphasis on the canonical approach in his *Jesus of Nazareth* (2007), thus lifting the topic to a much more visible stage as well as legitimizing (or delegitimizing, depending on one's point of view) the approach further through the association with his (then) office. Even if for that reason alone, it is worthwhile considering the functioning and heuristic potential of this particular approach to exegesis. Beyond this, however, and probably even more importantly, the study of the "canonical approach" to Scripture is of interest, as canonical criticism brings the exegesis of (biblical) texts in relation to, and exchange with, other disciplines that are concerned with the study of the establishment, transmission, and interpretation of bodies of literature (and/or practices) with a claim to authority, or to which such a claim is attributed. In particular, canonical exegesis leads to renewed attention to the relationship between communities of interpretation, processes of tradition(ing), processes of interpretation, and aspects of (theological group) identity. In this way, it also questions "traditional" historical-critical scholarship that often had little time for the question of the relevance of the canon in relation to the interpretation of the texts,[5] e.g. by stating that the Scriptural canon was without hermeneutical significance for biblical interpretation, as, for example, Barr did.[6] To be sure, the question of the historical development of a canon as such has hardly ever been considered an unimportant or uninteresting topic. With respect to the development of scholarship focusing on the

---

4   In this study, it is of some importance that he wrote his "Jesus books" while exercising the Petrine ministry; therefore, he will be referred to as "Pope Benedict XVI," as he was called at the time of writing, rather than "pope emeritus" as is his current title.

5   Whether canonical critics always do justice to "traditional" historical critical scholarship and do not set up a "straw man" remains to be seen. This, however, cannot be the main concern of this study, which is about the potential of the canonical approaches themselves.

6   James Barr, *Holy Scripture: Canon, Authority, Criticism* (Westminster, John Knox, 1983), 67. – A similar position was also taken by, e.g. Wolfgang Richter's 1971 *Exegese als Literaturwissenschaft. Entwurf einer alttestamentlichen Literaturtheorie und Methodologie* (Göttingen: Vandenhoeck & Ruprecht, 1971), 40: "Die Existenz des Kanons ist für den Interpreten der Texte bedeutungslos." See on Richter also: Georg Steins, "Der Bibelkanon als Text und Denkmal. Zu einigen methodologischen Problemen kanonischer Schriftauslegung," in: Auwers/De Jonge (ed.), *Canons*, 177–198, 179. – Note the contrast with the position of Christoph Dohmen, "Probleme und Chancen Biblischer Theologie aus alttestamentlicher Sicht," in: Thomas Söding/Christoph Dohmen (ed.), *Eine Bibel – Zwei Testamente. Positionen biblischer Theologie* (Paderborn: Schönigh, 1995), 9–17, 15, who argues that the importance of the (Old Testament) canon for exegesis and biblical theology can hardly be overestimated, which is striking to say the least.

role of the canon in exegesis in the 20th century, Von Lips has suggested that one could describe it in terms of a paradox: While at the beginning of the 20th century historical-critical scholars questioned the role of the canon in exegesis, towards the end of the 20th century, canonical critics began to question the merits of historical-critical exegesis.[7] This development also involves disciplinary boundary crossing, as Seckler noted:

> Während zuvor die Kanonfrage in den verschiedenen theologischen Disziplinen ziemlich isoliert und fächerspezifisch behandelt wurde – von den Biblikern traditionell als Teilgebiet der historisch orientierten biblischen Einleitungswissenschaft, von den Systematikern als Spezialthema der fundamentaltheologischen Prinzipienlehre – wird nun öfter der Blick über die Grenzen gewagt... Dieser Vorgang ist ein Indiz für eine immer häufiger zu beobachtende Öffnung der biblischen Kanonforschung für Fragestellungen, die man zuvor lieber den Systematikern überlassen hatte, ohne sich viel um sie zu kümmern.[8]

All of this, in turn, has much to do with, or is at least compatible with, the reemergence and (positive) reevaluation of the notion of the "canon" in literary

---

7 Hermann von Lips, "Kanondebatten im 20. Jahrhundert," in: Eve-Marie Becker/Stefan Scholz (ed.), *Kanon in Konstruktion und Dekonstruktion. Kanonisierungsprozesse religiöser Texte von der Antike bis zur Gegenwart. Ein Handbuch* (Berlin: De Gruyter, 2012), 109–126, 123: "Will man nun die Kanondebatten im 20. Jahrhundert auf eine Linie bringen, so könnte man zugespitzt zum paradoxen Ergebnis kommen: Hatte am Beginn des Jahrhunderts die historisch-kritische Exegese den Kanon in Frage gestellt, so wird am Ende des Jahrhunderts von der Kanon-Perspektive her die historisch-kritische Exegese in Frage gestellt."; see also Söding, "Kanon," xlviii–xlix, who calls it a veritable paradigm shift, and further P.D. Miller, "Der Kanon in der gegenwärtigen Diskussion," *JBTh* 3 (1988), 217–239, 217, who observes that no other topic had been discussed as much in American theology in the preceding years than that of the canon. A good place to appreciate the changing debate on the canon are the contributions to the 1988 volume of the *Jahrbuch für Biblische Theologie*, entitled *Zum Problem des biblischen Kanons* (ed. Ingo Baldermann; Neukirchen-Vluyn: Neukirchener Verlag, 1988). With regard to another volume (10[1995]), dedicated to the issue of the tension between a history of religions approach to the Old Testament and a theological approach, Brevard S. Childs, "The Canon in Recent Biblical Studies. Reflections on an Era," *Pro Ecclesia* 14 (2005), 26–46, 38, notes rightly that the alternative between these two approaches as it would be formulated for the New Testament by a scholar like Heikki Räisänen (notably in his *Beyond New Testament Theology* [Philadelphia: Westminster John Knox, 1990]), found little support, given that most contributors would favour a combination of the two approaches.

8 Seckler, "Problematik," 31.

and cultural studies with both a contemporary and historical focus,[9] not least as they are inspired by the work of Jan and Aleida Assmann.[10] This broader discussion, which has become part of literary and cultural studies for around 20–25 years, will not be the focus of this study, however. In spite of this, it is acknowledged as the contemporary context of the debate surrounding the exegetical and theological value of the canon and an important means for, to some extent, "de-theologizing" the canon debate, i.e. by pointing out the general cultural, social, and literary aspects of the construction of canons at large.[11]

---

9   See for an introduction to the contemporary debate e.g. the brief sketch of Stefan Scholz, "*Kanones* in Theologie, Literaturwissenschaften und Kulturwissenschaften. Einführende Bemerkungen zur Kanonforschung der Neuzeit und Moderne," in Becker/idem (ed.), *Kanon*, 33–38. See further also e.g. Jan Gorak, *The Making of the Modern Canon. Genesis and Crisis of a Literary Idea* (London: Athlone, 1991), idem (ed.), *Canon vs. Culture: Reflections on the Current Debate* (London: Routledge, 2001), and Aleida Assmann: "Kanonforschung als Provokation der Literaturwissenschaft," in: Renate von Heydebrand (ed.), *Kanon, Macht, Kultur. Theoretische, historische and soziale Aspekte ästhetischer Kanonbildungen* (Stuttgart: Metzler, 1998), 47–59. – On earlier developments regarding a literary canon, see e.g. Christoph Grube, "Die Entstehung des Literaturkanons aus dem Zeitgeist der Nationalliteratur-Geschichtsschreibung," in: Becker/Scholz (ed.), *Kanon*, 71–108.

10   See e.g. Jan Assmann *Das kulturelle Gedächtnis. Schrift, Erinnerung und politische Identität in frühen Hochkulturen* (München: Beck, 1992), Aleida Assmann/Jan Assmann (ed.), *Kanon und Zensur* (München: Fink, 1987), Aleida Assmann, *Einführung in die Kulturwissenschaft: Grundbergriffe Themen, Fragestellungen* (Berlin: Schmidt, ²2008), Jan Assmann, *Fünf Stufen auf dem Wege zum Kanon: Tradition und Schriftkultur im frühen Judentum und seiner Umwelt* (Münster: LIT, 1999), as well as Von Heydebrand (ed.), *Kanon*, Maria Moos-Grünewald (ed.), *Kanon und Theorie* (Heidelberg: Winter, 1997), and Gottfried Vanoni, "Der biblische Kanon. Institutionalisierte Erinnerung," *ThPQ* 151 (2003), 29–36. – See on canons, canonization, and cultural memory in antiquity further e.g. the contributions in: Margalit Finkelberg/Guy G. Stroumsa (ed.), *Homer, the Bible, and Beyond. Literary and Religious Canons in the Ancient World* (Leiden: Brill, 2003), in Becker/Scholz (ed.), *Kanon,* and in Loren T. Stuckenbruck/ Stephen C. Barton/Benjamin G. Wold (ed.), *Memory in the Bible and Antiquity* (Tübingen: Mohr Siebeck, 2007), esp.: Doron Mendels, "Societies of Memory in the Graeco-Roman World," 143–162; Anthony Le Donne, "Theological Memory Distortion in the Jesus Tradition: A Study in Social Memory Theory," 163–177, and James D.G. Dunn, "Social Memory and Oral Jesus Tradition," 179–194. – See in general also: Doron Mendels, *Memory in Jewish, Pagan and Christian Societies of the Graeco-Roman World* (London: T&T Clark, 2004). On various material aspects, see e.g. the essays collected by Craig A. Evans/H. Daniel Zacharias (ed.), *Jewish and Christian Scripture as Artifact and Canon* (London: Bloomsbury, 2011).

11   See also: Seckler, "Problematik," 33: "Die Fixiertheit der Theologie auf ihre eigenen Kanonprobleme bringt die Gefahr mit sich, die Formgesetze und Entelechien des Kanonphänomens allzu exklusiv als theologisches Spezifikum anzusehen, was leicht zu einer Art Inzucht, zu gewissen Mystifizierungen, zu einer verengten Sichtwiese und auch

Those approaches to Scripture, however, which started out under the heading "canonical," did not strongly interact with research on social or cultural memory in their day. In fact, crossovers only begin to be visible after the original work of Maurice Halbwachs was reframed and popularized by the Assmanns.[12] Therefore, in order to be able to study and evaluate the contribution of canonical critics themselves to biblical exegesis, it is more helpful to focus on contributions that predate the reception of Assmannian theory.

As will become clear from the discussion in this study, given the emphasis that canonical approaches to Scripture place on the interrelationship between text, community, and theology, it is apt that these approaches are considered in relation to specifically ecumenical hermeneutics/exegesis, as in this field, the same interrelationship plays a role of central importance. Beyond that, it will be demonstrated how the two approaches can also supplement one another, the one emerging out of exegetical and historical considerations regarding text, community, and theology, the other out of systematic theological considerations regarding the same, while both have the relationship between unity and diversity as one of their foci.

1.1   Research Question, Method and Structure

The purpose of this study is to inquire into the workings and heuristic potential of canonical exegesis and thus to be able to evaluate its advantages and disadvantages, while formulating further hermeneutical considerations by way of an outlook, specifically in relation to ecumenical hermeneutics. The connection between canonical and ecumenical hermeneutics is, surprisingly, very unfrequently made; the current study seeks to break new ground in this respect. Researching and evaluating the various canonical approaches will be

zu unnötigen apologetischen Reflexen führen kann. Die kulturphilosophische Reflexion der Kanonidee und die kulturwissenschaftliche Behandlung kanonischer Phänomene ist geeignet, den theologischen Diskurs zu entkrampfen und durch neue Perspektiven zu ergänzen. Auf jeden Fall wäre eine exklusiv binnentheologische Erklärung für die gegenwärtige Konjunktur der Kanondebatte."

12   On the entry of the notions of social and cultural memory into biblical exegesis, see e.g. Sandra Hübenthal, "Social and Cultural Memory in Biblical Exegesis," in: Kåre Berge/ Pernille Carstens (ed.), *Cultural Memory in Biblical Exegesis* (Piscataway: Gorgias, 2012), as well as Alan Kirk, "Social and Cultural Memory," in: Idem/Tom Thatcher (ed.), *Memory, Tradition and Text* (Atlanta: SBL, 2005), 1–24. See also the remarks of Söding. "Kanon," lviii-lvxi, as well as of Seckler, "Problematik," 32, rightly noting that the Assmann-reception has, at least for a long time, predominantly taken place among Old Testament scholars.

done by asking the question, "what are the advantages and disadvantages of the "canonical approach" as expressed in scholarly discussion, and how are they reflected in the actual use of this approach in the exegesis of the four New Testament gospels by five prominent representatives?" The focus on a particular part of the New Testament, i.e. the canonical gospels, facilitates a concentrated way of dealing with the amount of literature on canonical approaches to Scripture, especially given the peculiarity of the four-gospel canon, which immediately invites reflection on the canon. Most, if not all, of the questions raised in the discussion around canonical approaches to the gospels are also raised in discussions surrounding the canonical approach to other parts of the biblical canon, both Jewish and Christian. In this context, it may also be noted that given the fact that this study focuses on the New Testament gospels, the broader biblical theological question of the relationship between the two testaments of the Christian Bible will not be discussed on its own. To be sure, its importance is acknowledged, and aspects of the relationship do surface in the discussion of the overall canonical approaches of the scholars considered in this study.[13]

In terms of method, therefore, this study neither sets out to defend or attack canonical approaches to Scripture *a priori*, contested as they are; rather, its aim is an evaluation of such approaches by drawing out both their (potential) strengths and weaknesses. Its aim is to provide, in an essayistic manner, an inquiry into the heuristic potential and disadvantages of canonical exegesis of the New Testament gospels. In this study, priority has been given to actual examples of the canonical exegesis of gospel passages, rather than to, for example, theories about the hermeneutical relevance of the four-gospel-canon. While such theories do have their value, they are seldom accompanied by sample exegeses. The approach chosen in this study keeps exegetical theory and practice together and analyzes both, which has clear heuristic advantages and is innovative in terms of approach (most studies on canonical hermeneutics consider either hermeneutical theory or exegetical practice, but hardly analyze both).

In terms of method and structure, the study will first of all clarify the terminology as it is used in this study, and then it will present a brief sketch of the emergence and origins of canonical criticism. Subsequently, the canonical

---

13 See for a brief enumeration of questions that this issue provokes e.g. Söding, "Kanon," liii–lvi, and Jörg Barthel, "Die kanonhermeneutische Debatte seit Gerhard von Rad: Anmerkungen zu neueren Entwürfen," in: Bernd Janowski (ed.). *Kanonhermeneutik: Vom Lesen und Verstehen der christlichen Bibel* (Neukirchen-Vluyn: Neukirchener Verlag, 2007), 1–26, 3–4.

approaches of five prominent representatives will be presented,[14] i.e. of Brevard S. Childs, James A. Sanders, Peter Stuhlmacher, Joseph Ratzinger, and the so-called "Amsterdam School" of exegesis.[15] Each presentation will also include the analysis of a representative example of a scholar's canonical exegesis of a passage from the New Testament gospels. On the basis of the study of these scholars' respective theoretical considerations and examples from their praxis of canonical exegesis, its functioning and heuristic potential will be evaluated. Focusing on these canonical approaches on their own is legitimized by the fact that (at least) four of them predate the broader rediscovery of the canon as a topic of scholarly interest in literary and cultural studies. In addition, it is also worthwhile seeing what they have to offer in terms of heuristic potential on their own as a complete program of both canonical theory and praxis. In other words, the approaches considered here are hermeneutical trailblazers and worthwhile considering on their own, without immediately subsuming them to, for example, paradigms for the study of the canon deriving from cultural studies (even if compatibilities will be noted in this study as well). Furthermore, by focusing on acknowledged key representatives of canonical exegesis, the discussion around canonical criticism as a whole can be accessed efficiently, given that these key representatives function as crystallization points of the broader discussion. The analysis of these authors and their work will be followed by a more systematic consideration of the questions that their work gives rise to, leading into a discussion of insights from these various canonical approaches to Scripture in relation to ecumenical hermeneutics, for reasons already stated.

In every analysis of the canonical approaches and the appertaining "canonical" exegeses of gospel passages that will be presented here, the following (sub)

---

14   These key representatives, as may be noted, are all male, Western, white and heterosexual. An explanation for this fact may well be found in the sociology of religion and of biblical scholarship, but other issues may well be at stake too. For a feminist response to canonical exegesis, see, for example, the contribution of Nancy R. Bowen, "Canon and the Community of Women: A Feminist Response to Canonical Criticism," in Richard D. Weiss/David M. Carr (ed.), *A Gift of God in Due Season* (FS James A. Sanders: Sheffield: Sheffield Academic Press, 1996), 237–252. See also: Ilse Müllner, "Dialogische Autorität. Feministisch-theologische Überlegungen zur kanonischen Schriftauslegung," in: G Steins/E. Ballhorn (ed.), *Der Bibelkanon in der Bibelauslegung. Beispielexegesen und Methodenreflexion* (Stuttgart: Kohlhammer, 2007), 74–84, as well as Claudia Janssen/Ute Ochtendung/Beate Wehn/Luise Schottroff (ed.), *GrenzgängerInnen: Unterwegs zu einer anderen biblischen Theologie* (Mainz: Grünewald, 1999).

15   For the selection of these representatives, see below, 1.4.

questions will be answered in order to assist in answering the main question of this study:

- What sort of understanding of "canon" and "canonical exegesis" is being used?
- How is this approach applied, i.e. what sort of role does the canon play in exegesis?
- What effect does it have on the outcome of the exegesis, i.e. how is the canon appealed to in order to make decisions about interpretation and meaning?
- What is, for this exegesis, the heuristic and epistemological value of a "canonical approach?"

In answering these questions and considering canonical approaches, issues concerning communities of interpretation, specifically the church, authority, and the history of exegesis and biblical interpretation will also surface, given that the issue of the canon is closely related to all of these matters. On the basis of this, a number of further considerations will be developed, notably in relation to ecumenical hermeneutics and exegesis, about which a final chapter has been incorporated.

Finally, it should be noted that a canonical approach to Scripture, as it is understood here, is a phenomenon that has its roots in Western post-enlightenment Christian theological scholarship and has emerged in response to (modern) historical-critical exegesis and with the aim to do justice to the Scriptural texts in relation to the faith community. This is not to deny that there are other (often pre-modern) ways of doing exegesis that can very well be termed canonical. Examples of these include Jewish approaches to Scripture[16] and certainly (Eastern) Orthodox exegesis,[17] as it draws on patristic exegesis.

16 See e.g. Moshe Halbertal, *People of the Book, Canon, Meaning, and Authority* (Cambridge, MA: Harvard University, 1997). Note also the essays from a Jewish perspective in: Christine Helmer/Christof Landmesser (ed.), *One Scripture or Many? Canon from Biblical, Theological, and Philosophical Perspectives* (Oxford: Oxford University, 2004).

17 See e.g. Petros Vassiliadis, "The Canon of the Bible: Or the Authority of Scripture from an Orthodox Perspective," in: J.M. Poffet (ed.), *L'Autorité de L'Écriture* (Paris: Cerf, 2002), 113–135; see also Vasile Mihoc, "Basic Principles of Orthodox Hermeneutics," in: Moisés Mayordomo (ed.), *Die prägende Kraft der Texte. Hermeneutik und Wirkungsgeschichte des Neuen Testaments* (Stuttgart: Katholisches Bibelwerk, 2005), 38–64, Savas Agouridis, "The *regula fidei* as Hermeneutical Principle Past and Present," in: *L'Interpretazione della Bibbia nella Chiesa, Atti del Simposio promosso dalla Congregazione per la Dottrina della Fede* (Vatican: Libreria editrice Vaticana, 2001), 225–231, and John Breck, *Scripture in Tradition: The Bible and its Interpretation in the Orthodox Church* (Crestwood, NY: SVS Press, 2001).

Furthermore, various kinds of "identity-based" hermeneutics could also be described as canonical.[18] However, these kinds of exegesis, interesting as they are, stand in a different relationship to "classical" historical-critical exegesis and should therefore not be counted as part of the group of canonical approaches that are considered here. This notwithstanding, the interrelationship between community identity and exegesis will play a role of significance in the final part of this study. Specifically, this question will also be addressed in a chapter on ecumenical hermeneutics and canonical criticism.

1.2 What is Canonical Criticism? A Note on Terminology

The terminology that is used to describe canonical exegesis or canonical criticism varies, also among the practitioners of the various approaches commonly associated with the term. Therefore, the terminology used with regard to the approaches and with respect to some other topics should be briefly discussed here.

Canonical exegesis is sometimes referred to as "canonical criticism," a term introduced by Sanders, which someone like Childs would protest against. The reason for this is that a term like "canonical criticism" would place the approach on the same level as other kinds of "criticism" (e.g. historical-critical criticism, etc.). Childs rejects this and describes his own program as a "canonical approach," or as reading the Bible as Sacred Scripture, wishing it to be a hermeneutical framework that governs the use of various kinds of "criticism." Other terms that exist include "canonical exegesis," a term used by Ratzinger, and "theological exegesis," as is used in the title of a *Festschrift* for Childs, and which is currently gaining broader currency.[19] What all of these descriptions have in common is

---

18   See for thoughts along these lines, in relation to the canonical exegesis as it is discussed in this study, e.g. Peter-Ben Smit, "Wegweiser zu einer kontextuellen Exegese? Eine Miszelle zu einem Nebeneffekt der kanonischen Hermeneutik von Brevard S. Childs," *ThZ* 62 (2006), 17–24, as well as the broad overview provided by William J. Abraham, *Canon and Criterion in Christian Theology. From the Fathers of Feminism* (Oxford: Clarendon, 1998).

19   The term itself is used by Childs as well, see e.g. Brevard S. Childs, *Biblical Theology of the Old and New Testaments. Theological Reflection on the Christian Bible* (Minneapolis: Fortress, 1992), 55; see also his "Towards Recovering Theological Exegesis," *Pro Ecclesia* 6 (1997), 16–26. For the *Festschrift*, see Christopher Seitz/Kathryn Greene-McCreight (ed.), *Theological Exegesis. Essays in Honor of Brevard S. Childs* (Grand Rapids: Eerdmans, 1999). On "theological exegesis" in general, see the brief account by Arie W. Zwiep, *Tussen Tekst en Lezer* II (Amsterdam: VU University, 2013), 113–117, and further: Daniel J. Treier, *Introducing Theological Interpretation of Scripture* (Nottingham: Apollos, 2008); Markus

an understanding of the Christian Bible,[20] including a particular canonical shape,[21] which functions as an authoritative witness to God and God's workings in the world, and a reading of this Bible in the context of the Christian faith and the faith community.[22] (Thus, in this study, what is understood as the "canonical approach" clearly goes beyond the study of the development of the canon of the Christian Bible.[23] This topic will, accordingly, play a role of limited importance in this study.[24]) It is this broad understanding of canonical criticism that will serve as a starting point in this study. Both "canonical

---

Bockmuehl, *Seeing the World: Refocusing New Testament Study* (Grand Rapids: Baker, 2006), Carl E. Braaten/Robert W. Jenson (ed.), *Reclaiming the Bible for the Church* (Grand Rapids: Eerdmans, 1995), Ellen F. Davis/Richard B. Hays (ed.), *The Art of Reading Scripture* (Grand Rapids: Eerdmans, 2003), David F. Ford/Graham Stanton (ed.), *Reading Texts. Seeking Wisdom: Scripture and Theology* (Grand Rapids: Eerdmans, 2004), Stephen E. Fowl, *Engaging Scripture. A Model for Theological Interpretation* (Oxford: Blackwell, 1998), idem (ed.), *The Theological Interpretation of Scripture: Classic and Contemporary Readings* (Oxford: Blackwell, 1997), Scott Hahn, *Letter and Spirit: From Written Text to Living Word in the Liturgy* (New York: Doubleday, 2005), Ephraim Radner/George Summer (ed.), *The Rule of Faith: Scripture, Canon and Creed in a Critical Age* (Harrisburg: Morehouse, 1998), and Francis Watson, *Text, Church and World: Biblical Interpretation in Theological Perspective* (Grand Rapids: Eerdmans, 1994). – Most recently, see also the following volume on Childs and his work: Christopher R. Seitz/Kent Harold Richards (ed.), *The Bible As Christian Scripture: The Work of Brevard S. Childs* (Atlanta: Society of Biblical Literature, 2013).

20   This term is used to indicate the various kinds of canons that include both an Old and New Testament and as it has become associated with Christianity as a further development of pre-70 CE Judaism.

21   Not all those using a canonical approach to Scripture use the same canon, of course, given that the shape of the canon that one uses is (at least partially) determined by one's confessional context.

22   See also the following definition of Barthel, "Debatte," 5: "Kanonhermeneutik...ist die Reflexion der besonderen Verstehungsbedingungen und – problemen, die dadurch gegeben sind, daß die biblischen Schriften die Gestalt und Funktion eines Kanons, d.h. einer (relativ) abgeschlossenen Schriftensammlung mit normativer und/oder formativer Funktion für die Glaubensgemeinschaft(en) haben."

23   See with this emphasis rightly: Barthel, "Debatte," 5; see also: Bernd Janowski, "Die kontrastive Einheit der Schrift. Zur Hermeneutik des biblischen Kanons," in: idem (ed.), *Kanonhermeneutik*, 27–46, 45–46.

24   Even if it will become clear that the discovery of the historical circumstance that canonicity, in the sense of being part of a canonical process, is not foreign to the New Testament texts (or any Scriptural texts, for that matter), has played an important role in the legitimization of the use of notions such as canonicity and canon as interpretative tools, given that they could be shown to be historically connected to the processes that produced these texts and not, or at the very least not exclusively, a later ecclesial imposition upon the texts.

approach" and "canonical criticism" will be used as terms to indicate this particular way of interpreting Scripture; the content of this term is always determined by the scholar's work to which it refers.[25]

The above considerations concerning the definition of canonical criticism, canonical approach, and canonical exegesis, have their point of departure in an understanding of the "canon" as a normative collection of texts, e.g. as Theißen utilizes it: "Ein Kanon besteht aus normativen Texten, die geeignet sind, das Zeichensystem einer Religion immer wieder neu zu rekonstruieren und durch Auslegung für eine Gemeinschaft bewohnbar zu machen."[26] However, it should be noted that the term "canon" can also refer to other rules or measuring rods in the early church, apart from disciplinary canons, including the rule of faith. As is well known, such usage of the term far predates the usage of the term as a collection of texts.[27]

Nonetheless, the terms "Scripture" and "canon" are both used in a relatively loose sense in this study. While "Scripture" often primarily refers to an authoritative body of texts and "canon" often refers to a fixed list of texts,[28] the discussion of the canonical critics considered here needs some terminological flexibility, as one of the questions will be precisely what "canon" means for them, and also what it means for them to read biblical texts as Scripture. In general, the term "Scripture" will be used to refer to a set of texts, i.e. the Bible, that is regarded as authoritative, while the term "canon," as will become clear, can refer to both a list of books and to much more than just that (c.q., the rule of faith).

Furthermore, the capitalization of terms like "church" and "gospel" will follow the rule that only when a specific gospel or church is indicated a capital is

---

25   In fact, the terminological issue seems to be the most important when comparing Childs and Sanders; however, as will become clear from the example of Sanders' exegesis discussed below, his "canonical criticism," conceived as a sub-discipline of exegesis, can also function in a way that is very akin to Childs' "canonical approach," as it offers a vision of what texts are and of how they function as well.

26   Gerd Theißen, *Die Religion der ersten Christen. Eine Theorie des Urchristentums* (Gütersloh: Gütersloher Verlagshaus, [3]2003), 341–342, see in general: 339–344.

27   On the history of the term "canon," see esp. Heinz Ohme, *Kanon ekklesiastikos. Die Bedeutung des altkirchlichen Kanonbegriffs* (Berlin: De Gruyter, 1998).

28   See e.g. Lee M. McDonald, *The Biblical Canon: Its Origin, Transmission, and Authority* (Peabody, MA: Hendrickson, [3]2007), 55–58, and his distinction between a "canon 1" and "canon 2." See also the remarks of Childs, "Reflections," 29, drawing on A.C. Sundberg, *The Old Testament Canon of the Early Church* (Cambridge, MA: Harvard University, 1964), see further also e.g. Dwight Moody Smith, *The Fourth Gospel in Four Dimensions: Judaism and Jesus, the Gospels and Scripture* (Columbia: University of South Carolina, 2008), 181. See also e.g. Barthel, "Debatte," 4–5.

used, e.g. Roman Catholic Church, but "biblical interpretation in the church," and the New Testament gospels, but "the Gospel of Matthew." "Scripture" and "Bible" are always capitalized as references to (relatively) specific books or bodies of literature.

1.3   The Emergence of the Canonical Approach

The "canonical approach," as is currently being discussed, emerged in the late 1960s and early 1970s in the context of the search for new approaches to biblical theology.[29] Thus, unlike the canon and its scholarly study itself, the canonical

---

29   See e.g. the overviews by Mary C. Callaway, "Canonical Criticism," in: Stephen Haynes/Steven McKenzie (ed.), *To Each its Own Meaning* (Louisville: Westminster/John Knox, 1993), 142–155, Gerald T. Sheppard, "Canonical Criticism," ABD 1 (1992), 861–866, Söding, "Kanon," Steins, "Bibelkanon," Bernd Janowski, "Kanonhermeneutik: eine problemgeschichtliche Skizze," *BThZ* 22 (2005), 161–180, Von Lips, "Kanondebatten," Hermann von Lips, "Was bedeutet uns der Kanon?: Neuere Diskussion zu theologischen Bedeutung des Kanons," *VuF* 51 (2006), 51–56, Hermann von Lips, *Der neutestamentliche Kanon. Seine Geschichte und Bedeutung* (Zürich: TVZ, 2004), Karl-Wilhelm Niebuhr, "Die Gestalt des neutestamentlichen Kanons. Anregungen zur Theologie des Neuen Testaments," in: Steins/Ballhorn (ed.), *Bibelkanon*, 95–109, Robert W. Wall/Eugen E. Lemcio (ed.), *The New Testament as Canon: Reader in Canonical Criticism* (Sheffield: JSOT, 1992), Robert W. Wall, "Reading the New Testament in Canonical Context," in: Joel B. Green (ed.), *Hearing the New Testament. Strategies for Interpretation* (Grand Rapids: Eerdmans, [2]2010), 372–396, idem, "Canonical Criticism," in: Stanley E. Porter (ed.), *Handbook to Exegesis of the New Testament* (Leiden: Brill, 2997), 291–312, Seckler, "Problematik," 34–49, Henning Graf Reventlow, *Hauptprobleme der biblischen Theologie im 20. Jahrhundert* (Darmstadt: Wissenschaftliche Buchgesellschaft, 1983), 125–137, Ruth Scoralick, "Kanonische Schriftauslegung," *BiKi* 38 (2009), 645–647, D.A. Carson/John D. Woodbridge (ed.), *Hermeneutics and Canon* (Grand Rapids: Baker, 1995), Christoph Dohmen, "Der Biblische Kanon in der Diskussion," *ThRv* 91 (1995), 451–460, Christoph Dohmen/ Manfred Oeming, *Biblischer Kanon warum und wozu?* (Friedberg: Herder, 1992), John Barton, *The Spirit and the Letter* (London: SPCK, 1997), Gerhard Maier (ed.), *Der Kanon der Bible* (Giessen: Brunnen, 1990), Baldermann (ed.), *Problem,* Theo K. Heckel, "Neuere Arbeiten zum neutestamentlichen Kanon I-II," *ThR* 68 (2003), 286–312, 441–459, Childs, "Reflections," Katharina Greschat, "Die Entstehung des neutestamentlichen Kanons: Fragestellungen und Themen der neueren Forschung," *VuF* 51 (2006), 56–63, Dieter Böhler, "Der Kanon als herme- neutische Vorgabe biblischer Theologie. Über aktuelle Methodendiskussionen in der Bibelwissenschaft," *ThPh* 77 (2002), 161–178. On the New Testament canon, see further e.g.: Henk Jan de Jonge, "The New Testament Canon," in: Auwers/De Jonge (ed.), *Canons*, 309–319, Luc Zaman, *Bible and Canon* (Leiden: Brill, 2008), 13–211, 538–596, McDonald, *Canon,* 431–521, Gerd Theißen, *Die Entstehung des Neuen Testaments als literaturgeschichtliches Problem* (Heidelberg: Winter, [2]2011), Martin Ebner, "Der christliche Kanon," in: Idem/Stefan Schreiber

approach to Scripture is a relative novelty.[30] Brevard S. Childs, who was to be one of the main proponents of a "canonical approach" to Scripture, published his *Biblical Theology in Crisis* in 1970, while James A. Sanders' *Torah and Community* came two years later, only to be followed by Childs' first major attempt at a "canonical approach" to part of the Christian Bible, *Introduction to the Old Testament as Scripture* (1979).[31] Five years later, in 1984, its New Testament counterpart appeared.[32] The momentum produced by these books soon showed that dismissive remarks, such as James Barr's 1983 comment that the Scriptural canon was without hermeneutical significance for biblical interpretation, were no longer self-explanatory.[33] The discussion has not abated since Sanders and Childs pioneered the approach, as the canonical approach has been able to establish itself as a significant hermeneutical perspective in biblical scholarship. The broad reception of the approach is evidenced by a lively discussion in both Protestant and Roman Catholic quarters. The latter is indicated by the Pontifical Biblical Commission's document, *The Interpretation of the Bible in the Church*,[34] as well as by Joseph Ratzinger/Pope Benedict XVI's

---

(ed.) *Einleitung in das Neue Testament* (Stuttgart: Kohlhammer, 2008), 9–52, Bruce M. Metzger, *The Canon of the New Testament: Its Origin, Development and Significance* (Oxford: Clarendon, 1987), F.F. Bruce, *The Canon of Scripture* (Downers Grove: InterVarsity, 1988), H.Y. Gamble, *The New Testament Canon: Its Meaning and Making* (Philadephia: Fortress, 1985), Hans Freiherr von Campenhausen, *The Formation of the Christian Bible* (Philadelphia: Fortress, 1972), the appertaining contributions in Einar Thomassen (ed.), *Canons and Canonicity: The Formation and use of Scripture* (Copenhagen: Museum Tusculanum, 2010), Michael Bird/Michael Pahl (ed.), *The Sacred Text: Excavating the Texts, Exploring the Interpretations, and Engaging the Theologies of the Christian Scriptures* (Piscataway: Gorgias, 2010), Lee M. McDonald/James A. Sanders (ed.), *The Canon Debate* (Peabody, MA: Hendrickson, 2002), William R. Farmer/Denis Farkasfalvy, *The Formation of the New Testament Canon* (New York: Paulist, 1983), and the bibliography provided by J.A.M. Snoek, "Canonization and Decanonization: An Annotated Bibliography," in: Arie van der Kooij/Karel van der Toorn (ed.), *Canonization Decanonization* (Leiden: Brill, 1998), 435–506.

30   John Barton, *Reading the Old Testament: Method in Biblical Study* (London: Darton, Longman and Todd, 1984), 79.

31   Brevard S. Childs, *Introduction to the Old Testament as Scripture* (London: SCM, 1979).

32   Brevard S. Childs, *The New Testament as Canon. An Introduction* (Valley Forge: Trinity International Press, 1984).

33   Barr, *Scripture*, 67.

34   Pontifical Biblical Commission, *The Interpretation of the Bible in the Church* (Città del Vaticano: Libreria Editrice Vaticana, 1993), C.1.; the document mentions two scholars by name: James A. Sanders and Brevard S. Childs. On the compatibility of Child's approach with Roman Catholic biblical scholarship, see also: Artur Sanecki, *Approccio canonico: tra storia e teologia, alla ricerca di un nnovo paradigm post-critico: l'analisi della metodologia canonical di B.S. Childs dal punti di vista cattolico* (Rome: Pontificia Università Gregoriana, 2004).

reception of the canonical approach in his books on Jesus of Nazareth. Such reception is further evidenced by broad academic discussions in both the German and English discourses on biblical studies.[35] Thus, the canonical approach to Scripture has firmly established itself on the map of biblical hermeneutics and its future still remains open.[36] This does not mean that all accept this approach, and if scholars do accept this approach, it does not mean that they do so in the same way. Aspects of all of this will be outlined below.

1.3.1   *The State of the Canonical Debate and the Current Study*

Impulses provided by scholars such as Childs, Sanders, and others, have led to a diverse reception, oftentimes in relation to insights from other fields of study that underline the importance of the interrelationship between text and inter-pretative community. This includes the work of a variety of "contextual" exegetes, and those engaged in various types of "postmodern" hermeneutics (influenced by thinkers such as Derrida, Fish, Gadamer, and many others), asking partly analogous questions concerning the construction and deconstruction of meaning by readers in relation to texts (and their de/construction) in a process also involving the de/construction of the reader her-/himself. The widely spread acknowledgement of the importance of this interrelationship has, broadly speaking, forged two different approaches. The first focuses on the (historical) study of the reception of the Bible, leading to a variety of initiatives by scholars and publishers alike, generally seeking to describe and understand the processes of interpretation that have taken and are taking place in relation to the (Christian) Bible as the authoritative canonical Scripture of various communities of faith or as an influential document in the history of human-kind. Studies in the nature of canonicity have their place here as well, e.g., in relation to insights from the field of cultural studies and often with reference to the work of Jan and Aleide Assmann. While this approach has a clear herme-neutical agenda and seeks to highlight the variety of interpretations of Scripture in history – especially by marginal/ized groups – it is not always explicitly theological in its outlook (implicitly, however, it virtually always involves an ethical and philosophical agenda). Instead, it seeks to chart a way for-ward for biblical interpretation in a confessionally "neutral" academic environ-ment, rather than to discuss in detail how Scripture could (or even: Should) function within a particular community of interpretation (i.e., one with a more or less clear rule of faith, which is none other than a rule of interpretation). The lat-ter, however, is precisely the focus of a second group of studies that understand

35   See the literature listed above.

36   See also Von Lips, "Kanondebatten," 123: "Der Weg der Kanondiskussion im neuen Jahrhundert ist also völlig offen."

themselves as being engaged in the "theological interpretation of Scripture," i.e. the interpretation of Scripture in explicit relation to (Christian) theological concerns, often stemming from a particular confessional tradition, and the development of rules for such a project. Included in the project of the "theological interpretation of Scripture" are also attempts to restate an understanding of the reliability of Scripture, both historically, but also and especially soteriologically, as a trustworthy guide for a life of faith, or, indeed, a sound means of grace. A good example of the latter is the work of Kevin VanHoozer.[37] To be sure, historical studies in the nature of the canon, its development, and functioning also continue to be produced; they have a bearing on (and are often influenced by) insights from both strands of contemporary biblical interpretation, be it more along the lines of reception history or more along the lines of the theological interpretation of Scripture.

The current study is situated somewhat in the middle of the two main currents just identified. While not a study in the hermeneutics of reception history, it does take into account the significance of processes of reception for the development of a meaning of a text and, while not a study in the theological interpretation of Scripture in a particular tradition (not withstanding its author's theological situatedness) it is interested in questions of (implicit) normativity in processes of interpretation. It is not, however, as representatives of the "theological approach" to Scripture oftentimes are, interested in Christian apologetics. Instead, by analyzing five influential representatives of "the" canonical approach to Scripture, considering what questions arise from their work for the broader exegetical enterprise, and relating this to insights from ecumenical hermeneutics, an independent contribution is made here. It seeks to further the exegetical debate as a whole, beyond the confines of either reception history or the theological interpretation of Scripture as such, building on insights deriving from the analysis of the five representatives of the canonical approach to Scripture in relation to ecumenical hermeneutics, and thereby arriving at insights for a historically, hermeneutically, and theologically informed approach to Scripture, both for the academia and

---

37   See, esp. Kevin VanHoozer, *Is There a Meaning in this Text? The Bible, the Reader, and the Morality of Literary Knowledge* (Grand Rapids: Zondervan, 1998), see esp. his conclusions, 453–468. VanHoozer's aim is to reformulate the role of Scripture in the Church and to gain a new understanding of its reliability for a life of faith. See also his further works: Remythologizing Theology: Divine Action, Passion, and Authorship (Cambridge: Cambridge University, 2010); *The Drama of Doctrine: A Canonical-linguistic Approach to Christian Theology* (Louisville: Westminster John Knox, 2005); *First Theology: God, Scripture & Hermeneutics* (Westmont: IVP, 2002).

beyond. The focus will be on questions relating to hermeneutics and the process and praxis of exegesis that are raised by discussing canonical hermeneutics in relation to ecumenical theology. The entire enterprise, as it is presented here, is heuristic in nature and seeks to further understand what exegesis is about and how it could function in a reflected and responsible way by drawing inspiration from canonical approaches to Scripture in dialogue with ecumenical hermeneutics. Rather than a new proposal for a canonical approach to Scripture, this study intends to utilize the questions raised by both canonical and ecumenical hermeneutics in order to further the enterprise of the interpretation of Scripture as such. To be sure, the direction that this study will point toward is obviously influenced and inspired by canonical and ecumenical insights, but also goes beyond them. In this way, the current study is interdisciplinary in outlook and in its conclusions, transcending disciplinary boundaries between, for example, biblical studies and ecumenical studies, while taking into account relevant developments in philosophical hermeneutics on the one hand and intercultural studies on the other.

As was just indicated in doing all of this, this study will also venture to make a connection between canonical and ecumenical hermeneutics. This connection is, in spite of many interests and convictions shared by both types of hermeneutics (especially their focus on the interrelationship between text and community of interpretation), not often made; by making it here, an attempt is made at pointing towards new horizons in both canonical and ecumenical hermeneutics.

1.4   Selection of Authors

The five representatives of a canonical approach to the New Testament that are being considered here have been chosen because they represent distinct as well as, generally, broadly received and discussed examples of canonical exegesis. Futhermore, most of them can be seen as representing what may be considered as the formative period of canonical criticism,[38] during which much of the approach's "DNA" was formed and the research agenda set. Also during this period, most critical issues and forms of resistance against the method became clear (and continue to be discussed during later stages of the development of this approach). All of this may be obvious in the case of Childs, given that he was one of the two figures that sparked off the entire debate about the role of

---

38   Ratzinger would seem to be the exception, but his work can well be regarded as representing the late literary output of the adoption of an earlier paradigm.

the canon in biblical studies from the 1970s onwards; the same applies to Sanders. Although both started out as Old Testament scholars, and remained active in this field during their entire career, both men have also made significant contributions to New Testament scholarship. The German New Testament scholar Peter Stuhlmacher is included here because in German New Testament scholarship his contribution is arguably the best known and most influential in terms of canonical exegesis.[39] The inclusion of Joseph Ratzinger/Pope Benedict XVI is necessitated not only by the fact that he is by far the most prominent and influential Roman Catholic scholar using a canonical approach to exegesis, but also because he has placed the issue much higher on the agenda for both the popular and scholarly debate surrounding biblical interpretation in recent years. He also receives the work of the three scholars mentioned previously and his work can, as was already indicated, well be regarded as the late literary reflection of an earlier adoption of a canonical approach to exegesis. Finally, the so-called "Amsterdam School of Exegesis," a unique Dutch development, will be considered, given that it utilizes a canonical approach and raises exegetical issues and questions related to this that are not addressed by the other representatives in the same way. As this "school" of exegesis developed over multiple decades, providing significant contributions to the (Dutch and German) exegetical debate(s), and cannot be reduced to merely one person, it will be considered as a school here, while focusing on the work on the New Testament gospels by one of its current prominent protagonists. Arguably, most of the other approaches to a canonical approach to Scripture have been developed in reaction or response to these five representatives of canonical exegesis, most notably to the work of Childs and Sanders.

Having outlined the above, it is now possible to proceed to the analysis of the five canonical critics, their approaches and exegetical practices.

---

39   On Stuhlmacher as a canonical critic, see below, 2.3.1. He is not identified as such by all, however, see e.g. Niebuhr, "Gestalt," 96.

CHAPTER 2

Canonical Exegesis of the New Testament Gospels: Five Cases

2.1 Brevard S. Childs

The Presbyterian scholar Brevard S. Childs (1923–2007) of Yale Divinity School was,[1] together with Sanders, the most prominent representative of "canonical exegesis" in the English-speaking world, and was, to a considerable extent, responsible for placing question of the canon back on the exegetical agenda.[2] Childs, like Sanders, endeavored to produce work on both the Old and the New Testaments, and was theologically strongly influenced by Karl Barth.[3] Here, however, only his work on the New Testament as well as his general approach will be discussed, even though it is only one part of Childs' scholarly endeavor. As is well known,

---

1 As Christoph Markschies, "Epochen der Erforschung des neutestamentlichen Kanons in Deutschland. Einige vorläufige Bemerkungen," in: Becker/Scholz (ed.), *Kanon*, 578–604, 578–579, observes, the question of the canon is, like questions having to do with the development of ecclesial ministries, often very tightly bound up with a scholar's ecclesial loyalties, hence, of all the scholars discussed here, the ecclesial tradition to which they belong will be mentioned.

2 See especially the following works: Childs, *Crisis*, a programmatic work including examples of his method (149–219), idem, *Old Testament*, idem, *New Testament*, and *Theology*. Childs also produced a number of commentaries in which he used his own exegetical approach: *The Book of Exodus. A Critical Theological Commentary* (Philadelphia: Westminster Press, 1974) and *Isaiah* (Louisville: Westminster John Knox, 2001); see further also: idem, *The Church's Guide for Reading Paul: The Canonical Shaping of the Pauline Corpus* (Grand Rapids: Eerdmans, 2008) and idem, *The Struggle to Understand Isaiah as Christian Scripture* (Grand Rapids: Eerdmans, 2004). An extensive bibliography can be found in Daniel R. Driver, *Brevard Childs, Biblical Theologian: For the Church's One Bible* (Tübingen: Mohr Siebeck, 2010), 293–299; on the reception of Childs in both Anglophone and Germanophone academia, see idem, *o.c.*, 35–79; another recent overview of Childs' program is: Chen Xun, *Theological Exegesis in the Canonical Context. Brevard Springs Childs' Methodology of Biblical Theology* (Frankfurt: Lang, 2010). See for this and the following also: Stefan Krauter, "Brevard S. Childs' Programm einer Biblischen Theologie," *ZThK* 96 (1999), 22–48, as well as the earlier brief treatment by Eckhard J. Schnabel, "Die Entwürfe von B.S. Childs und H. Gese bezüglich des Kanons. Ein Beitrag zur aktuellen hermeneutischen Fragestellung," in: Maier (ed.), *Kanon*, 102–152, and Smit, "Wegweiser."

3 See on this topic, e.g. Charles J. Scalise, "Canonical Hermeneutics: Childs and Barth," *SJT* 47 (1994), 61–81, Driver, *Childs*, 82–93, Barthel, "Debatte," 10.

© KONINKLIJKE BRILL NV, LEIDEN, 2015 | DOI 10.1163/9789004301016_003

Childs' main aim was to develop a consciously theological approach to the entire Christian Bible by emphasizing the biblical canon as the hermeneutical key to Scripture. Here, it will be outlined what this amounted to for Childs, both in theory and in terms of exegetical practice: A sketch of his hermeneutical theory will be followed by the analysis of an example of his exegesis.

2.1.1   *The Canonical Approach of Brevard S. Childs*
Childs began developing his approach at the backdrop of what he saw as the failure of the Biblical Theology Movement.[4] He first provided a full outline of his concerns and his program in his 1970 *Biblical Theology in Crisis*.[5] Here, he argued vehemently that "the canon of the Christian church is the most appropriate

---

4 On this movement, see e.g. Zwiep, *Tekst* II, 102–108. Sheppard probably formulates the issue between Childs and the biblical theology movement well, when he wrote: "as the more rigorous historical orientation of the modern period came to dominate, canonical issues seemed to belong only to the last steps in a long process, at great distance from the original historical events upon which the revelatory claims of a religion depends. Therefore, modern scholars, whether conservative or liberal on questions of biblical history, tended to shift the treatment of these subjects to the back of introductions, following the lead of such major orthodox interpreters as J.G. Carpzov (1721). This same priority of biblical history to biblical text informed much of the recent "Biblical Theology Movement," which often focused the theological worth of the Bible to the "acts of God in history" or defined the biblical witness in terms of an "actualized" report about a historical event. The canon could be viewed, according to this model, as merely a late and flawed pre-modern effort to preserve efficacious "confessions" about history. A canonical approach challenges the assumption that the earliest historical events play such a determinative role in the capacity of scripture to have authority or to render reality. Without denying the value of information gained by means of any critical investigation, a canonical approach seeks to understand a different issue: How a biblical text is normative with religious interpretation, that is to say, how the context of ancient traditions within scripture functions as an arena in which certain religious questions are asked and answered. In this approach, one seeks to recognize the textual warrants and rules whereby a scripture makes specific religious claims, perpetuates paradoxical and ambiguous expressions of faith, engenders the need for repeated interpretation, and imposes upon the reader a vision of the world that God has made." (Sheppard, "Criticism," 862).

5 See Childs, *Crisis*; for an earlier and briefer outline, see Brevard S. Childs, "Interpretation in Faith: The Theological Responsibility of an Old Testament Commentary," *Interpretation* 18 (1964), 432–449. On the context and backgrounds, see esp. Driver, *Childs*, 5–21, as well as e.g. Schnabel, "Entwürfe," 104–105, and the broader contextualization offered by William John Lyons, *Canon and Exegesis. Canonical Praxis and the Sodom Narrative* JSOT 352 (Sheffield: Sheffield Academic press, 2002), 5–33, and the documentary history provided by Ben C. Ollenburger (ed.), *Old Testament Theology: Flowering and Future* (Winona Lake: Eisenbraun, 2004), 117–267 (it may be noticed that James Sanders does not figure in this study). Childs, "Canon," provides a retrospective through Childs' own eyes.

context from which to do Biblical Theology."[6] This amounted to more than just a call for the re-appreciation of the biblical canon as a literary phenomenon; it aimed for the interpretation of the scriptures "in relation to their function within the community of faith that treasured them."[7] Needless to say, this caused controversy, given the widely spread notion of the canon's irrelevance for exegesis.[8]

A historical and exegetical starting point of Childs' canonical approach is that the biblical canon is not a late development, foreign to the texts involved and somehow forced upon them. Quite the opposite is the case for Childs, as the following two quotations may illustrate:

> The [biblical] material was transmitted through its various oral, literary, and redactional stages by many different groups towards a theological end. Because the traditions were received as religiously authoritative, they were transmitted in such a way as to maintain a normative function for subsequent generations of believers within a community of faith.[9]

> Emphasis was placed on the process [of canonization] to demonstrate that the concept of canon was not a late ecclesiastic ordering, which was basically foreign to the material itself, but that canon-consciousness lay deep within the formation of the literature.[10]

The biblical canon that has come into being in this way is much more than a collection of books for Childs: It is the normative body of scriptures of a community of faith. In fact: "The canonical shape provides the larger framework of scripture – a rule of faith – within which the interpretative function of exegesis is guided."[11] This rule of faith can function as a guideline for the interpretation of these scriptures and serves as a "summary of the truth" which is none other than the "faith of the church," referring to this faith in its totality and thus serving as "criterion of correct interpretation." The rule of faith represents the content of Scripture without being identical with it; the rule of faith contains that to which Scripture (also) points.[12]

---

6   Childs, *Crisis*, 99.

7   Childs, *Crisis*, 99.

8   See, e.g. Steins, "Bibelkanon," 179.

9   Childs, *Biblical Theology*, 70.

10   Childs, *Biblical Theology*, 71.

11   Childs, *Struggle*, 317.

12   Childs, *Biblical Theology*, 31–32: "[the rule of faith is] a summary of the truth, which compromises the faith of the church. It refers to the totality of the faith as the criterion of correct interpretation. It is the content of scripture, but not identical with the Bible; rather it is that to which Scripture points."

Therefore, for Childs, the notion of "canon," while describing a body of literature, also has to do with the rule of faith (*regula fidei*) of the early church,[13] and accordingly with the place of Scripture in a community.[14] Childs took over the notion of the *regula fidei* from Irenaeus of Lyon who developed it in his polemic with competing Christian groups ("Gnostics").[15] The most extensive formulation of a rule of faith offered by Childs in his work also consists of a paraphrase of parts of Irenaeus' Adversus Haeresus. Since a clear cut formation of this rule in Childs' own words is hard to find, it is worthing quoting Irenaeus in full:

> In opposition to the Gnostic scheme that salvation occurred when the spiritual was freed from the bondage of the material, Irenaeus sought to establish the unity of the one true God, creator of heaven and earth and the Father of Jesus Christ (*Adv. Haer.* III.1.2). The Holy Spirit knew no other God but the one creator God (III.6.1). Central for Irenaeus was the biblical emphasis that God's order for salvation had extended from creation to its fulfillment in Christ, as God progressively made himself known in creation, was a prophecy through the divine Logos. Christian

---

13   See Childs, *Biblical Theology*, 67.

14   See on this point also John Barton, "Canonical Approaches Ancient and Modern," in: Auwers/De Jonge (ed.), *Canons*, 199–209, who offers the following helpful clarifications of Childs' terminology: "in saying 'canon' Childs does not primarily mean the Bible considered as an official list, but the Bible considered as the authoritative word for the church. That is, it is the *binding* character of the canon he is concerned with, not its character as an authoritative *selection* of particular books." With regard to the same topic, see also the comments of Barthel, "Debatte," 7: "Vereinfacht gesagt betrachtet Childs den Kanon in einer vierfachen Dimension, die sich mit den Stichworten Funktion, Gestalt, Genese und Referenz erfassen lassen. Die Bibel als Kanon zu lesen, bedeutet für Childs zunächst, sie in ihrer normativen *Funktion* für die Glaubensgemeinschaft...zu lesen. In kritischer Wendung gegen die traditionelle historisch-kritische Bibelauslegung führt dieser Ansatz Childs zweitens zur Privilegierung der *Endgestalt*...des Kanons als des eigentlichen Gegenstandes und Kontextes der Auslegung. Die Endgestalt aber weist ihrerseits zurück auf die Wirksamkeit des kanonischen Bewußtseins schon in der *Genese* des Kanons, die Childs kanonischen Prozeß...nennt. Schließlich richtet er sein Augenmerk...auf die *referentielle Funktion* des Kanons als Zeugnis für die Wirklichkeit Gottes. Erst die Berücksichtigung dieser vierten Dimension macht aus dem *canonical approach* ein explizit theologisches Unternehmen. In der Betrachtung dieser vier Dimensionen des Kanons ist Childs repräsentativ für jede Form kanonischer Hermeneutik, die diesen Namen verdient." – See also Barthel, "Debatte," 7.

15   Notably through his reception of Bengt Hägglund, "Die Bedeutung der Regula fidei als Grundlage theologischer Aussagen," *STh* 12 (1958), 1–44.

scripture bore witness to Jesus Christ as God's son and savior who was from the beginning with God and fully active throughout this entire history (IV.20.lff.). All the economies of God reveal this history of revelation according to its stages which led the church from infancy to perfection. Indeed in his doctrine of "recapitulation" Irenaeus pictured Christ's joining the end of time with the beginning and thereby encompassing within himself fully the entire experience of Israel and the church (III.21.10-23.8). Because of the unity of God's salvation, it was absolutely essential to the faith that two testaments of the Christian Bible be seen as a harmonious witness to the one redemptive purpose in history.[16]

In Childs' view, Irenaeus' approach to biblical interpretation thus leads to a reading of the Gospel in a holistic way, which included in itself the "sum of tradition," i.e. that revelation which is the basis for faith and to which Scripture witnesses.[17]

Thus, the canonical approach of Childs provides a hermeneutical framework for the interpretation of scripture.[18] In other words, when read in the context of this framework or canon (i.e. *rule of faith* as it is related to the collection of books that the canon is also), Scripture can (again) "function normatively and not merely illustratively for the church."[19]

Accordingly, using a canonical approach means for Childs also to do away with a "false dichotomy between the book and the community."[20] In terms of biblical theology, this leads to the following definition: "Biblical Theology is... theological reflection on both the Old and New Testament."[21] Methodologically, this means reading single texts in light of ever larger textual complexeties, which also include the faith of the church and thus results in establishing a

---

16   Childs, *Biblical Theology*, 31.

17   Childs, *New Testament*, 28: "[A] holistic reading of the gospel which included the sum of tradition constituting the true revelation on which the faith was grounded and to which Scripture testified." Childs, while pioneering this approach, was well aware that this approach was not quite uncontroversial. He owned up to this and took up the Pauline term σκάνδαλον (1 Cor. 1:23) to justify it, as the content of this stumbling block is: "...that the witness of Jesus Christ has been given its normative shape through an interpretative process of the post-apostolic age." (Childs, *New Testament*, 28).

18   Driver, *Childs*, 252–253; Driver adopts the notion of framework from James Kugel/Rowan Greer, *Early Biblical Interpretation* (Philadelphia: Westminster, 1986), 151.

19   Childs, *Crisis*, 101.

20   Childs, *Crisis*, 103.

21   Childs, *Biblical Theology*, 55.

relationship of mutual interpretation between the two.[22] In this way, Childs seeks to move beyond the constraints of historical-critical scholarship, which he views as "incapable of either raising or answering the full range of questions, which the church is constrained to direct to its Scripture."[23] In other words, a more encompassing interpretative approach is needed, because of the very character of Scripture itself and the need of the church; with his canonical approach, Childs intends to provide just that.[24]

As will become clear further on when discussing Sanders' approach,[25] Childs differs from Sanders by not considering canonical exegesis as a particular sub-discipline of biblical studies (or a particular kind of "criticism"), but rather as determining the way canonical texts are seen and treated at large (hence, his canonical "approach"). He sums this up as follows: "In the end, I would rather speak of a new vision of the text than in terms of method."[26] This new vision serves his overarching aim of arriving at a new way of reading the Bible as sacred Scripture.[27]

At this point, it should also be maintained that at least formally, Childs does not make a clear decision in favor of any particular form of the canon, be it that of Tenakh or of the Septuagint.[28] Discussing the historical and – especially – the theological pros and cons of opting for either of these canons, he comes

---

22   Childs, "Interpretation."

23   Childs, *Crisis*, 141.

24   Childs, *Crisis*, 141.

25   See below, 2.2.

26   Childs, *New Testament*, xvii.

27   Childs, *Old Testament*, 82: "I am unhappy with this term (sc. 'canonical criticism'), because it implies that the canonical approach is considered another historical critical technique that can take its place beside source criticism, form criticism, rhetorical criticism, and similar methods. I do not envision the approach to canon in this light. Rather, the issue at stake in relation to the canon turns on establishing a stance from which the Bible can be read as sacred scripture." This remark, which is aimed against Sanders' use of the term "canonical criticism," is more a difference in form than in content, however, as Sanders reacted to Childs' remark as follows, expressing more agreement than disagreement: "Our common concern with canon cannot be reduced to another technique. It is indeed a stance from which to read the Bible. And that is the reason I say canonical criticism rather than canon criticism, because it, more than any mode yet developed for proper exegesis, includes a clear posture with regard to the Bible." James A. Sanders, *Canon and Community: A Guide to Canonical Criticism* (Philadelphia: Fortress, 1984), 18.

28   Childs also acknowledges, however, that "the exact nature of the Christian Bible both in respect of its scope and text remains undecided up to this day," (idem: *o.c.*, 63). See on this topic further: Driver, *Childs*, 68, Paul R. Noble, *The Canonical Approach. A Critical Reconstruction of the Hermeneutics of Brevard S. Childs* (Leiden: Brill, 1995), 152–155.

down to a position that refers to an ongoing "*search* [emphasis in original] for the Christian Bible," in which the discipline of biblical theology participates by offering insights into the content as well as the form of the canon.[29] Thus, he leaves the question of the extent of the canon and its literary shape open, in principle.

Notwithstanding this, Childs does have a preference for the canon of Tenakh. Reasons for this include (his understanding of) the relationship between "church and synagogue" and the wish to clearly distinguish between Scripture and tradition.[30] Furthermore, even if he leaves the issue open in theory – at least to some extent – he does not do so in practice, given that only the books of the shorter canon of the HB/OT are discussed in both his introduction to the Old Testament and his full-scale biblical theology. Of interest, in this context, is also Childs' view of textual criticism. In both his introductions to the Old and New Testaments, Childs mounts an argument in favor of a canonical approach to textual criticism.[31] This means that textual criticism should not strive to reconstruct the earliest possible form of the text, but rather the best form of the canonical, i.e. ecclesially received text. However controversial this proposal may be, it is fully in line with the rest of Childs' project, particularly to the

---

29 Childs, *Biblical Theology*, 67: "Perhaps the basic theological issue at stake can be best formulated in terms of the church's on-going *search* for the Christian Bible. The church struggles with the task of continually discerning the truth of God being revealed in scripture and at the same time she stands within a fully human, ecclesiastical tradition, which remains the trident of the Word. The hearing of God's Word is repeatedly confirmed by the Holy Spirit through its resonance with the church's Christological rule-of-faith. At the same time, the church confesses the inadequacy of its reception while rejoicing over the sheer wonder of the divine accommodation to limited human capacity.

Part of the task of a Biblical Theology is to participate in the search for the Christian Bible. The enterprise is not one which will be resolved once-and-for-all, but one which appears to be constitutive for Christian faith. The dialectical poles, historically represented by the Protestant and Catholic positions, chart the arena between Word and Tradition, which is reflected in the controversy over the extent of the Christian canon. Equally important is the critical tension between the form and the substance of the church's witness in scripture, which calls for a continual struggle for truthful interpretation. One of the purposes of this attempt at a Biblical Theology is to apply these hermeneutical guidelines in working theologically within the narrow and wider forms of the canon in search for both the truth and the catholicity of the biblical witness to the church and the world."

30 See Childs, *Old Testament*, 96–99. – See also e.g. Driver, *Childs*, 69–196. – See also Thomas Söding, "Entwürfe Biblischer Theologie in der Gegenwart," in: Hans Hübner/Bernd Jaspert (ed.), *Biblische Theologie. Entwürfe der Gegenwart* (Neukirchen-Vluyn: Neukirchener Verlag, 1999), 41–103, 76–77.

31 See: Childs, *Old Testament*, 84–106; idem, *New Testament*, 518–530.

extent that it places more emphasis on the (developing) meaning of a work than on the intention of its author.[32]

Childs' work is arguably the kind of canonical exegesis that has drawn the most responses, some accepting his work and applying it, some critiquing it,[33] and some seeking to re-conceptualize it in relation to other hermeneutical models e.g. from literary studies or philosophical hermeneutics. These various studies cannot be the topic of this study, but should be noted here for the sake of completeness.[34] Instead, having outlined Childs' approach, it is now possible to turn to an example of this exegesis of a gospel passage.

2.1.2   *Presentation of a Representative Exegesis*

The example that is chosen here is a sample of canonical exegesis that Childs has included in his *opus magnum* and consists of an exegesis of Matt. 22:33–46. Before turning to this passage, however, it is necessary to provide a broader contextualization of Childs' exegesis of the gospels, outlining Childs' view of them at large, as this has a significant bearing on his exegesis of Matt. 22:33–46.

---

32   Childs prefers the notation of the *intentio operis* to that of the *intentio auctoris*; this allows him to account for the fact that the meaning of significance of texts develops beyond the initial (and historical) intention of their authors (see e.g. Mark G. Brett, *Biblical Criticism in Crisis? The Impact of the Canonical Approach on Old Testament Studies* [Cambridge: Cambridge University, 1991], 147). In this way, Childs comes close to other text-centred (postmodern) hermeneutical approaches, even if Childs maintains (and emphasizes) the referential character of (Biblical) texts; see e.g. Lyons, *Canon*, 68–71. – See for Childs' consideration of the process of canonization e.g. Childs, *Old Testament*, 77–84, and idem, *New Testament*, 16–34.

33   The Childs-Barr debate merits special attention in this respect, especially given the recent archival researchers of Driver that shed some new light on the matter, see: Driver, *Childs*, 211–215. See for a sketch of Barr's view of Childs: James Barr, *The Concept of Biblical Theology: An Old Testament Perspective* (Minneapolis: Fortress, 1999), 37–39, 47–51, 400–451, as well as e.g. "The Theological Case against Biblical Theology," in: Gene M. Tucker/David L. Petersen/Robert R. Wilson, *Canon, Theology and Old Testament Interpretation. Essays in Honor of Brevard S. Childs* (Philadelphia: Fortress, 1988), 3–19.

34   See especially the following studies: Barton, *Reading*, 77–157, Lyons, *Canon*, Brett, *Criticism*, Noble, *Approach*, Manfred Oeming, *Gesamtbiblische Theologien der Gegenwart* (Stuttgart: Kohlhammer, 1985), 186–209, and Georg Steins, *Die "Binding Isaaks" im Kanon (Gen 22); Grundlagen und Programm einer kanonisch-intertextuellen Lektüre* (Freiburg: Herder, 1999), see also the attention that Rolf Rendtdorff gave Childs (overview provided by Driver, *Childs*, 65–68). For an extensive (and very critical) review of all of these responses, see the overview provided by Driver, *Childs;* for an overview focusing on the German discourse, see esp. Barthel, "Debatte." For an attempt to understand Childs' approach as a kind of contextual theology, see Smit, "Wegweiser."

Childs' treatment of the four canonical gospels starts off with a consideration of their formation.[35] He first considers the genre of the gospels, rejecting a classification of the New Testament gospels as Hellenistic biographies. For Childs, this is not only historically unlikely, as he classifies analogies with other ancient biographies as superficial at best, but also as theologically spurious, as such a classification obscures the uniqueness of these writings in terms of their theological content and their kerygmatic intention ("witness rather than biography of Jesus").[36] The discovery of the latter already "broke the back of liberal Protestant theology in the 1920s."[37] With regard to the structure of the gospels, Childs argues that this structure is not primarily historical, but kerygmatic and intended to shape and reshape the memory of the community to which a gospel was addressed in order to be able to preach the message of the resurrected one.[38] Next, Childs discusses Q, acknowledging the likelihood of its existence but rejecting a variety of reconstructions of its content and theological tendency. Finally, Childs arrives at his own view, namely that Q depicts Jesus principally as the one that proclaims the good news in line with Isa. 61, while it does not underline his role as "the suffering Son of man." Thus, Q is not gnostic in its outlook, but rather focuses on Jesus' words, which, in the canonical gospels, have been combined with his deeds.[39]

Subsequently, Childs returns to the question of the relationship between the early church's proclamation (*kerygma*) and the gospels. He argues that the discovery of the early form critics, that the *kerygma* is of central importance as a hermeneutical key to the gospels, should be acknowledged again. Accordingly, all four gospels should be seen as having their point of departure in this proclamation of Christ's resurrection and as seeking to relate this to the memory of the earthly Jesus. Childs sees this as a development in early Christian thinking that is particularly concerned with the relation between the "risen Christ" and the "earthly Jesus" and that is reflected in the development from Paul's (kerygmatic) letters to the gospels; the latter seek to connect the "risen Christ" and "earthly

---

35   Childs, *Biblical Theology*, 251–261. – See also the account of the gospels and their (canonical) relationships in his introduction to the New Testament, Childs, *New Testament*, 57–209.

36   Childs, *Biblical Theology*, 262. – On the importance of the notion of "witness" for Childs, see also e.g. Barthel, "Debatte," 7–9.

37   Childs, *Biblical Theology*, 253.

38   Childs, *Biblical Theology*, 253–254.

39   Childs, *Biblical Theology*, 256: "The focus of Q falls completely on the centrality of the person of Jesus, indeed not as the suffering Son of man, but as the proclaimer of the good news to the poor in accord with the message of Isaiah 61. The portrait of Q, far from being Gnostic in tendency, is one which is fully congruent with the actions of Jesus which the tradition of the canonical Gospels joined with his words." For the full discussion, see: idem. *o.c.*, 255–257.

Jesus." The answers to this question of the relationship between (risen) "Christ" and (earthly) "Jesus" are offered by the gospels, in a key passage they are summarized by Childs; it deserves quoting in full:

> What is most remarkable is the variety of approaches used by the Gospels to address the problem. On the one hand, all the Gospels were written from the confessional stance of the exalted Christ, and all read backward from the resurrection to the earthly Jesus. Again, all four Evangelists used the form of a Gospel, and did not write either a dogmatic tractate or a historical life of Jesus. Finally, all four set the traditions of the earthly Jesus firmly within the context of the Old Testament's messianic promise. On the other hand, each Gospel functioned in its own independent integrity without explicit cross-references. In spite of the use of much common material and sources, each Evangelist brought forth his own witness without expressing dependence on each other. Moreover, each Gospel set forth the relation of the exalted Christ to the earthly Jesus in a strikingly different manner and from a varied Christological perspective. Mark emphasized the mystery surrounding the earthly life of Jesus through the misunderstanding by his disciples of the suffering Son of man. Matthew laid stress on the presence of the exalted Lord of the church who fulfilled scripture's promise of a Messiah and whose teachings remained binding on his followers. Luke pictured a Jesus who fulfilled the Old Testament promise of a savior of the poor and whose spirit continues to guide the emerging church of the Gentiles. John testified to the eternal unity of the Son of God with the Father who draws into his fellowship those who remain faithful to his commands in love.[40]

Against this background, Childs now approaches the issue of historical trajectories in the early Christian witness and the interpretation of the gospels. What is at stake here is nothing other than the relevance of research into the historical Jesus for the interpretation of the canonical gospels. This relevance is very limited for Childs. He outlines his own position by stating two objections to the work that is, in his view, aimed too much at historical reconstruction. First, he notes that there is always a "prior judgement" involved in one's determination of what belongs or could belong to the original proclamation of Jesus, and second, that moving from the witness of a gospel that views Jesus in the light of

---

40   Childs, *Biblical Theology*, 259–260.

faith to a level prior to that means making a major hermeneutical decision that is not always unproblematic.[41]

Nevertheless, Childs does see a role for research into earlier levels of gospel tradition as a tool to better understanding the final literary product.[42] However, this does not include the level of the "real" historical Jesus. Taking issue with Hoskyns and others, Childs states that he is not convinced that:

> [H]istory and revelation can be critically brought into a congruence with-out any appeal to faith. Such a move is to effect a metamorphosis in kind. Rather it is an essential function of the fourfold form of the canonical Gospels to resist all such attempts of a critical reductionism which would fuse the diverse witnesses into one portrait. I do not hold it to be histori-cally possible or theologically legitimate to seek an abstraction of the teachings of the earthly Jesus from the earliest levels of each Gospel, which in the end is a portrait of Jesus apart from his reception through the faith of the early church.[43]

The distinction between witness and historical research (or historical sources) that Childs introduces here is of fundamental importance to him: "The whole point of the Christian canon is to maintain such a distinction and thereby to acknowledge the special authority of sacred scripture."[44] In other words, the historical Jesus is not available apart from the witness of the early church.

When further developing his thoughts on this topic, Childs emphasizes a second interpretative lens that was used by the early church to shape its mem-ory of the earthly Jesus, while "reading" his memory from the perspective of the *kerygma* and thus, turning it into witness rather than into biography: The Scriptures of Israel. Even though these are, from Childs' point of view, often disregarded by those researching the historical Jesus, they are of fundamental importance for understanding him, at least according to the witness of the early church, for which the Old Testament provided "the context for interpreting the

---

41 Childs, *Biblical Theology*, 262: "First, the critic invariably presupposes a prior judgment of what belongs to the authentic message – whether Bultmann, Jeremias, or Dodd is irrelevant – which is essentially a form of theological reductionism. Secondly, an impor-tant hermeneutical shift is involved when the interpreter attempts to move from the evangelist's witness to a prior level in which Jesus is accessible apart from the evange-list's testimony, that is, apart from its perception in faith."

42 Childs, *Biblical Theology*, 262–263.

43 Childs, *Biblical Theology*, 263.

44 Childs, *Biblical Theology*, 264.

significance of Jesus in which both the earthly and the exalted Jesus are pro-
phetically interpreted from the perspective of God's redemptive will for the
world."[45] This has considerable consequence for the way in which traditions
concerning the historical Jesus are received, given that Childs understands the
Old Testament (in his formulation) as a continuing commentary on the events
in Jesus' life as described in the Gospels, to such an extent that is becomes very
hard to distinguish commentary from historical event. Childs views this as an
indication that the New Testament, when it is not understood within the context of the Old Testament, ceases to operate as gospel.[46]

The above amounts to a summary of Childs' general view of the gospels. On
this basis, it is possible to turn to his treatment of Matt. 21:33–46 immediately.
He also offers a separate discussion of the Gospel of Matthew,[47] but a discussion of it is superfluous for the purposes of this study, given that the most significant aspects of Childs' treatment of the Gospel of Matthew also return in
his more detailed exegesis of Matt. 21:33–46; discussion of both texts would
lead to much repetition.

When analyzing Childs' exegesis of the "parable of the wicked tenants," the
following may be observed. Childs first states where the parable can be found
(i.e. Matt. 21:33–46, Mark 12:1–12, Luke 20:9–18, and Logion 65 in the Gospel of
Thomas). On this statement, a synoptic analysis follows, which points to small
but – for Childs – significant differences.[48] Notably, Matthew maintains the
explicit Markan allusions to the Song of the Vineyard from Isa. 5, while, unlike
Mark, he also speaks of groups of servants being sent to the vineyard and that
some of those in these groups were beaten, killed, and stoned. Unlike in Luke
and Mark, the son that is eventually sent to the vineyard in Matthew is not
called "beloved," but like in Luke and unlike in Mark, he is first thrown out
of the vineyard and then killed. Finally, Childs notes the use of Psalm 118 in all of

---

45   Childs, *Biblical Theology*, 264.

46   Childs, *Biblical Theology*, 264–265: "Not only does the Old Testament provide a running
       commentary on how to understand a particular event in his life, but Scripture forms the
       very warp and woof of the gospel to such an extent that frequently historical event and
       scriptural warrant blur indissolubly together. Although critical historical reconstruction
       can often demonstrate that the use of the Old Testament in the Gospels extends back to
       the earliest levels of Christian tradition, it is quite impossible often to distinguish which
       elements derive from Jesus himself and which from the Evangelist's witness. From a canon-
       ical perspective the authority of a Gospel logion is not derivative of this distinction. The
       theological point to emphasize is that the Old Testament provides the kerygmatic context
       for the New Testament's witness without which the tradition does not function as gospel."

47   Childs, *Biblical Theology*, 270–276.

48   See for this and the following: Childs, *Biblical Theology*, 337–338.

the canonical accounts, while for him Matthew's addition, "The Kingdom of God will be taken away from you and given to a nation producing the fruits of it," (v. 43) stands out as the most important variation vis-à-vis the other versions of the parable. Furthermore, Childs notes that some manuscripts of Matthew add a further "stone metaphor" derived from Daniel (probably by way of Luke 20:18) after this verse (i.e. as v. 44).

Having provided this overview, Childs turns to the "demise of the allegorical interpretation"[49] of parables in general and of the one under discussion particular. This allegorical interpretation, *en vogue* since Irenaeus of Lyons (see esp. *Adversus Haereses* 4.36.2), saw "a point for point correspondence...between the text and an assumed sequence of historical events."[50] This tradition was received by, for example, Thomas Aquinas, and lasted at least until the work of Archbishop Richard Trench (*Notes on the Parables of our Lord*, 1861). However, this approach came to an end with the work of Jülicher (*Die Gleichnisreden Jesu*, 1888–1889), who distinguished between parables and allegories, with the former having only one point to make and not lending themselves for establishing the sort of "point or point correspondence" that allegories encourage. Jülicher's approach was further developed by Dodd and Jeremias, who, unlike Jülicher, thought that the parable was originally Jesuanic and had an eschatological message, while it appropriately reflected a "Palestinian milieu."[51] Childs concludes this overview of the history of interpretation of this pericope from Matthew by mentioning the work of Fiebig (*Altjüdische Gleichnisse*) and others (Klauck, Crossan, Flusser, and Weder), noting that Jülicher's clear-cut distinction between parable and allegory cannot be maintained, because precisely rabbinic parables (*meshalim*) combined elements of parable, simile, and allegory. This leads to a situation in which allegory cannot be "dismissed out-of-hand as an early church distortion."[52] Instead, it is acknowledged that "allegory has emerged as an extended narrative form of metaphor with its own integrity and particular function."

Having outlined aspects of the history of interpretation of Matt. 21:33–46, particularly concerning form criticism, Childs turns to the question of its tradition history, noting from the start that one of the issues is that one's view of this "depends on a variety of other problems, which are involved, such as the general Synoptic problem, the redactional history of each gospel, and a judgment regarding the relation of the Synoptic tradition to the Gospel of Thomas."[53]

---

49   Childs, *Biblical Theology*, 338–339.
50   Childs, *Biblical Theology*, 338.
51   Childs, *Biblical Theology*, 339.
52   This and subsequent quotations are taken from Childs, *Biblical Theology*, 339.
53   Childs, *Biblical Theology*, 339.

Then, Childs addresses a "now classic" paper by John Dominic Crossan on the parable, in which Crossan attempted to trace the original form of the parable to the form of it now found in the Gospel of Thomas; Childs describes the approach of Crossan (and others) as being very subjective and characterized by a "continuing concern to recover the teaching of the historical Jesus, which was set at some distance from its Synoptic representation."[54] Instead, Childs proceeds to reject this and other attempts to reconstruct the parable's origins and original meaning. From his perspective, the results are either trivial or merely tedious illustrations of what a scholar considers to be Jesus' original message anyway, heavy with ideological ballast, or still allegorical in nature. Next, Childs addresses the question of the setting of the parable, confessing frustration with the discussion, given that critical scholars demand too much from the parable in terms of, for example, logic. By contrast, scholars of a more conservative bend focus too much on the historical accuracy of the parable. Thus, both kinds of scholars run the risk of missing the point of the parable.[55] At its core, Childs' frustration with all of this scholarship has to do not so much with questions of historical reconstruction as such, but rather with another hermeneutical issue: The relationship between early Christian traditions and the *kerygma*. Opposed to recovering supposedly non-kerygmatic original layers in a text, he argues that, with regard to questions about the historical development of a text, the (tradition-)historical issue that matters is that of "the nature of the trajectory [*sc.* of a text's development]," which needs to be seen "within the context of the church's kerygmatic understanding of the subject matter constituting the gospel." In other words: Historical research into earlier stages of a text can only serve to illuminate the *Letztgestalt* of the text; the question "wie es eigentlich gewesen" is of very limited (theological) significance.

Childs then turns to the exegesis proper of the parable, beginning with a consideration of Matthew's use of the Old Testament in this pericope. He notes that all three synoptic gospels make use of Isa. 5, unlike the Gospel of Thomas; Childs considers it likely that the reference to Isa. has been removed from the latter version of the parable "in a redactional move to thoroughly de-allegorize the text."[56] Touching briefly on the meaning of Isa. 5:1–7 as a juridical parable, inviting the hearer to condemn himself (i.e. "the house of David which commits bloodshed and violence," and that will be punished accordingly by God),[57] Childs then addresses the way Matthew uses this text. For him, it is immediately

---

54   Childs, *Biblical Theology*, 339–340.

55   Childs, *Biblical Theology*, 340–341.

56   Childs, *Biblical Theology*, 342.

57   Childs, *Biblical Theology*, 342.

obvious that, in Matthew's use of the parable, the vineyard can no longer refer to the house of Israel, but must refer to the kingdom of God, as verse 43 would indicate. Also, unlike in Isaiah, in Matthew the addressees consist no longer of the leaders of the people, but rather of the people at large. In this way, the Matthean parable further develops the language of Isaiah, picking up where he left off and continuing the use of the vineyard as a metaphor.[58]

On this basis, Childs argues that another shift from the Isaian original to the Matthean use of the text is that the the focus is no longer on the productivity of the vineyard, but the behavior of the tenants. Furthermore, and also significantly, the Matthean parable shows an on-going allegorical application of Isa. 5, for which license was found in Isaiah's initial metaphorical use of the vineyard as one thing that stood for another. On this basis, the allegorical connections of the text were expanded, notably to include Jesus. This view of Matthew's use of Isaiah also has consequences for those who "attempt to find a *Sitz im Leben Jesu* for this parable free of all allegorical features," given that "they are forced to speculate on a level which is not represented by the canonical gospels and is no longer directly pertinent for understanding its witness."[59] Interestingly, Childs then decides to pursue the inverse trajectory by looking at its reception in order to discover the parable's meaning, thus utilizing later (but still early) Christian tradition to uncover the meaning of its Matthean version:

> Actually, the key to understanding how the parable was understood within the early church lies in pursuing the various ways in which the story was extended figuratively in an effort to clarify and increase the analogy of the story with the mission of Jesus. Whereas Mark has a sequence of single messengers, Matthew's description of two groups of servants serves to portray an analogy with the Old Testament prophets – the former and latter – whose mishandling culminated in the death of the Messiah (Acts 7.51ff.). Again, the identification of the son as the Messiah is made explicit by the reference to the "beloved son" (Mark 12.6; Luke 20.13) who was first cast out of the vineyard and then killed (Matt. 21.39) to match more closely the passion tradition. Finally, the citation of

---

58   Childs, *Biblical Theology*, 342: "The effect is that the New Testament parable has been initially introduced in an analogy to the Old Testament context by explicitly picking up its imagery of the vineyard, but then immediately its function has been transformed. Specifically, the New Testament begins where the Old Testament left off. The vineyard in the Gospels is a metaphor from the outset, which distinguishes it from Isaiah's use where the literary impact turns on the surprise move from concrete reality to metaphor."

59   Childs, *Biblical Theology*, 343.

the "rejected stone" passage (Ps. 118.22f.) extends the history of Jesus' passion to the victory of the exalted Christ at the resurrection (Acts 4.11; I
Peter 2.7, etc.) and confirms the context from which the parable was uni-
versally heard within the early church...[60]

Having argued this, Childs places the parable in the broader horizon of
Matthew's gospel as a whole, noting that the parable and its meaning are well
in line with Matthew's presentation of Christ as "the way of righteousness."
This includes the parable's punch line in verse 43, which refers to the kingdom
being taken away from some and given to others. Rejecting historicizing interpretations that would find an indication of the replacement of Israel by the
church here, Childs considers the message of the parable in its Matthean context, addressed originally to the leaders of the people, as addressed to later
generations of Christians to produce fruits of righteousness.[61]

Having outlined his interpretation of the parable, Childs also offers a further hermeneutical reflection that again addresses the relationship between
historical reconstruction and *kerygma*. Again, Childs indicates that the parable's meaning is found in its relationship, not only to historical developments,
but also – and especially – to the church's proclamation. In fact, one needs
knowledge both of Jesus' (historical) ministry and of the church's faith and
practice in order to fully do justice to the parable as recounted by Matthew.
Both the perspective of the historical Jesus and that of the Christ of faith, so to
speak (in terminology that Childs would decidedly not use), are needed.[62]
This hermeneutical position is of key importance for Childs.

Childs concludes his exegesis of Matt. 21:33–46 with a theological reflection from the perspective of both testaments. Here, he first indicates that the

---

60   Childs, *Biblical Theology*, 343.

61   Childs, *Biblical Theology*, 343.

62   Childs, *Biblical Theology*, 343–344: "The hermeneutical issue at stake lies in recognizing
      that the various forms of the parables in the Gospels all are shaped from the perspective
      of Jesus' death and resurrection as the rejected Messiah of Israel and have allowed this
      understanding to structure the text. This implies that one cannot derive the whole para-
      ble from Jesus' messianic consciousness, nor conversely can one completely sever the
      parable from Jesus' own teaching, because of the presence of allegory at its earliest level.
      The crucial point to emphasize is that the ability of the modern interpreter to determine
      how much of the parable stems from Jesus himself and how much from the church's con-
      textualization is not decisive for an understanding of the New Testament text, rather its
      exegetical significance has been greatly relativized. Indeed, only to the extent that such
      critical reconstructions aid in charting the trajectory of the church's kerygmatic witness
      does it make a genuine exegetical contribution."

parable is clearly and consciously set in an Old Testament context, even if the New Testament departed from this Old Testament context and matrix and rewrote the parable in the light of the witness to Jesus Christ: "This new story of the gospels was developed by means of a lengthy process of the early church's reflection on the meaning of the parable by extending its witness back into the Old Testament and at the same time, forward to the resurrection."[63] Childs contrasts this with the gnostic approach to the parable (i.e. Gospel of Thomas 65), in which all metaphorical extensions of the parable and its references to the Old Testament have been removed, which reflects a very different stance towards the Old Testament and a view of the relationship between Israel and the church that is just as different. How then, should the use of the Old Testament in this parable in Matthew's gospel be characterized? Childs does not think that allegory is the proper term, nor midrash, rather he sees the New Testament parable as picking up a shared narrative starting point, i.e. the planting of the vineyard (Isa. 5:1–7), and as subsequently proceeding to tell a completely different story. Childs outlines what is taking place here in a way that is best represented by his own words:

> A typological relation emerges from the juxtaposition, which the New Testament develops in terms of its shared content far beyond that of a formal analogy. The care and attention of God to his vineyard is shared in both stories, as well as the search for the fruits of righteousness. Whereas in the Old Testament the response to God's care was received in disobedience and bloodshed was substituted for justice and righteousness (Isa. 5.7), the rebellion in the New Testament extended far beyond the killing of God's messengers even to the slaying of the promised Messiah. The effect of reflecting theologically on this parable from both testaments is further to uncover the ontological relationship between the two events. Isaiah's prophetic witness testifies to the same rebellious spirit of Israel of which the entire Old Testament speaks, but which now culminates in the rejection of the Son. A reading of the Old Testament in the light of the full reality of the Gospel serves, not to provide a facile allegorical correspondence between texts, but to point to the shared reality. The content with which both testaments wrestle is the selfsame divine commitment to his people and the unbelieving human response of rejection, the sin of which climaxed in the slaying of God's Anointed One. In this sense, the two testaments are part of the same redemptive drama of election and rejection.[64]

63   Childs, *Biblical Theology*, 344.

64   Childs, *Biblical Theology*, 345.

Then, Childs turns to another intertext of the Matthean parable, i.e. the song of the vineyard in Isa. 27:2–9, which has a very strong eschatological orientation. This eschatological perspective, pointing to the redemption of the people of God, provides a further connection with the New Testament parable and serves as an indication that the one plan of God is witnessed to by both testaments.[65] Childs' final point is to state that Matthew's intention is not to "champion Christianity over Judaism," but to present the offer of reconciliation by the exalted Christ, but to present the offer of reconciliation by the exalted Christ, regarding which the church and Israel are in analogous positions (!). Even if the church has already experienced God's miraculous intervention, turning the rejected stone into a cornerstone (Matt. 21:42), it still needs to answer to this offer positively time and again. In his own words: "It is this decisive existential note which resists linking the testaments in a rigid, historicized sequence from the past, but which continues to call forth a living voice from the entire scriptures of the church."[66]

2.1.3   Analysis

When turning to the analysis of Childs' canonical approach in theory and practice, the following may be remarked.

First, the sub-question should be answered: "What sort of understanding of 'canon' and 'canonical exegesis' is being used?" A number of observations can be made with regard to this. To begin with, while Childs has a clear idea of the canon of the New Testament (i.e. the twenty-seven-book canon), he seems to leave the question of the size of the canon of the Old Testament open to some extent, at least in theory. In fact, and while providing reasons for it, he does make a decision, however, by only discussing the books of the shorter HB/OT canon in both his introduction to the Old Testament and his full biblical theology. Furthermore, for Childs, canonical exegesis is exegesis that takes the canon as its point of departure and as the primary context of the texts contained in the canon, specifically in their *Letztgestalt*. Childs argues that canonicity is an integral aspect of the (canonical) texts, relating canonization and canonicity to the production of the texts themselves ("canonical consciousness"), and does not see the canon as a late ecclesiastical development. To this understanding of the canon also belongs a specific relationship between the text and the community in which it has come to exist and for which benefit it exists. The canon functions as the community's

---

65   Childs, *Biblical Theology*, 345.
66   Childs, *Biblical Theology*, 346.

rule of faith;[67] specifically, the Scriptures point toward the rule of faith of the community as it can be formulated in creedal form as well. Canonical exegesis is therefore exegesis that places the interpretation of the canonical texts in the context of the canon, i.e. of the community's rule of faith as it is derived from the church's canonical Scriptures. The canon is, therefore, for Childs, a literary fact, and canonicity is an inherent characteristic of the texts that belong to the canon. At the same time, the canon (and a text's canonicity) also points to the faith of the community to which the texts belong and which provides the natural setting for their interpretation. In this way, given that the rule of faith of the community is theological in nature, canonical exegesis is theological exegesis. Before moving on to the next sub-question, a further aspect of Childs' understanding of canon, rule of faith, and community/church should be addressed. These notions are of vital importance to Childs' project but, surprisingly, precisely these three notions remain very unclear and underdefined in Childs' work, even if they are used in a way that suggests that it is perfectly clear what they refer to. While the canon of the New Testament that Childs refers to is fairly clear, his view of the Old Testament canon is much less clear, at least in his *opus magnum*, even if he comes down on the side of the Hebrew Bible (not the LXX). And, while he does provide an argument for a "canonical" textual criticism, i.e. a textual criticism that searches for the best form of the received, canonical text, it is not always clear in his exegetical work how this plays out. Furthermore, Childs never gives a clear outline of what he understands to be the church's rule of faith, i.e. he does not move beyond paraphrases of Irenaeus of Lyon's *Adversus Haereses*. Finally, Childs never indicates clearly, at least not in his *Biblical Theology*, what precisely he means with the church, or whether he has any particular church in mind.[68]

---

67   Childs does not seem to fully equate the Scriptural canon and the rule of faith as Charles J. Scalise, *Hermeneutics as Theological Prolegomena. A Canonical Approach* (Macon: Mercer University, 1994), 76, does, "[the] canon came to be seen as the rule that these particular books, rather than others, were to be read as Holy Scripture." – Scalise seems to contradict himself somewhat, however, when he lays out a theological framework for the interpretation of Scripture and then argues that "the movement of thought must flow from Scripture to theology (doctrine) and not the reverse," (idem, *o.c.*, 78), subsequently going on to express his sympathy with Florovsky's position Georges Florovsky, *Bible, Church, Tradition: An Easter Orthodox View* (Belmont: Nordland, 1972), 72.

68   See also Ephraim Radner, "The Absence of the Comforter: Scripture and the Divided Church," in: Seitz/Greene-McCreight (ed.), *Exegesis*, 355–394, esp. 356: "The frequent and vague references Childs makes to the Christian 'community' and to the 'church' as the defining agent for whom Scripture's subject matter is given shape are never clearly

Second, when addressing the sub-question, "how is this approach applied, i.e. what sort of role does the canon play in the exegesis?" the following can be said with regard to Childs' approach. First, there is the aspect of the text itself and how it is identified and classified. Apart from considering the canonical texts as canonical and hence normative for the community of interpretation, this also means, at least for the gospels, that the texts are placed in such a relationship to the faith of the church and the historical events that they refer to that they appear as "witnesses" to events (rather than historical sources). As "witnesses", they are related to and expressive of the church's faith, or rather: *Kerygma*, with, at its core, the death and resurrection of Jesus Christ. This *kerygma* is, together with the Scriptural (i.e. Old Testament) matrix within which it is placed, the early church's hermeneutical lens and "pen" by means of which it shaped the gospels and the other New Testament texts. This has major consequences for the way the texts are read, because it allows questions of historicity to move into the background in favor of questions of a more theological nature (in Childs' understanding of the two terms). Having outlined this, as a second point related to the second sub-question, the following may be noted: The way in which Childs understands the canonical nature of the texts also determines the sort of issues that he addresses in their actual exegesis. This does not only concern his fight against – in his view – all too historically interested interpretations in favor of a more theological exegesis, but within this theological exegesis also the sort of questions that he addresses. In the example that was discussed above, questions such as the relationship between the Old and New Testament, the nature of God's actions, the reality to which the texts point, such as the "redemptive drama of election and rejection,"[69] figure prominently. All of these questions are related to classical fundamental theological and systematic theological issues. This is a direct consequence of Childs' understanding of what the canonical nature of the Scriptural texts means, specifically in its relationship to the church and its faith.

The answer to the third sub-question, "what effect does it have on the outcome of the exegesis, i.e. how is the canon appealed to in order to make decisions about interpretation and meaning?" is very closely related to the second

---

identified, nor need they be, according to a long post-Reformation Protestant tradition in which such ecclesial references are deliberately peripheral. But in the contemporary context of communal dispute over the very nature of what Scripture is and of its authority and meaning, this vagueness carries with it an aura of unease that is also not altogether missing from Childs' work. Confusions over Scripture have become linked with confusions over what the Christian church is or where it is to be found."

69   Childs, *Biblical Theology*, 345.

sub-question. Childs appeals to the canon in two ways, it seems, in order to steer his exegesis. On the one hand, he appeals to the canon and the canonical selection of texts in the early church in order to determine which texts are authoritative and which are not. On the other hand, he appeals to the canonical nature of texts to determine what their relationship to history, the community of faith, and the latter's rule of faith is. In terms of appeals to the canon in the actual exegesis of a text, this means, as became clear in the example discussed above, that the intertextuality between the Old and New Testaments (also in the sense of its theological importance) is emphasized strongly. At the same time, the genre of the text is determined by means of an appeal to its canonicity and to its relationship to the faith/*kerygma* of the early church, and the sort of questions that are and are not (to be) addressed are also determined by what is and is not related to this *kerygma*.

Finally, addressing the last sub-question, "what is, for this exegesis, the heuristic and epistemological value of a 'canonical approach?'" the following may be observed. The "canonical approach" that Childs favors provides a vision of the text that actually suits the text (according to Childs, of course): The text is seen both in its appropriate context (as part of the bipartite canon of the Christian Bible, related to the church and the rule of faith) and in its appropriate function (as a witness to Christ). For Childs, this has far-reaching consequences for the interpretation of the text, i.e. he can proceed to an interpretation of the text at stake as a witness to God's self-revelation in Christ while the text is automatically placed in relation to questions concerning the faith of the church (not least in relation to the "Synagogue" in this case). This means that some other questions that could be asked (such as the original *Sitz-im-Leben* of the text and its significance for the text's meaning) move into the background and other questions are clearly foregrounded. Specifically the question of how the text bears witness to Christ, and thus contributes to the church's witness to Christ, is foregrounded in Childs' approach. In other words, as was outlined above and has become evident in Childs' exegesis of Matthew 21:33–46, for Childs, only the canonical approach places the text in its correct context and provides an appropriate approach to understanding it by asking the right questions. This is of fundamental epistemological and heuristic importance, given that the "right approach" leads also to specific questions being asked of a text, while also what may or may not be found in a text (and is not of relevance) is determined by this (canonical) approach.

2.1.4   Conclusions
By way of conclusion, the following may be maintained with regard to Childs' canonical approach. First of all, it should be emphasized that Childs' approach

is indeed an approach, meaning that it offers a vision of what the canonical texts are at large, which also has methodological consequences,[70] but which principally offers a (hermeneutical) framework for understanding what the Scriptural texts are and along which lines and in which context they ought to be read. This context consists for Childs of the canon, a notion that indicates the authoritative body of texts in its relationship to the community for which it is authoritative and an indication of this community's broad understanding of the significance of this body of texts (c.q. "rule of faith"). Put differently: Scripture, as a canonical text (or as a body of canonical texts), comes together with the church and its rule of faith. Notably, however important these three concepts are for Childs, none of them is defined with much precision (even the extent of the canon and its text remains open, at least in Childs' theory). Given the nature of these constituents, however, the interpretation of the canonical writings guided by this approach turns out to be a kind of theological exegesis, a term indeed associated with Childs' approach. As far as the New Testament texts are concerned, particular attention is given to the relationship between the New Testament texts and the Old Testament on the one hand, and to the church's *kerygma* on the other. This approach also has as a consequence that the relevance of historical questions is strictly limited. Nothing can have any authority for the interpretation of texts except for the texts themselves, the church's rule of faith, and the broader body of intertexts provided by the Scriptural canon as a matrix for the interpretation of a text. In this way, Childs has indeed reached his aim of placing the Bible back into the life of the church (see above, 2.1.1.), albeit at the cost of the relevance of much historical research and intertexts of the New Testament beyond those provided by the canon. The notion of the "rule of faith" (or the *kerygma*) and the definition of "church" remain strikingly underdefined, which, at least in theory, also applies to the extent of the Old Testament canon.

2.2 James A. Sanders

While originally a textual critic, and like Childs, an Old Testament scholar, the Presbyterian academic James A. Sanders (*1927; Union Theological Seminary/ Claremont School of Theology), using his own distinct approach to and

---

70 See e.g. Childs, *New Testament*, 48–53; see also e.g. Roy F. Melugin, "Canon and Exegetical Method," in: Tucker/Peterson/Wilson (ed.), *Canon*, 48–61, and Krauter, "Programm," 27–30, 36–38.

understanding of canonical criticism,[71] has also made a contribution to the (canonical) exegesis of the New Testament.[72] For this reason, and because Sanders' approach has been formative for the development of canonical criticism at large, his contribution will be considered here. As he notes himself, his own contribution to this debate has its roots in the publication (by himself) of the Psalms Scroll found at Qumran,[73] which, together with other finds, challenged the then current (albeit already debated) consensus surrounding

71 See for outlines of his position e.g. James A. Sanders, *Torah & Canon* (Philadelphia: Fortress, 1972), 117–121, idem, *Canon*, as well as the essays collected in idem, *From Sacred Story to Sacred Text, Canon as Paradigm* (Philadephia: Fortress, 1987), especially "Biblical Criticism and the Bible as Canon," "Canonical Context and Canonical Criticism," and "From Sacred Story to Sacred Text" (75–86, 153–174, 175–191). See also the bibliography in Shemaryahu Talmon/Craig A. Evans (ed.), *The Quest for Context and Meaning* (Leiden: Brill, 1997), xxv–xxxvix. – Scholars that have taken up Sanders' approach include Mary Callaway, *Sing, O Barren One* (Atlanta: Scholars, 1986), Peter Pettit, *Shene'emar: The Place of Scripture Citation in the Mishna* (PhD dissertation: Claremont Graduate School, 1993), and James E. Brenneman, *Canons in Conflict: Negotiating Texts in True and False Prophecy* (Oxford: Oxford University, 1997), who expands Sanders' approach by taking into account community dynamics and power structures.

72 See e.g. James A. Sanders, "Dissenting Deities and Philippians 2:1–11," *JBL* 88 (1969), 279–290, "The Ethic of Election in Luke's Great Banquet Parable," in: J.L. Crenshaw/J.T. Willis (ed.), *Essays in Old Testament Ethics* (New York: Ktav, 1974), 245–271, "From Isaiah 61 to Luke 4," in: J. Neusner (ed.), *Christianity, Judaism, and other Greco-Roman Cults* I (Leiden: Brill, 1975), 75–106, "Torah and Paul," in: W.A. Meeks (ed.), *God's Christ and His People* (Oslo: Universitetsforlaget, 1977), "The Conversion of Paul," in: *A Living Witness of Oikodome* (Claremont: Disciples Seminary Foundation, 1982), 71–93, "A New Testament Hermeneutic Fabric: Psalm 118 in the Entrance Narrative," in: C.A. Evans/W.F. Stinespring (ed.), *Early Jewish and Christian Exegesis* (Atlanta: Scholars, 1987), 177–190, with Craig A. Evans, *Luke and Scripture: The Function of Sacred Tradition in Luke-Acts* (Minneapolis: Fortress, 1993), "Paul and Theological History," in: idem/C.A. Evans (ed.), *Paul and the Scripture of Israel* (Sheffield: JSOT Press, 1993), 98–117 and "Ναζωραῖος in Matthew 2.23," in: Craig A. Evans/W. Richard Stegner (ed.), *The Gospels and the Scriptures of Israel* (Sheffield: Sheffield Academic Press, 1994), 116–128, as well as the example discussed below in 2.2.2.

73 See Sanders' retrospective remarks in: James A. Sanders, "What's up now? Renewal of an Important Investigation," in: Lee M. McDonald/James H. Charlesworth (ed.), *Jewish and Christian Scriptures: The Function of "Canonical" and "Non-Canonical" Religious Texts* (London: T&T Clark, 2010), 1–7, 1. Sanders provides a similar review of his own scholarly career in relation to canonical criticism in "Scripture as Canon for Post-Modern Times," *Biblical Theology Bulletin* 26 (1995), 56–63. – See also his earlier contribution, "Cave 11 Surprises and the Question of Canon," in: D.N. Freedman/J.C. Greenfield (ed.), *New Directions in Biblical Archeology* (New York: Doubleday, 1969), 101–116. For the Psalms scroll, see: James A. Sanders, *The Dead Sea Psalms Scroll* (Ithaca: Cornell University, 1967) and idem, *Discoveries in the Judean Desert* 4 (Oxford: Clarendon, 1965). – See also Childs,

the formation of the canon of the Old Testament/Hebrew Bible. This study of the formation of the canon also led to the study of the question of the nature of canonicity itself, given that scant attention was being paid to the subject at the time. This is to say that the question regarding the dynamics of the use of a text in a different context than was obviously intended historically speaking, as is part and parcel of the functioning of canonical literature, was left without due attention.[74]

In Sanders' work, engaging these questions gave rise both to the field of "comparative midrash" and to theoretical reflecting on the recycling of texts, searching for meaning in them in new contexts, which influenced both the reception of older texts and the production of new ones. In interaction with insights from literary study, such as Kristeva's notion of *relecture*, a hermeneutical triangle was developed, which Sanders describes as follows:

> One angle of the triangle (#1) represents the older Scripture being cited or echoed, the second angle (#2) represents the historical/social situation the newer addressed; and the third (#3) represents the differing hermeneutics perceived in the later literature being compared.[75]

Thus, for Sanders, canonicity is an important aspect of biblical literature, both with regard to its authoring and its functioning; indeed, canonicity is, for him, part of the texts themselves. This will be further explored now, both regarding Sanders' hermeneutical approach and his exegetical practice. The latter will be achieved through the analysis of a sample exegesis.

2.2.1   *The Canonical Approach of James A. Sanders*

When comparing Sanders' method of canonical criticism to that of Childs, it will be observed that they share a significant similarity, namely that they want

---

"Reflections," 27, on the significance of the Qumran (and others) finds for the rekindling of the study of the canon.

74   Sanders, "What's," 2: "Still, it was important to deal with the issue of canon because no biblical discipline so far had done so. The focus shifted in our work to the problems arising out of how a piece of literature clearly intended by its authors to address one set of issues of a particular community went on to speak to other communities in other circumstances with quite different issues – the very nature of canonical literature." – See on the broader context and on the current situation e.g. Eileen Schuller, "The Dead Sea Scrolls and Canon and Canonization," in: Becker/Scholz (ed.), *Kanon*, 293–314.

75   Sanders, "What's," 3.

to relate the Bible again to the community of faith, and to take into account the canonical nature of the texts involved, i.e. the canon is not seen as something that was imposed upon the texts at a later stage, but as part and parcel of the texts themselves. In this way, Sanders, like Childs, does seek to correct a trend in biblical research dating back to, according to Sanders, Spinoza.[76] At the same time, there are also significant differences between the two scholars, as has often been noted.[77]

Sanders refers to his work on the canon as "canonical criticism" and considers it as one among the many subdisciplines of biblical studies. It is concerned with the dynamics of canonicity, i.e. the process of reception, application, rereception, collection of texts and traditions that are considered as authoritative, specifically in relation to the Bible as the book of the churches. Thus, rather than a history of the canon or a discussion of the authority of Scripture per se, canonical criticism aims at understanding the process that leads to a

---

76   See Sanders, "Scripture," 56–58.

77   See also, e.g. the following observations by Gorak, *Making* 40–41: "Childs reattaches to the idea of canon the narrative dimension described by Irenaeus and Augustine, the orderly canon of texts and religious practices which has aesthetic qualities we normally find in art. Similarly, for James A. Sanders, the Old Testament canon endures not as a collection of prohibitions "but because of its essential diversity, its own inherent refusal to absolutize any single stance as the only place where one might live under the sovereignty of God." When he emphasizes the experience of exile at the heart of the Jewish canon, Sanders conforms to the pattern of modern experience reported by a Kafka or a Raymond Williams. When he aligns *canon* with "the community's historic memory," he suggests its consonance with the deep hope for continuity in the midst of change that secular authorities from Mathew Arnold to Frank Kermode have associated with culture. When Sanders interprets canon as transmitting the eschatological fears and hopes of a particular community, he speaks of Scripture in terms that Northrop Frye and Walter Benjamin use to discuss the apocalyptic potential of art and mythology. Sanders' emphasis on its diversity not only validates the biblical canon for a plural society but renders it a potentially useful instrument for literary and cultural critics as well. Some of these critics may be surprised to hear the Bible described as "veritable textbook in contemporization of tradition." ...As a practitioner of what he calls "canonical criticism," Sanders discovers in the Bible the kinds of patterns earlier commentators found in church customs and laws. Sanders' canon conforms to the assumptions of a plural society, while the canons of Irenaeus, Gregory, and Augustin conform to their assumptions of a hierarchical universe. In both cases, however, the power of the canon lies in its ability to suggest the ultimate shape and destiny of Christian existence. All these writers agree that the Christian canon impresses on believers a set of values which scriptural narrative perpetually confirms," with which Sanders agrees in "Scripture," 61–62.

text becoming canonical and functioning as such.[78] As a result of his work on canonical criticism, he is able to state that "[t]he primary character of canon or authoritative tradition, whatever its quantity or extent, is its adaptability; its secondary character is its stability."[79] Sanders also moves beyond a primarily descriptive approach to the processes involved in a text's becoming canonical and functioning as canonical. For him, canonical criticism also leads to a particular hermeneutical position, that is to say: Having understood and reconstructed the dynamics involved in ancient canonicity, these very same dynamics should be used as a hermeneutical tool for the interpretation of the canonical texts, thereby doing justice both to their letter and to the spirit of the canonical process.[80]

This understanding of canonical criticism leads to a highly dynamic and creative approach to both biblical traditions and contemporary conventions, as Sanders puts it:

> Canonical criticism can liberate biblical study from the pervasive tendency to moralize upon reading all biblical texts thus absolutizing ancient Bronze Age or Iron Age or Hellenistic customs and mores. It stresses the ontology of the Bible as a paradigm of God's work from creation through re-creation out of which we may construct paradigms for our own works, rather than as a jewel box of ancient wisdom to be perpetuated. It seeks

---

78   Sanders, *Story*, 82: "Canonical criticism should be viewed as another sub-discipline of biblical criticism and complementary to the earlier developments. It takes seriously the authoritative function of the traditions that compose the Bible in the believing communities that shaped its various literary units, compiled and arranged its several parts in the conditions received, and continues to adapt its traditions in their ongoing lives. The Bible is the churches' book (in Christian terms) in every sense of the expression. The early believing communities created and shaped it and passed it down to their successors today – hence the term 'canonical criticism' and not history of canon."

79   Sanders, *Canon*, 83. – See also idem, "Adaptable for Life: The Nature and Function of the Canon," in: F.M. Cross/W.E. Lemke/P.D. Miller Jr. (ed.), *Magnalia Dei: The Mighty Acts of God* (New York: Doubleday, 1976), 531–560, as well as idem, "Stability and Fluidity in Text and Canon," in: C.J. Norton/S. Pisane (ed.), *Tradition of the Text: Studies Offered to Dominique Barthélemy in Celebration of His 70th Birthday* (Göttingen: Vandenhoeck & Ruprecht, 1991), 203–217.

80   Sanders, *Canon*, 83: "Hermeneutics is the midterm between canon's [sic] stability and its adaptability. Discerning the hermeneutics used by the ancient biblical thinkers and authors in adapting the early authoritative tradition to their contexts, for their people, is the essence of canonical criticism. And those hermeneutics cannot be discerned without as much knowledge as possible of the ancient historical (cultural, economic, political, etc.) contexts addressed. Hence, responsible use of all the tools available from biblical criticism is necessary."

the biblical hermeneutics whereby we may adapt the new wisdoms of our age just as they back then adapted the wisdom of the ancient Near East from many peoples.[81]

Building on his work on "comparative midrash," the development of the canon and the appertaining text (the "canonical process"), becomes of central importance, both theologically and hermeneutically, in Sanders' understanding of a canonical approach to Scripture. In this context, he understands "Midrash" in the broad sense of rereading old Scriptures for new situations. This approach differs significantly from that of Childs.[82]

In developing his theory with regard to this, building up on his work in comparative midrash and the functioning of sacred texts, he takes his point of departure in the historical observation that "a canon begins to *take shape* first and foremost because a question of identity or authority has arisen, and a canon begins to *become unchangeable* or invariable somewhat later, after the question of identity has for the most part been settled."[83] From this, Sanders deduces that "canonical criticism starts by defining the hermeneutics of that generation which gave the canon its basic shape."[84] Sanders' aim in doing "canonical criticism" is, on the one hand, to uncover the process that led to the canonization of particular texts and on the other hand, to find a way of using this process in the present. In other words, "to apply the Bible's own 'unrecorded hermeneutics,' which lie between the lines of most of its literature."[85] Thus, Sanders seeks to uncover a particular hermeneutical process that continues in the present.[86]

---

81   Sanders, *Canon*, 84.

82   As indeed noted by Sanders, see *Canon*, 101: see for Sanders' view of Childs' *Introduction to the Old Testament as Scripture:* Sanders, "Context."

83   Sanders, *Guide*, 21.

84   Sanders, *Guide*, 21.

85   Sanders, *Canon*, 46.

86   See: James M. Robinson, "Foreword," in: Weiss/Carr (ed.) *Gift*, 14–15, 14: "At the core of canonical criticism as developed by Sanders is the perception that to call a tradition, text, or collection of texts canonical or authoritative is to recognize that it is enmeshed in a symbiotic relationship with communities of believers to whom the tradition, text, or collection, 'gives life,' and who at the same time 'give life' to it. Canonical or authoritative materials give such communities life by providing a source for a communal identity that enables the establishment of maintenance of communal integrity in a particular historical context. The believing communities give life to such traditional materials as each new generation grants them authority to name the community's life, thus selecting, transmitting and elaborating them for succeeding generations." See in this volume also various studies interacting with the approach of Sanders.

In developing his model of canonical criticism, Sanders emphasizes both the historical fact of a process of the traditioning of authoritative texts and traditions and the continuation of such processes today, with all the pluralism that this implies.[87] This means both a full validation of the historical critical method *and* a recognition of the formative role of communities in the interpretation of texts. For this reason, Sanders is also able to integrate textual scholarship and canonical criticism. In fact, his work on the canon is a direct result of his work as a textual scholar.[88]

2.2.2 *Presentation of a Representative Exegesis*

The example of Sanders' (canonical) approach to the canonical gospels that will be considered here is an essay published in the 1990, concerning John 8:1–11, the *pericopa adulterae*. Specifically, the challenge put to Jesus in v. 5.[89] Right from the start, Sanders notes a number of problems that are all related to the interface between the canon, canonical process, exegesis, and to some extent also to textual criticism, which makes the passage a good test case for canonical exegesis as understood by Sanders, given that it raises all sorts of questions concerning its form, its place in the canon of Scripture, its function in its literary context, what Jesus wrote in the sand, and the fact that, although text-critically dubious, it has survived in the Christian tradition.

In his exegesis of the pericope, Sanders starts off with some form-critical observations that allow him to structure the narrative as well, namely, following a transitory passage in John 7:53–8:2, in three scenes: 8:3–6a, identified as a "controversy passage," 8:6–9a, identified as a "prophetic symbolic act," and 8:9b–11, which is a "concluding scene."[90] Next, Sanders gives a paraphrase of the contents of John 8:1–11, noting how, instead of an argument based on the Law, in Jesus' case "a prophetic and symbolic act thwarts the controversy raised

---

87   See e.g. Sanders, "Scripture," 61–62; the ultimate meaning of the text is eschatological for Sanders.

88   See: James A. Sanders, "Text and Canon: Concepts and Method," in: idem, *Story*, 125–151 (published earlier in *JBL* 98 [1979], 5–29, as Sanders' 1978 SBL presidential address).

89   James A. Sanders, "'Nor do I...': A Canonical Reading of the Challenge to Jesus in John 8," in: B.R. Gaventa/R.T. Fortna (ed.), *The Conversation Continues: Studies in Paul and John in Honor of J. Louis Martyn* (Nashville: Abingdon, 1990), 337–347. – On Sanders' view of the gospels and the canonical process at large, see his earlier contribution "The Gospels and the Canonical Process: A Response to Lou H. Silberman," in: W.O. Walker Jr. (ed.), *The Relationships Among the Gospels: An Interdisciplinary Dialogue* (San Antonio: Trinity University, 1978), 219–236.

90   Sanders, "Reading," 336–339.

by the Pharisees."[91] To be sure, this controversy was introduced by Pharisees who must have been very certain of their case in this setting, especially against the backdrop of John 7, where a failed attempt to arrest Jesus is narrated. Subsequently, Sanders discusses in which context the pericope fits best, which may be seen as a comment on the canonical context of this particular text:

> The question of which Gospel most enhances the point of the story seems almost to be a non-question. While it is true that the story is syn-optic in tone and vocabulary, includes non-Johannine expressions, and may well have circulated independently or in another now lost context before being attached either to John (after 7:36, after 7:52, or after 21:25), or to Luke (after 21:38 or after 24:53), or omitted from the New Testament altogether (the majority of manuscripts and early witnesses), one must say that nowhere else is the story's main point so enhanced as in the con-text of John 7 and 8. The prophetic charge in 7:19 that no one keeps the law would be contextually sufficient to highlight the story. That charge is variously complemented: In 7:24 by the challenge not to judge by appear-ances; in 7:51 by Nicodemus' question about a fair and just hearing before a condemnation; in 8:13 by the charge that "you are your own witnesses;" in 8:15 by the charge that "you pass judgment by human standards; I judge no one;" in 8:18 by the affirmation that "I give testimony on my own behalf and the Father...gives testimony for me;" and finally in 8:21, 24 and 46 that Jesus' interlocutors, in contrast to himself, are sinful indeed.[92]

Having argued this, Sanders goes on to state that there are three aspects of the story that may be helpfully analyzed by means of the "method of Canonical Criticism:" (1) "the question of what understanding of Jesus' writing would most advance the thrust of the story;" (2) "the question of the significance of a prophetic symbolic act as the response Jesus chooses to the challenges by the Scribes and Pharisees;" (3) "the issue of the canonical context and hermeneu-tics by which to understand Jesus' response."[93] Sanders proceeds to discuss them all.

To begin with, Sanders discusses the question of Jesus' writing with his fin-ger in the dust – Sanders emphasizes all three elements: Writing as such, writ-ing in the dust, and writing with a finger. He does so by considering a number of possible intertextual connections. For example, he points out (a) a "midrashic

91   Sanders, "Reading," 339, see also 340.
92   Sanders, "Reading," 340.
93   Sanders, "Reading," 340–341.

reference to Jer. 7:13: 'O Lord, the hope of Israel, all who abandon thee will be ashamed; those who turn away from thee shall be written in the earth..., for they have abandoned a spring of living water, the Lord;'" (b) references to Exodus 23:1b ("You shall not join hands with the wicked to act as a malicious witness") and 23:7 ("Keep far from a false charge, and do not kill the innocent and those in the right, for I will not acquit the guilty"); (c) a link with the Susanna-narrative in Daniel (an indication that Sanders is open to the LXX canon), specifically in relation to the ninth commandment;[94] (d) a connection with Daniel 5:24, specifically with the writing on the wall mentioned there.[95] Sanders rejects all of these intertexts, and states that the intertexts that suit Jesus' writing in the dust with his finger best are Deut. 9:10 and/or Ex. 31:18, the hinge is especially God's writing with a finger in these passages. All this "would indicate that Jesus was scratching some form of the Decalogue 'in the ground.'"[96] In this context, Sanders makes reference to early (rabbinic) traditions surrounding the abbreviation of the "Ten Commandments" that could serve to provide a (historical) context for Jesus' behavior in John 8:1–11. The focus remains on the Decalogue, then, rather than on a particular commandment. For Sanders, referring to an interpretation of Jesus' kneeling twice in order to write in terms of his writing two "tablets," an interpretation becomes plausible that confronts Jesus' audience with the full weight of the two tables with each five commandments, making it impossible for them to escape the awareness of their own sinfulness. To this observation, Sanders adds, by way of narrative (and historical) contextualization that the story is set at the climax of the Jewish high holidays, in which human sinfulness and the study of Torah play such an important role.[97]

Having argued this, Sanders moves on to a discussion of the broader canonical setting and context of John 8:1–11, arguing that there are canonical dimensions that have not yet been recognized. Specifically, this concerns the relationship between law, lawgivers, and the latter's keeping of the law (or not), as "[t]he Torah and the Prophets very realistically demonstrate time and

---

94   Sanders, "Reading," 341.

95   Sanders, "Reading," 341–342.

96   Sanders, "Reading," 342.

97   Sanders, "Reading," 343: "[t]he story is set on the morrow of the celebration of *Shemini 'Azaret*, the climax of the high holy days when both human sinfulness and joy in Torah are brought to mind in the most poignant of ways at *Rosh ha-Shanah, Yom Kippur,* and *Succot.* Consciousness raising about general human sinfulness precisely by contemplating Torah, as Jesus is presented as doing, would not be difficult; and this unbelabored, cursory, abbreviated reminder summarizes the significance of the whole."

again how those charged with administering law were themselves sinners."[98] This background, Sanders argues, is what Jesus evokes by his writing with his finger in the dust, making the "universal human point that those whose responsibility it is to execute justice in any society may simply be unindicted trespassers themselves, not yet "caught" as the woman had been."[99] Thus, Jesus in fact plays the role of one of the prophets of old, taking the side of the poor, and, in particular, reaching out to sinners, or even identifying with them, as the prophets had identified with them.[100] Therefore, when Jesus says that he does not condemn the woman either, "[t]he story is open to the interpretation that Jesus, perhaps like Isaiah, was a man of unclean lips living among a people of unclean lips. Jesus, being himself without sin, according to the gospel tradition at this point in its development, still would not cast the stone."[101] Thus, Jesus continues a prophetic tradition, specifically one consisting of "[c]riticism of applying the law by those charged with its administration, and even criticism of points of the law itself."[102] To this, Sanders adds a further layer of historical and theological reflection by arguing that one of the distinctions between true and false prophecy in biblical tradition is that, unlike false prophecy, true prophecy always underlined God's identity as both creator and redeemer, thus safeguarding his freedom as sovereign Lord of all.[103] In John 8 (and related controversy passages in the gospels), Jesus continues this line of thought, by indicating through his actions and words that God is free to forgive sinners and is, unlike human beings, above the law. God follows God's own agenda of grace (which from a human point of view may look like injustice), rather than the agenda of those that are in charge of the administration of sacred tradition and law.[104] Subsequently, after noting that this story does not abolish the Law or the

---

98   Sanders, "Reading," 343.

99   Sanders, "Reading," 343.

100   Sanders, "Reading," 343–344.

101   Sanders, "Reading," 344.

102   Sanders, "Reading," 344.

103   See on prophecy also: James A. Sanders, "Hermeneutics of True and False Prophecy," in: G.W. Coats/B.O. Long (ed.), *Canon and Authority: Essays in Old Testament and Authority* (Philadelphia: Fortress, 1977), 21–41.

104   Sanders, "Reading," 345: "God is free to forgive sinners. God only is above the law, not humans. As good theology has long recognized, from a human point of view grace may seem to be a form of divine injustice. While God's promises are sure, God is free to judge and forgive whom God wills. In the Prophets and the Gospels God's freedom to follow God's own agenda, and not the agenda of those charged institutionally with administration of law and tradition, is equally stressed."

administrators of law, Sanders ends on a note about the canonicity of John 8:1–11, for which he adduces a theological rationale:

> Seen in the light of a pervasive canonical wrestling, in both testaments, with the realities of human life, this poignant story, without prejudice to its actual provenance or historicity, deserves inclusion – whether with or without brackets, asterisks, or obeli – in the Fourth Gospel right where the Codex Cantebrigiensis and later manuscripts place it – both for its sake and for the sake of the message of the Gospel.[105]

2.2.3   *Analysis*

When turning to an analysis of the above sample of Sanders' exegesis, the following observations may be made, following the four sub-questions as they were outlined above.[106]

First, with regard to Sanders' understanding of the canon and the notion of "canonical exegesis" (or in the case of Sanders: "Canonical criticism"), a number of things may be said. The question of the canon in terms of a list of books does not play a role of major importance in the example of Sanders' New Testament exegesis that was considered here (even though his reference to the Susanna-narrative from the book of Daniel at least suggests openness to the LXX-canon). However, given the fact that it is an example of New Testament exegesis, one may relatively safely assume the generally accepted New Testament canon as far as lists of books are involved. However, a focus on this question alone would also mean to miss the point that Sanders makes in general, in his canonical approach and specifically in this essay. First, Sanders places much emphasis on the development of various canons and is less interested in the creation of one valid canon (which would invalidate all others). Second, the text that Sanders has chosen for his exegesis is a text that is on the brink of the canon, given that its position in the New Testament text is much disputed. Sanders' exegesis, therefore, is a very good example of what he means with the canonical process that continues even after the "conclusion" of the canon, in this case because the canonical text has remained alive, so to speak. Given that Sanders' canonical approach originated in his work as a tex-

---

105   Sanders, "Reading," 345 – See for considerations about a somewhat analogous case, the longer ending of Mark, also Camille Focant, "La canonicité de la finale longue (Mc 16, 9–20) vers la reconnaissance d'un double texte canonique?" in: Auwers/De Jonge (ed.), *Canons*, 587–297.

106   See above, 1.1.

tual scholar is of special significance: For Sanders, the development of the text and with that of the canon is in principle open-ended, or even eschatologically oriented, just as the interpretation (through the canonical process) of Scripture is.[107] Unlike others, Sanders is not a theologian of the finalized text or canon, he is one of a living text and a canon that continues to develop its form and meaning. Beyond this, however, Sanders does apply some other aspects of canonicity to his exegesis. For example, he makes decisions with regard to his choice of intertexts with which he brings John 8:1–11 into conversation: It turns out that these are texts from the canon of the Old Testament and from non-canonical materials, such as rabbinic texts. He thus privileges these texts with regard to the interpretative process. Here, Sanders operates with a different canon of sorts, i.e. of texts that he understands to be of particular relevance for the interpretation of the (New Testament) text at hand.

With regard to the second sub-question, "what sort of understanding of 'canon' and 'canonical exegesis' is being used," a relatively straightforward answer can be given. Sanders operates with the notion of an evolving canon that can take on different forms and meanings in interaction with the community of interpretation to which it belongs. This "canonical process" has its roots in Sanders' understanding of "comparative midrash" with the hermeneutical triangle (text, context, hermeneutical rule) that was outlined above. The canonical process plays a major role in the example of his exegesis of a gospel text as it was considered above. While Sanders uses on the one hand, and quite uncontroversially, various canonical texts to elucidate the meaning of John 8:1–11, he also appeals to the canonical process and its characteristics drawing his final exegetical conclusions, which is a much less common way of proceeding. Specifically, Sanders takes recourse to an outline of a canonical process with regard to the interpretation of the law and the call to faithfulness to it, by prophets in particular, vis-à-vis those charged with guarding the law and administering it with righteousness. With regard to this, he discerns a canonical hermeneutic at play in which texts are re-contextualized and read in a new way under new circumstances in order to safeguard the notion that law leads to justice and not to its abuse. On this basis, Sanders is able to argue that, despite its highly uncertain textual status, John 8:1–11 ought to remain part of the New Testament canon, given that it stands in the tradition of this canonical hermeneutics of the reinterpretation of the law in order to ascertain that justice is achieved.

Therefore, with regard to the third sub-question ("how is this approach applied, i.e. what sort of role does the canon play in the exegesis?"), Sanders does not use a canon as such in his exegesis, as he makes use of the canonical

---

107   See e.g. Sanders, "Scripture," 61–62.

process, or the canonical hermeneutics that he has identified in his study of the formation and interpretation of scripture at large. The canon (in whatever form) is both the product of (a particular stage of) this canonical process and also its new starting point. With regard to Sanders' exegesis of John 8:1–11, this means that based on the canonical process due to which John 8:1–11 may have come into being, and because of its agreement with a main strand of dynamics within the (already existing) canon, it can be made part of the canonical text, thus providing a starting point for a next round of the canonical process (the stages which, to be sure, can never be as neatly separated from one another as it would seem they are here).

A very clear answer can be given with regard to the fourth sub-question, "what effect does it have on the outcome of the exegesis, i.e. how is the canon appealed to in order to make decisions about interpretation and meaning?" Sanders makes a direct appeal to the canon twice, once in order to establish, in a relatively common way, the most likely intertextual connections of John 8:1–11, and once in order to argue, based on the canonical process, for the inclusion of the pericope into the Gospel of John. As was noted, the latter is distinctive of Sanders' approach, whose understanding of canonicity does not depend much on a formal or factual closure of the canon (an impossibility for him), or even on formal text critical arguments, but on a text's agreement with (aspects of) the innercanonical hermeneutics of the Scriptures.

In line with the previous paragraph, it may also be clear that, for Sanders' exegesis, the heuristic and epistemological value of his canonical approach (as the fourth sub-question addresses it) consists of the discovery of appropriate intertextual connections. This is both in order to facilitate the interpretation of the text at hand, and to argue an interpretative case based on a particular aspect of the content and theological characteristics of the canonical process and the hermeneutics that can be found in the canonical scriptures.

2.2.4   Conclusions

For Sanders, canonicity in relation to exegesis has two main aspects. On the one hand, his "canonical criticism" is the academic study of the processes of canonization and of the functioning of canonical literature in new contexts, particularly in relation to the production of new (potentially canonical) texts on the basis of earlier canonical texts. The field of "comparative midrash" is dedicated to this kind of research, to which Sanders has contributed substantially. This kind of research, a sub-discipline of biblical studies, also takes into account the relationship between the community and the (canonical) texts when it comes to the re-adaptation of such texts for new contexts. By drawing attention to these aspects of canonical texts, Sanders has helped to place the canon back onto the scholarly agenda and to recognize that canonicity (both in the sense of being canonical and having canonical claims, i.e. being oriented towards authoritative texts and their reception) is, in many instances, a very real aspect of the texts themselves and not a concept that was imposed upon the texts at a later stage. On the other hand, as became apparent in the example of Sanders' exegesis, which was discussed above, the kind of canonical hermeneutics, i.e. hermeneutical tendencies that can be found in the authoritative texts of Christianity, also have consequences for the way in which these texts continue to be received and adapted to new circumstances. At the very least, Sanders is able to argue for the inclusion of a historically clearly secondary pericope into the canonical Gospel of John, based on his observation that it continues the canonical hermeneutics present in Scripture in a legitimate way. The boundaries between Scripture and tradition, therefore, also seem to be relatively porous in Sanders' approach and interpretation, or rather: The discovery of the meaning of Scripture is principally open-ended (until the eschaton). The discussion of Sanders' theory and exegetical practice here also gives reason to think that the distinction between his "canonical criticism" (i.e. an exegetical sub-discipline) and Childs' "canonical approach" (an overall approach to the texts) is, at least in actual practice, limited Sanders' canonical criticism also offers a total vision of the text and how it ought to be read in order to do it justice and understand it adequately.

2.3   Peter Stuhlmacher

Peter Stuhlmacher (*1932), a Lutheran scholar, lastly of the University of Tübingen, is the next canonical critic that will be considered. He published a large number of works,[108] ranging from a work on New Testament hermeneutics, published

---

108   See the bibliography in: Jostein Ådna/Scott J. Hafemann/Otfried Hofius (ed.), *Evangelium – Schriftauslegung – Kirche* (FS Peter Stuhlmacher, Göttingen: Vandenhoeck & Ruprecht, 1997), 419–438, as well as the thematic overview given by Daniel Graf, *Unterwegs zu einer Biblischen Theologie: Perspektiven der Konzeption von Peter Stuhlmacher* (Göttingen: Vandenhoeck & Ruprecht, 2011), 25–28, and his bibliography on 341–346. Graf also studies the development of Stuhlmacher's work, not least as it is reflected in various editions of the work of Stuhlmacher; here, focus will be on the latest phase of Stuhlmacher's work, in which he also produced his full-scale theology of the New Testament, rather than on its development.

in 1979,[109] by way of a full-scale New Testament theology,[110] to more topical studies and collections of sermons[111] and essays,[112] a brief outline of how to do biblical theology,[113] and finally, a number of commentaries.[114] During his long career, Stuhlmacher served at the University of Erlangen-Nürnberg and especially at his *alma mater*, the University of Tübingen.[115]

Even though Stuhlmacher's approach can be termed tradition-historical,[116] there are good reasons to regard him as a canonically oriented exegete. For example, Ulrich Luz considers him as such, by noting that the interrelatedness of both parts of the Christian canon is a central concern in Stuhlmacher's work, as are the question of the rule of faith and the quest for a hermeneutics that can do justice to the unique character of the Bible and to the expectations that its readers bring to it.[117] There is, therefore, good reason to consider

---

109 Peter Stuhlmacher, *Vom Verstehen des Neuen Testaments. Eine Hermeneutik* (Göttingen: Vandenhoeck & Ruprecht, 1979; 2nd edition: 1986) – See also the earlier work *Schriftauslegung auf dem Weg zur biblischen Theologie* (Göttingen, Vandenhoeck & Ruprecht, 1975). On his hermeneutical approach, see also e.g. Hans Weder, "Einverständnis. Eine Überlegung zur Peter Stuhlmachers Hermeneutik," in: Ådna/Hafemann/Hofius (ed.), *Evangelium*, 403–418.

110 Peter Stuhlmacher, *Biblische Theologie des Neuen Testaments* I–II (Göttingen: Vandenhoeck & Ruprecht, 2005). See also his two earlier studies idem, *Gerechtigkeit Gottes bei Paulus* (Göttingen: Vandenhoeck & Ruprecht, 1965), and idem, *Das paulinische Evangelium. I. Vorgeschichte* (Göttingen: Vandenhoeck & Ruprecht, 1968).

111 See e.g. Peter Stuhlmacher, *Jesus von Nazareth – Christus des Glaubens* (Stuttgart: Calwer, 1988), *Was geschah auf Golgatha?* (Stuttgart: Calwer, 1998), with Theo Sorg, *Das Wort vom Kreuz. Zur Predigt am Karfreitag* (Stuttgart: Calwer, 1996), *Die Verkündigung des Christus Jesus* (Wuppertal: Theologische Verlagsgemeinschaft, 2003), *Die Geburt des Immanuel. Die Weihnachtsgeschichten aus dem Lukas- und Matthäusevangelium* (Göttingen: Vandenhoeck & Ruprecht, 2005), *Das Evangelium von der Versöhnung in Christus* (Stuttgart: Calwer, 1979).

112 See Peter Stuhlmacher, *Biblische Theologie und Evangelium. Gesammelte Aufsätze* (Tübingen: Mohr Siebeck, 2002), with Helmut Claß (ed.), *Versöhnung, Gesetz und Gerechtigkeit. Aufsätze zur biblischen Theologie* (Göttingen: Vandenhoeck & Ruprecht, 1998).

113 Peter Stuhlmacher, *Wie treibt man Biblische Theologie?* (Neukirchen-Vluyn: Neukirchener Verlag, 1995).

114 Peter Stuhlmacher, *Der Brief an Philemon* (Neukirchen-Vluyn: Neukirchener Verlag, [3]2004 [1975]), idem, *Der Brief an die Römer* (Göttingen: Vandenhoeck & Ruprecht, [15]1998 [1989]).

115 For a biographical sketch, see: Graf, *Unterwegs*, 19–25. – Graf, *o.c.*, 1–245, also considers various theological and philosophical discussion partners of Stuhlmacher.

116 See e.g. Söding, "Entwürfe," 78–80.

117 Ulrich Luz, "Kanonische Exegese und Hermeneutik der Wirkungsgeschichte," in: Hans Gerny/Harald Rein/Maja Weyermann (ed.), *Die Wurzel aller Theologie: Sentire cum Ecclesia* (FS Urs von Arx; Bern: Stämpfli, 2003), 40–57, 40: "Für Peter Stuhlmacher...steht die Zusammengehörigkeit der beiden Testamente in dem einen christlichen Kanon im Vordergrund des Interesses. Aber es geht ihm nicht nur um die 'Beurteilung des kanonischen Prozesses

Stuhlmacher a canonical critic, given his fundamental orientation towards the canonical Scriptures *qua* canonical Scriptures, and his intention to take their canonical claim to authority and their relationship to the life and faith of the church seriously.[118] Stuhlmacher relates all of these topics explicitly to the canonical character of the Scriptures of the Old and New Testaments, which can only be understood properly, according to him, when their canonical character is taken into account; this is an aspect of the texts themselves.[119] Having outlined this, it is now possible to turn to an outline of his approach and an example of his exegesis. As with the discussion of all five approaches considered in this study, the focus will be on Stuhlmacher's own work principally, rather than on the (lively) discussion surrounding it; this discussion will first take into account his hermeneutical theory and then his exegetical practice by analyzing a sample exegesis of a New Testament text.

2.3.1 *The Canonical Approach of Stuhlmacher*

Between the publication of the first and second volumes of his *Biblische Theologie des Neuen Testaments* in 1992 and 1999, and well after the publication of the first edition of his main hermeneutical work (1979),[120] Stuhlmacher

---

und des aus ihm hervorgegangenen zweiteiligen christlichen Kanons,' sondern ebenso sehr um zwei weitere Fragen. Da ist mal die Frage nach dem κανών τῆς πίστεως ('Richtschnur des Glaubens'), welche die Alte Kirche mit dem Hinweis auf die Glaubensregel, die Reformation mit dem Hinweise auf Christus als Mitte der Schrift beantwortet hat. Seine dritte Frage ist die nach den besonderen Auslegungsweisen, welche die Bibel als kanonisches Buch seinen Auslegerinnen und Auslegern nahelegt, d.h. um die Frage nach einer besonderen, der Bibel als Kanon entsprechenden Hermeneutik. In ihr muss der ganze besondere Anspruch der biblischen Texte, 'eine Wahrheit zu bezeugen, welche aller menschlichen Erkenntnis voraus und überlegen ist,' aufgenommen und reflektiert werden.' The references in this quotation are to Stulmacher, *Theologie* II, 287, 323. – Ulrich Luz' own *Theologische Hermeneutik des Neuen Testaments* (Göttingen: Vandenhoeck & Ruprecht, 2014), appeared to late to be taken into consideration in this study.

118   See e.g. Stuhlmacher, *Theologie* I, 1–12, idem, "Der Kanon und seine Auslegung," in: idem, *Theologie und Evangelium*, 167–190, as well as the discussion by Graf, *Unterwegs*, 252–257.

119   See also Stuhlmacher, *Theologie* II, 322–336; his two-volume biblical theology of the New Testament, therefore begins and ends with hermeneutical considerations closely related to the role of the canon in exegesis and biblical theology. – Other, newer theologies of the New Testament that have appeared in German include Ferdinand Hahn, *Theologies des Neuen Testaments* I–III (Göttingen: Vandenhoeck & Ruprecht, 1990–1995), and Ulrich Wilckens, *Theologie des Neuen Testaments* I–II (Neukirchen-Vluyn: Neukirchener Verlag, 2002–2009) are much less explicitly oriented towards the canon.

120   See Stuhlmacher, *Verstehen.*

published a brief volume entitled *Wie treibt man biblische Theologie*.[121] As this presents, in a compact way, Stuhlmacher's main concerns and theses, it will serve here as a guide to his approach. It will show how Stuhlmacher seeks to combine insights of both ecclesial and historical-critical approaches to the interpretation of Scripture.[122] In this booklet, Stuhlmacher immediately outlines what he understands as the one main task of biblical theology and its three subordinate tasks. The main task of biblical theology is, according to Stuhlmacher, to unearth the original sense and the theological claims of the biblical texts. From this main task, three other tasks can be deduced. First, to practice a hermeneutical approach that is characterized by a receptive acceptance as well as by an identification with the texts and by a desire to get to know the reality that is presented to the reader by the texts. Second, to defend the texts whenever they are threatened by historical or dogmatic lack of expertise. Third, the exegete is called upon to engage the texts theologically.[123]

When considering his approach further, it appears that Stuhlmacher has much faith in sound historical and philological research in order to achieve the aims mentioned above, as well as the aim of unearthing a continuous, consistent, and reliable early Christian tradition in the New Testament writings.[124] Therefore, Stuhlmacher states that he has little time for a preoccupation with systematic-theological questions of interpretation or, what he considers to be

---

121   See also the English translation: *How to Do Biblical Theology* (Allison Park: Pickwick, 1995), here.

122   See e.g. Graf, *Unterwegs*, 154: "Durch Peter Stuhlmachers hermeneutische Arbeiten zieht sich wie ein roter Faden die Frage nach einer sowohl wissenschaftlich als auch kirchlich verantworteten Schriftauslegung." More specifically, Graf, *o.c.*, 145, notes "dass es Stuhlmacher um eine Verbindung von kirchlich-evangelikaler Frömmigkeit und wissenschaftlich-historisch-kritischer Exegese geht."

123   Stuhlmacher, *Wie*, 8–9: "Da Biblische Theologie meines Erachtens die Hauptaufgabe hat, den historischen Ursprungssinn und theologischen Anspruch der biblischen Texte herauszuarbeiten, wachsen ihr in dieser Situation drei Zusatzaufgaben zu: Sie muß bei der Exegese der Bibeltexte eine Hermeneutik einüben, die bestimmt ist von der annehmenden Anerkennung, vom historischen Sich-Identifizieren und vom Erlernen der Wirklichkeit, die die Tradition zu erkennen gibt; sie muß die ihr anvertrauten Texte in Schutz nehmen, wo immer historischer oder auch dogmatischer Unverstand sie verdunkelt; sie darf schließlich nicht scheuen, theologische Kritik zu üben, wo aus dem Blick gerät, daß die in einer Identitätskrise steckenden evangelischen Kirchen nur noch so lange Existenzrecht gegenüber den katholischen haben, als sie ernsthaft versuchen, creatura verbi zu sein und zu bleiben."

124   See with regard to this also Graf, *Unterwegs*, 271–302, on Stuhlmacher's view of unity and diversity in the New Testament.

the postmodern irrelevance of a historical original sense of a text.[125] In terms of hermeneutics, this means for Stuhlmacher a hermeneutic of consent or agreement ("Einverständnis"), which he has developed in various steps. His eventual position entails that a biblical theology of the New Testament has to be in hermeneutical agreement with the texts that it seeks to interpret, i.e. the texts need to be interpreted in the way in which they want to be interpreted. This means that the texts cannot only be read as historical sources, but also need to be read as witnesses to the faith that are part of the Holy Scriptures of Christianity. Historical and dogmatic theological perspectives both need to be involved in the interpretative process; the question of the interrelationship between the Old and New Testaments is, in this context, of much significance.[126] With regard to the latter question, Stuhlmacher defends a pronounced thesis that has programmatic value for his own biblical theology of the New Testament, given that he argues that Christian theology needs to be aware of the fact that Old and New Testament have belonged together in an intimate way since the inception of the Church. As a result, the New Testament cannot be understood without the Old Testament, while the Old Testament remains incomplete without the New Testament.[127]

---

125   Stuhlmacher, *Wie*, 9.

126   Stuhlmacher, *Wie*, 13: "Eine Biblische Theologie des Neuen Testaments, die mit Recht diesen Namen trägt, muß den biblischen Texten hermeneutisch entsprechen, d.h. sie muß sie sich bemühen, die alt- und neutestamentliche Überlieferung so auszulegen, wie sie selbst ausgelegt werden will. Sie darf die ihr vorgegebenen Texte deshalb nicht nur aus kritischer Distanz als historische Quellen lesen, sondern muß sie gleichzeitig als Glaubenszeugnisse interpretieren, die zur Heiligen Schrift der Christenheit gehören. Dementsprechend überschneiden sich bei der Abfassung einer Biblischen Theologie des Alten oder Neuen Testaments (oder auch zu beiden Testamenten gleichzeitig) historische und dogmatische Gesichtspunkte. Außerdem steht von Anfang an die schwierige und bis heute offene Frage zur Debatte, wie sich Altes und Neues Testament zueinander verhalten."– For the development of Stuhlmacher's understanding of "Einverständnis," see Graf, *Unterwegs*, 109–156, noting that Stuhlmacher develops this concept into the direction of a primary exegetical attitude of listening to the texts. See also the brief sketch by Zwiep, *Tekst*, 162–164.

127   Stuhlmacher, *Wie*, 14–15: "Für die christliche Theologie ist es...an der Zeit, sich auf die Tatsache zu besinnen, *daß Altes und Neues Testament vom Anfang der christlichen Kirche an aufs engste zusammengehört haben. Der Zusammenhalt ist so groß, daß man das Zeugnis des Neuen Testaments ohne das des Alten nicht angemessen verstehen kann und die Auslegung des Alten Testaments ohne Blick auf das Neue unvollständig bleibt.*"(Italics in original). He further elaborates and substantiates this position on 15–24, notably emphasizing the canonical process and the importance of the Septuagint to a much larger extent than Childs. See for his sketch of Stuhlmacher's view of the emergence of the canon, see: idem, *o.c.*, 60–68, concluding as follows: "Während der Streit um den Rang der

Stuhlmacher also considers the question of the "Mitte der Schrift," the (theological) center of Scripture, noting that while this question has only been asked with some intensity since the Reformation, it had in fact already been answered in the early church by means of the *regula fidei*.[128] From the perspective of this old tradition, he notes that some modern discussions about and approaches to the question of the center of Scripture are deficient in three ways: (a) Those refusing to determine such a center overlook the fact that some parts of Scripture are more important than others and that such an approach can never lead to a clear statement of doctrine; (b) attempts that seek to find both a New Testament and an Old Testament "Mitte der Schrift" overlook the fact that both corpora came into existence as part of one and the same canonical process; and (c) proposals that come down to declaring Pauline theology to be the true center of Scripture also miss the mark.[129] With these caveats in mind, Stuhlmacher proceeds to formulate his own center of Scripture, seeking to do justice to both Testaments, which is best quoted here in his own words:

> Der eine Gott, der die Welt geschaffen und Israel zu seinem Eigentumsvolk erwählt hat, hat in der Sendung, dem Werk, dem Tod, und der Auferweckung seines eingeborenen Sohnes Jesus Christus ein für allemal genuggetan für die Rettung von Juden und Heiden. Jesus Christus ist Herr und Hoffnung der ganzen Schöpfung. Wer an ihn als den Versöhner und Herrn glaubt und seiner Weisung gehorcht, darf der Teilhabe an der Herrschaft Gottes gewiß sein.[130]

Septuaginta-Apokryphen bis heute ungeschlichtet geblieben ist, gibt es über den Kernbestand des Alten und des Neuen Testament keine ernst zu nehmenden Auseinandersetzungen mehr. Es herrscht heute sogar unter evangelischen und katholischen Theologen Einigkeit darüber, daß die Kirchen die Bibel nicht einfach selbst geschaffen haben, sondern daß die biblische Offenbarung die treibende Kraft des kanonischen Prozesses war. *Die aus diesem Prozeß hervorgegangene Heilige Schrift aus Altem und Neuen Testament muß darum auch den Vorrang vor aller kirchlichen Lehre behalten."* (68).

128 Stuhlmacher, *Wie*, 68–69. See further also: Graf, *Unterwegs*, 289–294.

129 Stuhlmacher, *Wie*, 69–70.

130 Stuhlmacher, *Wie*, 70–71; italics in original. Stuhlmacher refers for support to the following texts: NT: John 11:25–26, 14:6, I John 2:1–2, 4:9–10, Rom. 1:1–6, 1:16–17 with 3:21–31, and I Tim. 2:5–6; OT: Exod. 20:1–6, Deut. 6:4–5, Hos. 11:8–9, Isa. 7:9, 9:5–6, 25:6–9, 43:1–7, 52:13–53:12, Jer. 31:31–34, Ps. 139:1–17, Prov. 8:22–36. On P. 24, Stuhlmacher also offers a formulation of the center of the New Testament: "Das Zentrum des Neuen Testaments, die Botschaft von Jesus Christus, ist durch und durch alttestamentlich formuliert und bezeugt das von dem einen Gott für Juden und Heiden gewirkte endzeitliche Heil. Dieses Zeugnis bindet das Neue Testament unlöslich an das Alte. Das Alte Testament gehört aufgrund dieser christologischen Klammer Juden und Christen gleichermaßen, und das Evangelium Gottes

For the actual interpretation of Scripture, six points are of central importance for Stuhlmacher, which are all related to his hermeneutics of consent and what he calls a biblical epistemology ("biblischer Erkenntnisweg").[131]

(1)   This biblical epistemology has two poles: (a) Prov. 1:7 ("The fear of the LORD is the beginning of knowledge; fools despise wisdom and instruction"): the mystery of God both makes human knowledge possible and determines its boundaries; and (b) Gal. 4:9 and 1 Cor. 13:13: God's knowledge of a human being precedes a human being's knowledge of God. This leads to an understanding of revelation with a strong pneumatological emphasis, given that the Spirit is part of "biblical epistemology." These considerations have their basis in the following conviction: "Man kann die Wahrheit der biblischen Texte nur ergründen und zur Mitte der Schrift nur vordringen, wenn man den biblischen Erkenntnisweg beachtet und gebührend berücksichtigt, daß diese Texte inhaltlich vor allem (Offenbarungs-) Weisheit mitteilen wollen, deren Wahrheitsgehalt erst dann voll ermessen werden kann, wenn er anerkannt und gelebt wird."[132]

(2)   The New Testament authors regard the "Holy Scriptures" as inspired and wish to have them interpreted in the spirit of the faith, which, already in the New Testament, was also applied to the witness of Jesus and the apostles.

(3)   As a consequence of the former point, authentic exegesis can only take place when the exegete participates in the same spirit that also permeates the various texts and traditions, while an interpretation can only be heard properly when the Spirit opens up the recipient for this. For New Testament authors, the logical place for such exegesis is the spirit-filled community of Jesus Christ, i.e. the church.

(4)   The third point can boast an impressive pedigree, including the early church, the Reformers, and Vatican II, specifically *Dei Verbum* 3.12 (esp.: "Holy Scripture must be read and interpreted in the sacred spirit in which it was written").

(5)   For contemporary exegesis, this means that these (Scriptural) rules for Scriptural interpretation need to be followed. As a consequence, historical

---

von Jesus Christus richtet sich "zuerst an den Juden, aber auch an den Griechen" (Röm 11, 16). Es lädt zu dem Bekenntnis ein, daß Jesus der Herr ist, den Gott von den Toten auferweckt hat (Röm 10, 9–10), und an diesem Bekenntnis entscheidet sich für Juden und Heiden ihre endzeitliche Rettung."

131   On the development of which, see: Graf, *Unterwegs*, 145–153.

132   Stuhlmacher, *Wie*, 72.

research as such, however important, is not sufficient, and analytical findings cannot be the final product of exegesis, but both exegetical findings and, by consequence, the exegetes need to become witnesses themselves.

(6) All of this means that Scriptural interpretation is the task of all theological disciplines. Exegetes merely have the special task of safeguarding and defending the texts and to discover their original meaning ("Ursprungssinn").[133]

In his two-volume New Testament theology, Stuhlmacher returns to most of these themes, for example, by emphasizing again a concern of most, if not all, forms of canonical exegesis, namely the relations between Scripture and the church. In particular he argues that the both the individual writings of the New Testament and the New Testament as a whole have had their place, from the moment of their inception until today, in the context of the ongoing and continuous life of the Church. Therefore, the texts of the New Testament and the life of the Church (understood as a "horizon of understanding") belong inextricably together. One hermeneutical insight deriving from this interrelationship is that knowledge of the revelation (to which the New Testament witnesses), at least in the existential sense of "knowledge," is only possible in the communal venture of an existence determined by and based on faith.[134]

In line with this, he formulates the four principles for his approach, laying out both his historical, hermeneutical and theological concerns. First, any theology of the New Testament needs to receive both its core theme and its way of presenting itself from the New Testament itself.[135] Second, a theology of the New Testament needs to take into account both the historical claim to communicate revelation as well the ecclesial importance of the New Testament canon.[136] Third, a theology of the New Testament is to be conceptualized as

---

133   Stuhlmacher, *Wie*, 71–76.

134   Stuhlmacher, *Theologie* I, 11: "Die neutestamentlichen Einzelschriften und das Neue Testament im Ganzen standen von Anfang an in einem kirchlichen Lebens- und Wirkungszusammenhang, der bis heute nicht abgebrochen ist. Die Texte des Neuen Testaments und dieser kirchliche Glaubens- und Lebenshorizont gehören wesenhaft zusammen. Wir haben deshalb die Texte des Neuen Testaments methodisch auf ihren Lebensbezug und ihre Erfahrungsdimension zu befragen und herauszustellen, *daß die existentielle Erkenntnis der Offenbarung erst im Vollzug und Wagnis gemeinschaftlicher Glaubensexistenz möglich ist.*"

135   Stuhlmacher, *Theologie* I, 2: "Eine Theologie des Neuen Testaments hat sich ihr Thema und ihre Darstellungsweise vom Neuen Testament selbst vorgeben zu lassen."

136   Stuhlmacher, *Theologie* I, 4: "Die Theologie des Neuen Testaments muß sowohl dem geschichtlichen Offenbarungsanspruch als auch der kirchlichen Bedeutung des neutesta-

deriving from the Old Testament and open towards that part of the Christian Bible; as a discipline, theology of the New Testament is to be understood as a subdiscipline of a biblical theology that encompasses both testaments.[137] Fourth, the message of the New Testament is to be understood primarily as the Christian witness of faith for the Greco-Roman world of the 1st-2nd centuries CE.[138]

He also states, quite succinctly, his view of the process of canonization and its (theological) consequences. First of all, with regard to the relationship between Scripture and (ecclesial) tradition, Stuhlmacher maintains that the New Testament has an advance, both historically and qualitatively, vis-à-vis all ecclesial teaching and tradition, which needs to remain visible in any presentation of biblical witness and ecclesial dogmatic tradition. Therefore, a theology of the New Testament should not be developed along dogmatic, but along historical lines, a project that should be open towards the Old Testament and lead to the formulation of a dogmatic position and an evaluation of the centre of Scripture ("Mitte der Schrift").[139]

In line with this emphasis on a historical approach to biblical theology, Stuhlmacher considers not the Hebrew Bible, but the Septuagint as the version of the Old Testament that ought to be the point of reference in a Christian biblical theology.[140]

Furthermore, with regard to the process of canonization, Stuhlmacher holds a position according to which the Church has not determined the scope of the New Testament on its own authority ("eigenmächtig"), but rather only

---

mentlichen Kanons Rechnung tragen."

137   Stuhlmacher, *Theologie* I, 5: "Die Theologie des Neuen Testaments ist als eine vom Alten Testament herkommende und zu ihm hin offene Theologie des Neuen Testaments zu entwerfen und als Teildisziplin einer Altes und Neues Testament gemeinsam betrachtenden Biblischen Theologie zu begreifen."

138   Stuhlmacher, *Theologie* I, 11: "Die Botschaft des Neuen Testaments ist historisch primär als christliches Glaubenszeugnis für die griechisch-römische Welt des 1./2. Jh.s n. Chr. zu begreifen."

139   Stuhlmacher, *Theologie* I, 12: "Daß das Neue Testament einen geschichtlichen und qualitativen Vorsprung vor aller kirchlichen Lehre und Tradition hat, muß bei der Darstellung die Differenz von biblischem Zeugnis und kirchlicher Lehrüberlieferung sichtbar werden und bleiben. Unter diesen Umständen empfiehlt sich für eine Biblische Theologie des Neuen Testaments kein dogmatischer, sondern *ein zum Alten Testament hin offener geschichtlicher Aufriß, der in eine dogmatische Stellungnahme und Wertung der 'Mitte der Schrift' ausmündet.*"

140   Stuhlmacher, *Theologie* I, 6–8. Two lines of thought concerning historicity seem to meet here: on the one hand the history of Israel is of significance, a history that can be reconstructed using the available sources, on the other hand, however, the canonical record of this history as such, i.e. the Septuagint, is of significance for Stuhlmacher.

established ("festgestellt") it in a long process of preserving the authentic and warding off the unauthentic.[141]

This all leads to Stuhlmacher following succinctly formulated demands for a biblical theological exegesis of the New Testament – or a New Testament text. Such an exegesis needs to be done (1) in a way that deals with the New Testament adequately in terms of historical research; (2) it needs to be open vis-à-vis the claim to revelation of the Gospel; (3) it needs to be related to the ecclesial experience of faith and life; (4) it needs to be rationally transparent and verifiable.[142]

How Stuhlmacher practices this approach will now become clear from the next section.

2.3.2 *Presentation of a Representative Exegesis*

The representative exegesis that has been chosen in order to demonstrate and subsequently analyze Stuhlmacher's approach and method is his discussion of the Gospel of Mark in his *Biblische Theologie des Neuen Testamentes*. The exegesis of this gospel follows Stuhlmacher's general criteria for canonical exegesis, or biblical theological exegesis, and stands in the context of his large-scale synthesis of the theology of the New Testament. The structure of his discussion follows that of a general outline also found in introductory textbooks, i.e. discussing authorship, date, provenance, structure, and then major themes and characteristics.

Stuhlmacher starts out by identifying that the work is written by a "Mark," who is otherwise not mentioned in the book, and that it sounds like an expanded sermon of Peter as e.g. found in Acts 10:36–43. The work itself, i.e.

---

141 Stuhlmacher, *Theologie* I, 3: "*Die Kirche hat das Neue Testament nicht eigenmächtig festgelegt, sondern in einem jahrhundertelangen Prozeß von Bewahrung des Ursprünglichen und Abgrenzung gegen Sekundäres und Fremdes festgestellt.* Man sieht dies am besten daran, daß sich während der Geschichte der Kanonbildung gegen die Hauptschriften des Neuen Testaments, d.h. die vier Evangelien, die Apostelgeschichte, die wesentlichen Paulusbriefe und den 1. Petrusbrief so gut wie kein Widerstand erhoben hat. Auseinandersetzungen sind nur um einige Nebenschriften geführt worden, und zwar vor allem die Johannesoffenbarung und den Hebräerbrief. Die Hauptbücher des Neuen Testaments verdanken ihre kanonische Autorität als nicht erst einem dogmatischen Entscheid der Kirche, sondern sind ihr geschichtlich und inhaltlich *vorgegeben.* Das von diesen Büchern bezeugte Evangelium und das dieses Evangelium begründende Heilswerk Gotts in und durch Christus sind im geschichtlichen und dogmatischen Sinne für die Kirche grundlegend (vgl. Röm 5, 6–8)."

142 Stuhlmacher, *Theologie* I, 11: "[Das Vorhaben] muß (1) dem Neuen Testament historisch angemessen, (2) für den Offenbarungsanspruch des Evangeliums offen, (3) auf die kirchliche Glaubens- und Lebenserfahrung bezogen und (4) rational durchsichtig und kontrollierbar sein."

Gospel of Mark, was intended to be read out in the congregation (see Mark 13:14).[143] As far as the identification of the author is concerned, Stuhlmacher follows the view of the early church that this Mark is the Mark of Acts 12:12.25, 13:5.13, 15:37.39, Phlm. 24, Col. 4:10, 2 Tim. 4:11, and 1 Peter 5:13, as well as of the relevant Papias-fragment (VI). With Mark as Peter's interpreter, Stuhlmacher believes that it is:

> Historisch durchaus glaubhaft, daß Petrus die hermeneutischen Dienste des Markus in Anspruch genommen hat. Der Apostel sprach zwar Griechisch, war aber rhetorisch ungeschult und hat sich deshalb bei der Formulierung (und Weitergabe?) seiner Lehre von Markus helfen lassen. Josephus ist bei der Abfassung seiner Bücher ähnlich verfahren (vgl. Ap I 50).[144]

With regard to the date of this gospel, Stuhlmacher opts for the second half of the 60s, following Peter's death (64, see 1 Clem. 5:4, Irenaeus, *AH* 3.1:1) and before the destruction of Jerusalem, given that Mark nowhere alludes to it (diff. Luke 19:43–44, Matt. 22:7). As far as readership and location are concerned, Stuhlmacher considers the author to be a Jew writing for a non-Jewish audience, probably in Rome.

Next, Stuhlmacher turns to the structure and content of the Gospel according to Mark. First, he notes the large amount of striking and probably Petrine material that can be found in the book, specifically the account of Jesus' ministry in Capernaum (2:1–3:6), a collection of parables (4:1–34), a collection of miracle stories (4:35–6:52), an eschatological discourse (13:1–37), and the strictly chronologically structured account of the passion (14:1–16:8). Furthermore, Mark, as narrator and witness, has combined three elements (that he received from tradition): (a) a predetermined "Erzählmuster vom Evangelium Gottes" (Acts 10:36–43) and its contents; (b) already existing references to the Holy Scriptures that Mark expanded; and (c) the references to the messianic secret that surrounded Jesus. In terms of structure this means that Mark consists of a title in 1:1-2a, followed by a prologue 1:1b–15, and subsequently of three main parts: (I) Jesus' ministry in Galilee and beyond (1:16–8:26); (II) Jesus' way towards his death and the imitation of the way of the cross (8:27–10:52); and (III) Jesus' ministry in Jerusalem, his passion and resurrection (11:1–16:8).

---

143   Stuhlmacher, *Theologie* I, 131.

144   Stuhlmacher, *Theologie* II, 132. Stuhlmacher notes also that arguments against authorship by this particular Mark are not convincing because in the course of a canonical process the attribution of a work to an unknown person would be unlikely.

Next, Stuhlmacher notes that Mark has made some innovations with regard to the term εὐαγγέλιον, given that until Mark, it indicated "die den Aposteln offenbarte und von ihnen zu verkündigende Missionsbotschaft von Jesus Christus" (Acts 15:7, 20:24, Rom. 1:16, etc.), but Mark changed its meaning to include a reference to the "Christus-Botschaft," which is closely connected to the (hi)story of Jesus, while in the Markan narrative Christ himself preaches this gospel. In his own words: "Markus will also mit seinem Buch der Verkündigung des Evangeliums von Jesus Christus, dem Sohn Gottes, dienen, und zwar so, daß er diese Verkündigung fest mit Jesu eigener Botschaft und Geschichte verbindet."[145] This connection between Jesus' proclamation and the proclamation of Jesus Christ safeguards against spiritualizing tendencies and arbitrariness in terms of content ("inhaltliche Beliebigkeit"). Simultaneously, Mark gives all of this a theological context: God has made the beginning of this gospel, i.e. by promising it through Isaiah – this constitutes the "heilsgeschichtliche Tiefendimension" of Mark. This dimension is also evidenced by other quotations from the Old Testament.[146] God realized this promise through the sending of Jesus, while God has also determined the goal and end (τέλος) of it all: The παρουσία of the Son at a time determined by God himself. With regard to the Holy Scriptures (i.e. the Old Testament), Mark presents "Die Geschichte des Christus Jesus als messianisches Erfüllungsgeschehen."[147]

Subsequently, under the heading "Die Geschichte des Gottessohnes," Stuhlmacher treats Mark's Christology, starting with the (Christological) predicates used with regard to Jesus in Mark. This includes the fact that from the start, Mark presents a "Präexistenzchristologie" (1:1a), with Jesus Christ in the role of the messianic "Son of God" that fulfills his divine work on earth,[148] which consists of the establishment of a new eschatological people of God through Jesus' death and resurrection.[149] In this context, the title "Son of Man" can be interpreted along the same lines as the title "Son of God."[150] Having argued this, Stuhlmacher next discusses Jesus as a miracle worker, placing Mark's account of Jesus' miracles in the context of the messianic expectation that began to be fulfilled in Jesus and as forms the counterpart to Jesus' proclamation of the gospel of God's rule in his preaching.[151]

---

145   Stuhlmacher, *Theologie* II, 134.

146   Stuhlmacher, *Theologie* II, 135–136.

147   Stuhlmacher, *Theologie* II, 136.

148   Stuhlmacher, *Theologie* II, 137. It may be noted that the reference to Christ's pre-existence may betray an anti-adoptionist stance on the part of Stuhlmacher.

149   Stuhlmacher, *Theologie* II, 136–137.

150   Stuhlmacher, *Theologie* II, 138.

151   Stuhlmacher, *Theologie* II, 139–140.

Concerning the "Weg des Gottessohnes," i.e. the narrative of Jesus' life and death in Mark, Stuhlmacher notes Jesus' proclamation of the gospel of God's rule after his baptism and his overcoming of temptations, the calling of the Twelve, and the unfolding of this proclamation in Jesus' parables, exorcisms, and healings. The healings evidence Jesus' divine authority, which is also the case in the (Old Testament inspired) gift miracles and epiphanies.[152] With many others, Stuhlmacher identifies Peter's confession at Caesarea Philippi as the turning point of Mark, in which the reader learns to discern in Jesus the Christ who will accomplish the salvation of Jews and Gentiles by means of his substitutionary suffering.[153] The latter is the focus of the final part of Mark, in which Jesus engages more in direct discussions, has a stronger focus on eschatological matters, and is more outspoken about his messianic claims. This more pronounced public ministry climaxes in the triumphal entry into Jerusalem and the cleansing of the Temple, after which the events of the passion occur. Stuhlmacher's interpretation of part of this is worth quoting in full:

> Im Verlauf des Abschiedspassa mit den zwölf Jüngern gibt er seinen Tischgenossen im Voraus Anteil an der heilbringenden Frucht seines Sterbens (vgl. 14, 22–24 mit Ex 24, 8 und Jes 53, 10–12), bezieht beim anschließenden Gang zum Ölberg Sach 13, 7 auf sich selbst und nimmt in der Wegentscheidung in Gethsemane…das Leiden, das Gott über ihn verhängt hat, ohne Fluch oder Gegenwehr auf sich. Vor dem Synhedrium bekennt er, der messianische Gottessohn zu sein, und kündigt seinen Richtern an, ihnen in Bälde als der zur Rechten Gottes erhöhte Menschensohn-Weltenrichter erscheinen zu wollen (14, 61–62). Auf diese in den Augen seiner Gegner gotteslästerliche Äußerung hin wird er des Todes schuldig befunden, am nächsten Morgen bei Pilatus als messianischer Aufwiegler angezeigt und von diesem nach kurzem Verfahren zum Kreuzestod verurteilt. Die auf der Grundlage von Ps 22 und 69 gestaltete Geschichte von Jesu Passion deutet seinen Tod als das stellvertretende Sterben des messianischen Gerechten, durch dessen Geschick Gott seine Herrschaft Aufrichten und die Bekehrung der Heidenvölker herbeiführen will (vgl. Ps 22, 29–30). Das Zerreißen des Vorhangs vor dem Allerheiligsten nach Jesu Sterben weist die Leser darauf hin, daß die durch Jesu Tod ein für allemal erwirke

---

152   Stuhlmacher, *Theologie* II, 140–141. See also with regard to the transfiguration on p. 142; this specifically introduces Jesus as both God's beloved Son and as follower ("Nachfolger") of Moses. – Of interest is the historical note that the transfiguration indicates that Peter (and other disciples) recognised in Jesus already the Son of God before Easter.

153   Stuhlmacher, *Theologie* II, 143.

> Sühne den Tempel als Ort der Sühne obsolet gemacht hat. In dem 15, 39
> folgenden *Bekenntnis* des römischen Hauptmanns: "Wahrhaftig, dieser
> Mensch ist Gottes Sohn gewesen!" darf und soll sich die (vorwiegend hei-
> denchristliche) Lesergemeinde des Markus wiederfinden.[154]

Subsequently, Stuhlmacher briefly treats the bodily resurrection of Jesus (reading up until Mark 16:8 – Stuhlmacher does not discuss the textual issues at
stake here), stating that the reason that there are no direct resurrection appearances in the Gospel of Mark has to do with the fact that until the παρουσία the
Jesus-anamnesis on earth and the belief that he was raised from the dead by
God were what mattered. Finally, Stuhlmacher considers the Markan "messianic secret," relating it both to Jesus' historical ministry, in which much was
mysterious, while only after his death the resurrection appearances enabled
the disciples to understand "das göttliche Sein und die überirdische Würde
Jesu,"[155] and to Mark's literary intention to make clear that "Jesu Auferstehung
und seine messianischen Heilstaten mit der Leidensbereitschaft und dem in
äußerster (Gott-) Verlassenheit erlittenen Kreuzestod des Gottessohnes,"
should be seen together.

Finally, Stuhlmacher turns to discipleship and community in Mark. With
regard to this, he highlights a number of issues, most fundamentally that Mark
calls upon his audience – initiated Christians with a good knowledge of baptismal catechesis and the Holy Scriptures – to think their own "Zeugnisexistenz"
together with the "Geschichte des Sohnes Gottes."[156] At the same time, there is a
notable difference between the time of Jesus and the (Markan) community,
given that the latter lives in a time of eschatological distress. Simultaneously,
Mark presents the disciples of Jesus a mirror and a model for their discipleship
– with all the flaws that the disciples of Jesus have in his gospel. Beyond this, the
following applies: "Durch die Jünger (sc. die Zwölf) war für Markus selbst die
Kontinuität von Jesuszeit und Zeit der Gemeinde gegeben. Er hat sein Evangelium
auch deshalb verfaßt, um diese Kontinuität über das Petrusmartyrium hinaus zu
gewährleisten."[157] The identity of the community consists of being Jesus' true
family, made up of people that do the will of God as Jesus had taught it.
Stuhlmacher considers this an anticipation of the Pastoral Epistles. While
the community does pay its (Roman) taxes, it does not follow the norms of the
Roman Empire, but rather its own, i.e. Jesus', such as an ethos of servanthood

---

154   Stuhlmacher, *Theologie* II, 143.
155   Stuhlmacher, *Theologie* II, 146.
156   Stuhlmacher, *Theologie* II, 147.
157   Stuhlmacher, *Theologie* II, 148.

and the "Doppelgebot der Gottes- und Nächstenliebe."[158] Faithfulness to Jesus is a requirement for this community and a soteriological necessity; although Mark does not use terms like πίστις or πιστεύω, trusting Jesus and entrusting oneself to him is of fundamental importance for Mark. In sum:

> Die Leser-Gemeinde darf sich nach Markus auf dem Weg, den sie durch die messianischen Wehen hindurch auf ihren kommenden Herrn zugeht, der Vergebung getrösten. Denn Jesus ist als Lösegeld für Vielen in den Tod gegangen, zu denen auch sie gehört (vgl. 10, 45), und sie darf immer wieder das Herrenmahl mit dem (Tisch-) Herrn feiern, der für sie in den Tod gegangen ist und ihr an der himmlischen Tafel Platz geschaffen hat (vgl. 14, 22–25). In dem gekreuzigten und erhöhten Gottessohn ist den Lesern die Vergebung von Sünden und die Errettung im Endgericht verbürgt.[159]

2.3.3   Analysis

Having outlined Stuhlmacher's canonical approach and presented an example of his exegesis of the New Testament gospels, now both can be analyzed together, paying specific attention to the role of the canon in the whole of it.

First, the question what sort of understanding of the "canon" and "canonical" exegesis is used by Stuhlmacher? With regard to the New Testament, somewhat unsurprisingly, the twenty-seven-book canon is normative for Stuhlmacher. His position with regard to the Old Testament is somewhat unusual, certainly for a protestant exegete, given that he views the LXX, not the Tenakh, as the first part of the Christian Scriptures. Although the latter is not the subject of this study – concerned as it is with the canonical approach to the New Testament gospels – it does illustrate an important aspect of Stuhlmacher's approach, i.e. its strong emphasis on historical studies: His preference for the LXX instead of the Tenakh as the Christian "Old Testament" has its basis in historical considerations. In fact, Stuhlmacher's argument throughout is that what he presents is proper historical-critical exegesis, while other kinds of historical-critical exegesis, i.e. those that do not follow his hermeneutical considerations, in fact fall short of their own aim. In a similar – and characteristic – attempt to relate historical developments to the significance of texts and their relationship to their community of interpretation, Stuhlmacher also considers the development of the New Testament canon and its relationship to the church, at least as far as its emergence is concerned. In this context, Stuhlmacher

---

158   Stuhlmacher, *Theologie* II, 148.
159   Stuhlmacher, *Theologie* II, 149.

takes a position with regard to the emergence of the New Testament canon that echoes particular ecclesiological (and fundamental theological) concerns – or, more neutrally put: Hermeneutical concerns, as he states that the church has not "eigenmächtig festgelegt" (i.e. in a "dogmatic decision") what should and should not be part of the canon, but has rather "festgestellt" what the canon amounts to "in einem jahrhundertelangen Prozeß von Bewahrung des Ursprünglichen und Abgrenzung gegen Sekundäres und Fremdes."[160] While this acknowledges, on the one hand, historical insights with regard to the development of canon, this also safeguards the authority of Scripture vis-à-vis that of the church.

Building on this view of the development of the New Testament canon, Stuhlmacher understands canonical exegesis, for him: proper historical-critical exegesis, as exegesis that acknowledges the fact of the canon and the selection process of the church, seeking to position the exegete in such a way that s/he can understand the meaning of the Scriptures by identifying with them. It is here that Stuhlmacher's notion of a "Hermeneutik des Einverständnisses" begins to play a role. In order to understand the writings of the New Testament as – canonical! – writings of the New Testament, their authority as sources of revelation and their place in the church has to be taken into account and identified with, in order to achieve a proper interpretation of the texts as they understand themselves. According to Stuhlmacher, to the extent that this identification means sharing the faith of the church, the believing exegete has an epistemological advantage over the non-believing interpreter of Scripture.

The canon, as a historical and literary fact that determines what the writings of the New Testament amount to, what their claim is, and in which community of interpretation they are at home, thus governs the interpretation of these writings to a very considerable extent, specifically with regard to the proper attitude of the exegete. Notably, all of this arises – at least according to Stuhlmacher's own presentation of things – not so much from a theological or dogmatic conviction, but from a historical-critical consideration of the New Testament texts, seeking to understand what sort of texts they are indeed.

When turning to the question of how Stuhlmacher applies his approach, or rather: What role it plays factually in his exegesis, the following observations may be made. First of all, when turning to Stuhlmacher's historical contextualization of the Gospel of Mark, i.e. as written by Peter's secretary, one may get the sense that the witness of the early church does play an important role for Stuhlmacher's decision regarding Mark's historical origins. Here also, a certain willingness to agree with ecclesial tradition, as it is part of his hermeneutical

---

160   Stuhlmacher, *Theologie* I, 3.

approach in general, can be sensed. Stuhlmacher refers to a variety of sources (i.e. Acts 12:12.25, 13:5.13, 15:37.39, Phlm. 24, Col. 4:10, 2 Tim. 4:11, 1 Peter 5:13, and Papias-fragment VI) that do constitute a tradition, but are certainly not seen by all to constitute evidence of the existence of one single Mark, the author of the Gospel of Mark and Peter's secretary.[161] All of this is of major significance for Stuhlmacher's interpretation of Mark, given that his dating of this gospel (around 64, i.e. shortly after Peter's death in Rome and well before the destruction of the Jerusalem Temple in 70) depends on it, as well as his attribution of traditional material in the gospel to "Petrine" traditions. A canonical tendency also appears towards the end of his exegesis of Mark, where Stuhlmacher both places Mark into a historical line that leads towards the Pastoral Epistles, and also attempts to rephrase Mark's point of view in terminology that is better known from other New Testament writings (see above, his discussion of Mark's non-use of πίστις or πιστεύω, but the agreement of Mark's story with other New Testament texts that do use these concepts to refer to trust or faith in God). Furthermore, Stuhlmacher's conviction that the New Testament texts are fairly traditional, both in the sense that they transmit early Christian material faithfully and in that they are very closely related to the Old Testament (i.e. Septuagint), plays a role in his exegesis, given that he places significant emphasis both on Mark's transmission of, for example, Petrine traditions and on Mark's "heilsgeschichtliche Tiefendimension," evidenced by Mark's use of the Old Testament and the way in which he writes his Jesus story in general.[162]

What is probably more striking is what is not found in Stuhlmacher's exegesis of Mark: Indications as to how the "Einverständnis" with the text for readers today needs to take place, i.e. how readers today should receive the text's meaning in the way in which Stuhlmacher has outlined in his description of biblical hermeneutics and his canonical approach to Scripture. In fact, because Stuhlmacher *does* provide an outline of what sort of message Mark had for its first readers and to what attitude he called them, one wonders whether Stuhlmacher expects contemporary readers of Mark just to step into the shoes of these first readers – and forget about their own context?

When addressing the third sub-question, "what effect does the canon and the canonical approach have on the outcome of the exegesis, i.e. how is the canon appealed to in order to make decisions about interpretation and meaning?" again a few observations can be made. While Stuhlmacher presents his research as just historical research, he does nevertheless operate with a very particular view of which aspects of such research, and particularly which

---

161 Stuhlmacher, *Theologie* II, 132.
162 Stuhlmacher, *Theologie* II, 135–136.

sources, need to be taken into account. This became clear with regard to his decisions as to the identity of Mark – in many ways Stuhlmacher can be said to operate with a "canonical" Mark that is equated with the historical Mark – as well as with regard to the salvation historical trajectory in which he places Mark. This trajectory is at the very least co-determined by the place that Mark occupies in the canon of the Christian Bible, which as such provides the shape of this history of salvation at large. Mark's canonical setting, therefore, determines the intertextual connections of the work. This also applies, it seems, to the tradition-historical trajectory in which Stuhlmacher places Mark, i.e. as originating in Peter's preaching, such as it is, for example, presented in Acts 10:36–43.[163] For Stuhlmacher, these exegetical decisions all have their origins in his wish to understand the texts as they wish to be understood, i.e. as canonical texts. Another aspect of this is his focus both on Christological and ecclesiological questions throughout Mark; he is trying to uncover what Mark had to say to the church of the first century regarding Christ and the church, as much as he is trying to uncover what that might mean for the church today.

When turning to the fourth and last sub-question, i.e. "what is, for this exegesis, the heuristic and epistemological value of a 'canonical approach?'" the following may be maintained. While for Stuhlmacher the goal of (canonical) exegesis, which, in turn, is for him simply proper historical-critical exegesis on a sound hermeneutical basis, is very specific and certainly at odds with the aims of many fellow exegetes, the results of this approach to Mark remain fairly traditional. Certainly, he is able to draw information that he considers historical from other (quasi-)canonical sources with more ease than (many) other historical-critically oriented exegetes would (e.g. the Peter-Mark connection), and he is able to place Mark with great ease into a salvation-historical trajectory that is determined by the canonical shape of the Christian Bible. However, it remains relatively unclear at which point his exegesis of Mark does a better job of understanding the text as it wishes to be understood than other historical-critical approaches to the same text that are less (explicitly) committed to the hermeneutical program that Stuhlmacher propagates. Also, given his hermeneutical program, Stuhlmacher is able to claim that Mark wishes to be listened to as a proclamation of the good

---

163   An obvious problem with this particular connection is not addressed by Stuhlmacher: In Acts 10:36–43 Jesus' post-resurrection appearances play a major role, while Mark stands out among the evangelists precisely (and mysteriously) for not containing such appearances.

news, yet this could also be said without a hermeneutics of "Einverständnis" in the background.

2.3.4   Conclusions

In summary, therefore, Stuhlmacher lays out an impressive program of canonical exegesis, which in its core has the intention of understanding texts as they wish to be understood. While this can be taken as a general hermeneutical point – and as such certainly has its merits – it has a particular relevance for the writings of the Christian Bible, including the New Testament gospels. Given that Stuhlmacher considers the canonical context and the canonical claims of these writings to be authoritative witnesses to God's acting in the world as part of what they are – and not as some extraneous aspect that was somehow forced upon these texts – they must be read differently than they often are by other exegetes (according to Stuhlmacher). For example, they ought not to be read as windows into the world of early Christianity, or as sources for the reconstruction of the life of Jesus, given that this would be using the texts in a different way than originally intended (given their *intentio operis* and/or *intentio auctoris*). Instead, they ought to be read as witnesses to God's work in Christ. This, Stuhlmacher argues, is a more correct historical-critical exegesis than an exegesis that does not listen to what the texts were intended to communicate originally, but uses the texts for other purposes. As the texts are found in a canonical context, which reflect a particular salvation-history, this must also be regarded as an appropriate context for understanding the texts of the New Testament. Thus, the canonical approach of Stuhlmacher leads to an emphasis on the theology of the New Testament writings themselves, understood as part of a salvation-historical trajectory provided by the entire Christian Bible. This means that both the claim to authority made by (canonical) texts and their claim to provide an authentic witness to the events that they refer to also needs to be taken into account in their exegesis, which, accordingly, is to be related to the life of the church with an eye to the church's, or in general: The reader's "Einverständnis" with what the work has to say. In the analysis of Stuhlmacher's exegesis of Mark, as provided above, it was noted that the integration of Mark into a canonical context, and the emphasis on searching for the message of the work, as well as the theologically oriented exegesis of Stuhlmacher (i.e. exegesis that emphasizes theological topics and therefore, relates well to matters of faith), are readily discernable. It does, however, remain unclear how his exegesis really differs from that of other historical-critical scholars (of a somewhat conservative bend). What remains unclear as well is how the "Einverständnis" with Mark's witness has to take place, i.e. how the reader has to respond to what Mark wishes to say.

2.5   Joseph Ratzinger/Pope Benedict XVI

Of the scholars considered here, the Roman Catholic scholar Joseph Ratzinger (*1927), after his election on 19 April 2005 and until his resignation on 28 February 2013, Pope Benedict XVI, who taught at the universities of Bonn, Münster, Tübingen, and Regensburg, is in a number of ways a unique representative of the canonical approach. First, Ratzinger comes to a canonical approach as a systematic theologian, not as a biblical scholar by training;[164] second, he did so as a Pope, even if he published the book under his Christian name as well;[165] and third, he did so in a way that decidedly aimed at reaching a very broad audience, in the academia and beyond.[166] Furthermore, Ratzinger clearly interacts with some of the other scholars discussed here, e.g. Sanders and Childs are mentioned in the Pontifical Biblical Commission's *The Interpretation of the Bible in the Church*,[167] which came into being under Ratzinger's supervision, while he invited Stuhlmacher for a discussion of his own work on the historical Jesus during his pontificate.[168] Having thus sketched

---

164   See e.g. the (positive) comments with regard to this by Jörg Frey, "Historisch-kanonisch-kirchlich: Zum Jesusbild Joseph Ratzingers," in: Thomas Söding (ed.), *Das Jesus-Buch des Papstes. Die Antwort der Neutestamentler* (Freiburg: Herder, 2007), 43–53, 43, as well as Seckler, "Problematik," 31, who notes that the crossing of borders between theological (and other) disciplines is characteristic of the newer discussion about the canon. – That Ratzinger brings substantial systematic-theological concerns to bear, specifically with regard to the nature of the historical-critical method, is apparent from his essay, "Schriftauslegung im Widerstreit. Zur Frage nach Grundlagen und Weg der Exegese heute," in: Joseph Ratzinger (ed.), *Schriftauslegung im Widerstreit* (Freiburg: Herder, 1989), 15–55, *in nuce* the method that he uses in his "Jesus-books" can be found there on 40–42. See also his *Theologische Prinzipienlehre* (München: Wewel, 1982), 343–348.

165   Frey, "Historical-kanonisch-kirchlich," 43, overestimates the significance of this fact; as the title of the volume indicates in which Frey published his essay, Ratzinger's work will remain the Pope's book on Jesus.

166   As may be evidence by a veritable wave of reviews and reactions, among which are: Söding (ed.), *Jesus-Buch*, and further: Jan Heiner Tück (ed.), *Annäherungen an "Jesus von Nazareth," Das Buch des Papstes in der Diskussion* (Mainz: Grünewald, 2007), Karl Lehmann (ed.), *"Jesus von Nazareth" kontrovers* (Münster: LIT, 2007), as well as, e.g., Rainer Riesner, "Der Papst und die Evangelien-Forschung," in: Thomas Pola/Bert Roebben (ed.), *Die Bibel in ihrer vielseitigen Rezeption* (Münster: LIT, 2010), 35–49. It cannot be the task of the present study to engage with all of this discussion extensively.

167   The Pontifical Biblical Commission, *Interpretation*, C.1.

168   See: Peter Kuhn (ed.), *Gespräch über Jesus. Papst Benedikt XVI. im Dialog mit Martin Hengel und Peter Stuhlmacher* (Tübingen: Mohr Siebeck, 2010), see also: Peter Stuhlmacher, "Joseph Ratzinger's Jesus-Buch – ein bedeutsamer geistlicher Wegweiser," *Communio* 36 (2007), 399–407.

Ratzinger's profile with some broad strokes, a more detailed discussion of his canonical approach and appertaining exegetical practice follows.

2.5.1   *The Canonical Approach of Joseph Ratzinger*

In the first part of his book on Jesus of Nazareth,[169] Joseph Ratzinger/Pope Benedict XVI, publishing under his own name and under the name that he had adopted on his election to the See of Rome, offers some reflections on his method.[170] He begins with some very positive comments on the application of the historical-critical method to biblical texts. This method is necessary due to the intrinsically historical character of the Christian faith. However, Ratzinger also stakes out the limits of this method, namely that it leaves whatever it researches in the past and is not able to unearth any "deeper value" in the writings to which it is applied.[171] Ratzinger then proceeds to emphasize, to a considerable extent, the significance and fruitfulness of "canonical exegesis," referring to unidentified "American scholars" that had developed this approach (likely, he thinks of Sanders and Childs here primarily).[172] He describes this kind of exegesis as follows: "The aim of this exegesis is to read individual texts within the totality of the one Scripture, which then sheds new light on all the individual texts."[173] Ratzinger connects this definition to the teachings of the Second Vatican Council, which, in its Constitution on Divine Revelation (*Dei Verbum*), had identified this, i.e. what canonical exegesis aims at, as "a fundamental principle of theological exegesis: If you want to understand the Scripture in the spirit in which it is written, you have to attend to the content and the unity of Scripture as a whole."[174] He then proceeds to add that the Second Vatican Council went on "to stress the need for taking account of the living tradition of the whole church and of the analogy of faith (the intrinsic correspondences within the faith)."[175] In the

---

169   Benedict XVI/Joseph Ratzinger, *Jesus of Nazareth. The Illustrated Edition* (New York: Rizzoli, 2009; first edition: 2007). It should be noted that the book has been published in different editions, some with extensive pictorial material; this material, in all likelihood, should be seen as part of the book's message and as a witness to the unfolding of the message of Scripture. See for the further volumes on Jesus by Ratzinger: *Jesus of Nazareth: Holy Week: From the Entrance Into Jerusalem to the Resurrection* (San Francisco: Ignatius, 2011), and *Jesus of Nazareth. The Infancy Narratives* (New York: Image, 2012). – Only the first volume will be considered here, as in it, the most fundamental hermeneutical issues are discussed.

170   Ratzinger, *Jesus*, 5–17. See also his earlier "Schriftauslegung."

171   Ratzinger, *Jesus*, 5–10.

172   Given that these two scholars are mentioned in The Pontifical Biblical Commission, *Interpretation*, C.1.

173   Ratzinger, *Jesus*, 10.

174   Ratzinger, *Jesus*, 10.

175   Ratzinger, *Jesus*, 10.

context of his discussion of method, Ratzinger also comments on the unity of Scripture, noting that the coherence of the writings that make up Scripture is not something that foreign to them, but inherent to the way in which they came into being (i.e., the canonical process). In this process, the potential for meaning of words unfolds itself gradually. For understanding the writings that came into being in this way, the life, death, and resurrection of Jesus Christ provide a hermeneutical key that allows it to access the various writings as the unified Scriptures of the church.[176] Therefore, "'Canonical exegesis' – reading the individual texts of the Bible in the context of the whole – is an essential dimension of exegesis. It does not contradict historical-critical interpretation, but carries it forward in an organic way toward becoming theology in the proper sense."[177]

Having stated this, Ratzinger goes on to outline two further aspects of his methodology, specifically as to how the meaning of a statement evolves in history. He first notes that whenever a word transcends its original communicative setting, it has a "deeper value," the person that speaks or writes a word originally, therefore, says more than she or he is actually aware of; her or his words are richer than they initially seem to be and this richness is unfolded in the course of history.[178] Second, Ratzinger argues that the Scriptures of the

---

176   Ratzinger, *Jesus*, 11: "[I]t [*sc.* the unity of Scripture] is not simply imposed from the outside on what is in itself a heterogeneous ensemble of writings. Modern exegesis has brought to light the process of constant rereading that forged the words transmitted in the Bible into Scripture: Older texts are reappropriated, reinterpreted, and read with new eyes in new contexts. They become Scripture by being read anew, evolving in continuity with their original sense, tacitly corrected and given added depth and breadth of meaning. This is a process in which the word gradually unfolds its inner potentialities, already somehow present like seeds, but needing the challenge of new situations, new experiences and new sufferings, in order to open up. This process is certainly not linear, and it is often dramatic, but when you watch it unfold in the light of Jesus Christ, you can see it moving in a single overall direction; you can see that the Old and New Testaments belong together. This Christological hermeneutic, which sees Jesus Christ as the key to the whole and learns from him how to understand the Bible as a unity, presupposes any prior act of faith. It cannot be the conclusion of a purely historical method. But this act of faith is based upon reason – historical reason – and so makes it possible to see the internal unity of Scripture. By the same token, it enables us to understand anew the individual elements that have shaped it, without robbing them of their historical originality."

177   Ratzinger, *Jesus*, 11.

178   Ratzinger, *Jesus*, 11: "When a word transcends the moment in which it is spoken, it carries within itself a 'deeper value.' This 'deeper value' pertains most of all to words that have matured in the course of faith-history. For in this case the author is not simply speaking for himself on his own authority. He is speaking from the perspective of a common history that sustains him and that already implicitly contains the possibilities of its future, for the further stages of its journey."

church are the product of the interaction between three living subjects: The historical authors, the collective subject "people of God," and finally, God.[179]

For Ratzinger, therefore, canonical exegesis is to read the individual biblical text in the context of the whole of Scripture and to read the whole of Scripture in light of the evolving faith of the church, one of the Scripture's authors, which, in fact, can be conceived of as the evolving meaning of Scripture. In this way, Ratzinger seeks to do justice to both the historical dimension of Scripture, valuing historical-critical research for theological reasons,[180] and to its theological dimension, by simultaneously developing a hermeneutic that views the meaning of a text as something that develops in the context of an on-going dialogue with the community that produced it, thus, combining aspects of what may be found elsewhere as a hermeneutic of reception history or as elements of community-based hermeneutics. The latter aspects of Ratzinger's hermeneutical model secure that later interpretations (or readings) of a text can still be seen as authentic interpretations of this text, which is exactly what unfolds in the remainder of his study.

2.5.2   *Presentation of a Representative Exegesis*

As a representative exegesis, Ratzinger's interpretation of the temptation of Jesus in the wilderness, as it occurs in the synoptic gospels, has been chosen.[181] Ratzinger discusses this event after his discussion of the baptism of Jesus, which precedes the temptations in all relevant narratives. At the start of his treatment of the temptation in the wilderness, Ratzinger links the two events closely by stating that the Spirit's decent upon Jesus is to be seen as a formal

---

179   Ratzinger, *Jesus*, 11: "Neither the individual books of Holy Scripture nor the Scripture as a whole are simply a piece of literature. The Scripture emerged from the heart of a living subject – the pilgrim People of God – and lives within this same subject. One could say that that the books of Scripture involved three interacting subjects. First of all, there is the individual author or group of authors to whom we owe a particular scriptural text. But these authors are not autonomous writers in the modern sense; they form part of a collective subject, the 'People of God,' from within whose heart and to whom they speak. Hence, this subject is actually the deeper 'author' of the Scriptures. And yet likewise, this people does not exist alone. Rather, it knows that it is led, and spoken to, by God himself, who – through men and their humanity – is at the deepest level the one speaking."

180   See however Seckler, "Problematik," 51–53, who emphasizes much more strongly the theological value of the results of diachronic exegesis; Ratzinger seems to follow the lead of (e.g.) Childs more strongly than that of Seckler, whose essay originated in a paper read at a symposium on the subject of "Die Interpretation der Bibel in der Kirche," (see Seckler, *o.c.*, 30), organized by the Congregation of the Doctrine of the Faith in 1999, i.e. during the time that Ratzinger was perfect of this congregation.

181   Mark 1:9–13, Matt. 3:13–4:11, Luke 3:21–4:13. See Ratzinger, *Jesus*, 51.71.

institution of Jesus as Messiah, an event which in patristic exegesis was correctly related to the anointing of Israelite kings and priests when they took office.[182] The anointing at stake at the beginning of Jesus' public ministry takes place with the Holy Spirit, in line with Old Testament tradition (e.g. Isa. 11:1–2, a text referring to the future and true "Anointed One"), while Ratzinger sees this interpretation confirmed by Jesus' use of Isa. 61:1 in Luke 4:18: "The Spirit of the Lord is upon me, for he has anointed me." In other words, the baptismal scene indicates that Jesus is the "awaited Anointed One" on whom kingly and priestly dignity were formally bestowed. Upon this, and to the reader's surprise, Ratzinger notes,[183] Jesus is first led into desert "to be tempted by the devil," (Matt, 4:1 – the Matthean text speaks for all three synoptic accounts). This, Ratzinger already interprets in advance by arguing that it expresses Jesus' entering into the "drama of human existence" in order to penetrate it and thus be able to redeem it. For this, it is necessary that Jesus, like any human being, has to struggle with the demands associated with his mission.[184]

Following this, Ratzinger relates the temptations to Jesus' "descent into hell" as it occurs in the Apostles' Creed, noting that this descent was not a particular port-mortal adventure of Jesus, but in fact something that "accompanies him along his entire journey," which itself is understood as a recapitulation of the entirety of human history.[185] Notably, Ratzinger finds support for these claims in Heb. 2:17–18 and 4:15.[186] Thus, following Jesus' baptism, which indicated his solidarity with sinners, by way of the temptations in the

---

182   Ratzinger, *Jesus*, 51: "[t]he descent of the Holy Spirit upon Jesus, which concludes the baptismal scene, is to be understood as a kind of formal investiture with the messianic office. The Fathers of the Church therefore, rightly saw this event as analogous to the anointing by which kings and priests in Israel were installed in office."

183   Ratzinger, *Jesus*, 51.

184   Ratzinger, *Jesus*, 51–52: "The action is prefaced by interior recollection, and this recollection is also, inevitably, an inner struggle for fidelity to the task, a struggle against all the distortions of the task that claim to be its true fulfillment. It is a descent into the perils besetting mankind, for there is no other way to lift up fallen humanity. Jesus has to enter into the drama of human existence, for that belongs to the core of his mission; he has to penetrate it completely, down to its uttermost depths, in order to find the 'lost sheep,' to bear it on his shoulders, and to bring it home."

185   Ratzinger, *Jesus*, 52.

186   Ratzinger, *Jesus*, 52; "Therefore he had to be made like his brethren in every respect, so that he might become a merciful and faithful high priest in the service of God, to make expiation for the sins of the people. For because he himself has suffered and been tempted, he is able to help those who are tempted." (Heb. 2:17–18) "For we have not a high priest who is unable to sympathize with our weaknesses, but on who in every respect has been tempted as we are, yet without sin." (Heb. 4:15).

wilderness and the agony on the Mount of Olives, temptations are with Jesus on every step of his journey.

Ratzinger begins to expound how this plays out after these considerations, which, *in nuce*, already contains the main aspects of his view of the significance of Jesus' temptation in the wilderness. To begin with, Ratzinger notes that the account of the temptation in Mark 1:13 draws on a parallel between Adam and Jesus. Jesus enters into the wilderness, a symbol of the rebellion of creation against God, and then, in an act of "suffering through the quintessential human drama,"[187] turns the desert into a place of "reconciliation and healing," given that Jesus was with the wild beasts and with angels ministering to him.[188] Ratzinger draws explicitly on Isa. 11:6 and Rom. 8:19 in order to indicate both the expectation of and the longing for a redeemed creation.[189] He associates this with the "oases of creation" around monasteries, e.g. in the Benedictine tradition, that can be seen as expressing the anticipation of a reconciled creation, while he refers to nuclear disaster of Chernobyl as an expression of what happens to creation in the absence of God.[190]

Next, Ratzinger focuses on the accounts of Jesus' temptation in the Gospels of Matthew and Luke, specifically as accounts that "reflect the inner struggle over his, i.e. Jesus', own particular mission and, at the same time, address the question as to what truly matters in human life."[191] The latter is, for Ratzinger, related to the issue of a transcendent God's presence in the world and of the relevance of God for the world, and therefore, to a question about what is really real and about what really matters. Temptations are those things that "speak for true realism: What's real is what is right there in front of us – power and bread. By comparison, the things of God fade into unreality, into a secondary world that no one really needs."[192]

---

187   Ratzinger, *Jesus*, 52.

188   As noted in Mark 1:13 and Matt. 4:11; seen by Ratzinger as a possible reference to Ps. 91:11, a text that is quoted in Matt. 3:6 and Luke 3:10.

189   Ratzinger, *Jesus*, 52–53, Isa. 11:6: "The wolf shall dwell with the lamb, and the leopard shall lie down with the kid," Rom. 8:19; creation, which "waits with eager longing for the revealing of the sons of God."

190   Ratzinger, *Jesus*, 53: "Are not the oases of creation that sprang up, say, around the Benedictine monasteries in the West foreshadowings of this reconciliation of creation brought about by the children of God – just as, conversely, something like Chernobyl is a shocking expression of creation's enslavement in the darkness of God's absence?"

191   Ratzinger, *Jesus*, 53.

192   Ratzinger, *Jesus*, 53. – The illustration on p. 55, William Blake, *The First Temptation* (Cambridge, Fitzwilliam Museum) underlines this forcefully: Jesus, the true human being, is a tall figure, standing upright, pointing towards heaven, his halo bursting through

Furthermore, when turning to the three temptations themselves, Ratzinger decides to follow their sequence as they appear in the Gospel of Matthew, as Matthew's "arrangement reflects a logic that intensifies from temptation to temptation."[193] First, Ratzinger considers Jesus' fast of forty days, which is related to Israel's forty years' sojourn in the wilderness, the forty days that Moses spent on Mount Sinai, as well as to a rabbinic tale about Abraham's forty days' journey to Mount Horeb (where he was to sacrifice Isaac), during which his only sustenance was "the vision and words of the angel that accompanied him."[194] This, in turn is related to a summary of patristic exegesis that runs as follows. In this summary, Ratzinger notes that the "Fathers of the Church" considered 40 to be a number that referred to the cosmos, i.e. as a number representing the world. In this way, Jesus' 40 days in the wilderness indicate his living through the entire drama of the cosmos' history, seeking to embrace it entirely.[195]

Subsequently, Ratzinger quotes and discusses Matt. 4:3, "If you are the Son of God, command these stones to become loaves of bread," focusing on the notion of challenge and (implied) mockery that he also finds in Matt. 27:40 ("If you are the Son of God, come down from the Cross") and in Wisdom 2:18 that Ratzinger applies to this situation ("If the righteous man is God's son, he will help him"). Ratzinger views the demand that Jesus "finally" prove his identity as a constant issue during his earthly life and also states that, "[w]e make this same demand of God and Christ and his church throughout the whole of history."[196] In a brief comparison between Luke 4:3 and Matt. 4:3, Ratzinger notes that Luke focuses on Jesus' own hunger, whereas Matthew understands

---

the mountain range in the background, while Adam, with whom Jesus is contrasted, is a stooping figure of a much heavier build than Jesus, pointing downwards, to the earth as that what really matters and remaining well below the rim of the mountains in the back.

193   Ratzinger, *Jesus*, 53. The difference in order, however, is not the only difference between the two texts with regard to which Ratzinger follows Matthew rather than Luke, e.g. with regard to the forty days' fast, he also follows Matthew, given that in that gospel the temptations begin after Jesus' abstinence from food, while in Luke, they take place during it.

194   Ratzinger, *Jesus*, 54.

195   Ratzinger, *Jesus*, 54: "The Fathers of the Church, stretching number symbolism in an admittedly slightly playful way, regarded forty as a cosmic number, as the numerical sign for this world. The four 'corners' encompass the whole world, and ten is the number of the commandments. The number of the cosmos multiplied by the number of the commandments becomes a symbolic statement about the history of this world as a whole. It is as if Jesus were reliving Israel's Exodus, and then reliving the chaotic meanderings of history in general; the forty days of fasting embrace the drama of history, which Jesus takes into himself and all the way through to the end."

196   Ratzinger, *Jesus*, 56.

the issue in a broader sense, i.e. in relation to the suffering of the entire world –
and hence, in relation to the *theodicy*, specifically in the shape of the demand
that the Redeemer and his church ought to solve world hunger if they really are
what they claim to be. This, Ratzinger adds, would be exactly the kind of salvation that Marxism promised.[197] These considerations lead to a further consideration of two other narratives involving food in the New Testament, the
multiplication of loaves for the thousands who followed Jesus and the Last
Supper.[198] With regard to the first, Ratzinger wonders, why (the Matthean?)
Jesus now does what he refused to do earlier during the according temptation,
i.e. to provide food for a hungering multitude. His answer is that it is a question
of disposition: The people in the multitude had "opened their heart[s] to God
and to one another."[199] On this basis, Ratzinger argues that there are three
dimensions to the miraculous feeding: There is the aspect of searching for God,
given that this precedes the actual miracle (people come to Jesus); furthermore, it is significant that God is called upon to provide for the people; finally,
there is an element of being willing to share with one another. Thus, searching
for God and entrusting one to God leads into the discovery of the other as a
"neighbor."[200] Following this, Ratzinger turns to the Last Supper, which he
interprets as an expansion and amplification, both in terms of (theological)
quality and quantity, of the miraculous feeding: Now Jesus himself becomes
bread, in a way that provides an endless supply of bread, while this bread also
feeds the believer with the idea of being in communion with God.[201] In this
context, he approvingly quotes German Jesuit Alfred Delp, who was executed
by the Nazis, who state that: "Bread is important, freedom is more important,

---

197 Ratzinger, *Jesus*, 56.

198 Ratzinger, *Jesus*, 56–58.

199 Ratzinger, *Jesus*, 57.

200 Ratzinger, *Jesus*, 57: "This miracle of the loaves has three aspects, then. It is preceded by
the search for God, for his word, for the reading that sets the whole of life on the right
path. Furthermore, God is asked to supply the bread. Finally, readiness to share with one
another is an essential element of the miracle. Listening to God becomes living with God,
and leads from faith to love, to the discovery of the other. Jesus is not indifferent towards
men's hunger, their bodily needs, but he places these things in the proper context and in
the proper order."

201 Ratzinger, *Jesus*, 57: "Jesus himself has become the grain of wheat that died and brought
forth much fruit (cf. Jn. 12:24). He himself has become bread for us, and *this* multiplication
of the loaves endures to the end of time, without ever being depleted. This gives us the
background we need if we are to understand what Jesus means when he cites the Old
Testament in order to repel the tempter: "Man does not live by bread alone…but by everything that proceeds out of the mouth of the Lord." (Deut 8:3)."

but most important of all is unbroken fidelity and faithful adoration."[202] On this basis, Ratzinger argues that as soon as this ordering of goods is no longer respected, ruin, even of material goods, follows. This applies to Marxism just as well as to development aid that is material only.[203] Thus, Ratzinger emphasizes most of all the order of things, and in that context also the primary of God and the good.[204]

Ratzinger then moves on to the second temptation, in which the devil places Jesus on the pinnacle of the Temple (Mt. 4:5, Luke 4:9), which Ratzinger considers more difficult to penetrate. In the end, he views it as a warning against possible aberrations of (scholarly) theology, given that Jesus and the devil enter into a debate about Scripture here, which shows that "scriptural exegesis can become a tool of the Antichrist."[205] This has an immediate relation to contemporary issues in theology and exegesis, given that Ratzinger notes that the Antichrist, with the attitude of a modern scholar, uses one of the the dogmas of modernity, i.e. that God cannot act in history, as the measuring rod of all authentic exegesis, or even as its starting point. Therefore, any exegesis which is open to God's acting in history must be considered as unscientifict and fundamentalist in nature.[206] Thus, the question of the way in which Scripture

---

202   Ratzinger, *Jesus*, 57.

203   Ratzinger, *Jesus*, 57–58.

204   Ratzinger, *Jesus*, 58: Here, Ratzinger also briefly addresses the related question of the theodicy, having outlined that what makes a human life good is an orientation towards God and an according ordering of itself: "Of course, one can still ask why God did not make a world in which his presence is more evident – why Christ did not leave the world with another sign of his presence so radiant that no one could resist it. This is the mystery of God and man, which we find so inscrutable. We live in this world, where God is not so manifest as tangible things are, but can be sought and found only when the heart sets out on the 'exodus' from 'Egypt.' It is in this world that we are obliged to resist the delusions of false philosophies and to recognize that we do not live by bread alone, but first and foremost by obedience to God's word. Only when this obedience is put into practice does the attitude develop that is also capable of providing bread for all."

205   Ratzinger, *Jesus*, 60.

206   Ratzinger, *Jesus*, 60: "The common practice today is to measure the Bible against the so-called modern worldview, whose fundamental dogma is that God cannot act in history – that everything to do with God is to be relegated to the domain of subjectivity. And so, the Bible no longer speaks of God, the living God; no, now we alone speak and decide what God can do and what we will and should do. And the Antichrist, with an air of scholarly excellence, tells us that any exegesis that reads the Bible from the perspective of faith in the living God, in order to listen to what God has to say, is fundamentalism; he wants to convince us that only *his* kind of exegesis, the supposedly purely scientific kind, in which God says nothing and has nothing to say, is able to keep abreast of the times."

ought to be interpreted is finally also a question about God, Christ, and their role in the world. In the end, the second temptation of Jesus is, for Ratzinger, about one's way of relating to God, either in an objectifying way, by making God an object and imposing one's own "laboratory conditions" on him, or by surrendering one to God and thus knowing God, rather than tempting God.

Ratzinger then turns to the third temptation, which receives by far the most space in this work. Now, the devil takes Jesus up to a mountain (Matt. 4:8, Luke 4:5 – Ratzinger refers to neither text explicitly), and as Ratzinger puts it, the temptation consists of fulfilling the messianic mission in a particular way, namely by unifying "the whole earth in one great kingdom of peace and well-being."[207] Ratzinger relates this scene to another scene at a mountain top in the Gospel of Matthew, namely the "Great Commission" in Matt. 28:16–20. He notes that the devil offers Jesus only earthly power, whereas Jesus claims both heavenly and earthly power for himself in the latter text – and only heavenly power has true soteriological relevance.[208] This power of Christ, however, is based on his resurrection, which in turn presupposes his humiliation and crucifixion. As Ratzinger notes, the temptation to use power to establish the rule of the powerless Lord has often prevailed in the history of Christianity. He also sees this temptation reflected in the choice of the "robber" (i.e. messianic resistance fighter) Barabbas over Jesus in the passion narrative.[209] Thus, in line with Origen's interpretation, Ratzinger notes that Jesus, the Son of the Father, and Barabbas, whose name also means "son of the father," can be seen as alter egos, or rather, alternatives. That this alternative is not hypothetical, Ratzinger illustrates by means of a reference to Soloviev's *Antichrist*, in which the Anti-Christ presents a book *The Open Way to World Peace and Welfare*, a kind of new Bible, the real message of which is "the worship of well-being and rational planning."[210] Thus, the third temptation asks the fundamental question of what the task of the savior is, which turns out to be the inauguration of "the new community of faith based on Christ," "the radically different community that comes into being through the Cross."[211] This, then, also differs from modern concepts of Christianity, as "a recipe for progress and the proclamation of universal prosperity as the real goal of all religions."[212] These concepts amount

---

207 Ratzinger, *Jesus*, 64.
208 Ratzinger, *Jesus*, 64.
209 Ratzinger, *Jesus*, 65.
210 Ratzinger, *Jesus*, 66.
211 Ratzinger, *Jesus*, 66.
212 Ratzinger, *Jesus*, 69.

to modern forms of that old temptation. Ratzinger places this in the context of two Old Testament expectations, namely one of a (worldly) utopia, and one of a suffering servant, the latter of which came to fulfillment in Jesus' life. However, this leads to the question: What good does this Jesus bring to the world, if not world prosperity and the like? Ratzinger answers this question as follows:

> The answer is very simple: God. He has brought God. He has brought the God who formerly unveiled his countenance gradually, first to Abraham, then to Moses and the Prophets, and then in the Wisdom literature – the God who revealed his face only in Israel, even though he was also honored among the pagans in various shadowy guises. It is this God, the God of Abraham, Isaac, and Jacob, the true God, whom he has brought to the nations of the earth. He has brought God, and now we know his face, now we can call upon him. Now we know the path that we human beings have to take in this world. Jesus has brought God and with God the truth about our origin and destiny: Faith, hope and love. It is only because of our hardness of heart that we think this is too little. Yes indeed, God's power works quietly in this world, but it is the true and lasting power. Again and again, God's cause seems to be in its death throes. Yet over and over again it proves to be the thing that truly endures and saves. The earthly kingdoms that Satan was able to put before the Lord at that time have all passed away. Their glory, their doxa, has proven to be a mere semblance. But the glory of Christ, the humble, self-sacrificing glory, has not passed away, nor will it ever so.[213]

Returning to the temptations, this means for Ratzinger that throughout all temptations Jesus points towards God, rather than to worshipping the well-being of people. He points to the fact that God is God and God is "man's true Good."[214] Similarly, when invited to worship power, Jesus states that only the Lord is to be worshipped. Hence, "the fundamental commandment of Israel is also the fundamental commandment for Christians: Only God is to be worshipped."[215] Ratzinger concludes with a comment on Mark 1:13 and Matt. 4:11, where angels are mentioned that minister to Jesus at the end of temptations. Here, he argues, Psalm 91:11 finds its fulfillment: The angels serve the one that has proven himself to be the Son of God and thus one to whom the heavens

---

213   Ratzinger, *Jesus*, 70.

214   Ratzinger, *Jesus*, 70.

215   Ratzinger, *Jesus* 70. – Ratzinger sees also fundamental continuity between the ten commandments and the Sermon on the Mount (which he considers next in his book).

above stand open, like it was the case with Jacob; Jesus is the "Patriarch of a universalized Israel."[216]

2.5.3   Analysis

On the basis of the above considerations, Ratzinger's approach to canonical exegesis can now be analyzed, following the matrix that is used throughout this study, focusing in particular on the heuristic potential and functioning of the canon in his exegesis.

First of all, the question "what sort of understanding of 'canon' and 'canonical exegesis' is being used?" will be addressed. To begin with, it may be noted that Ratzinger understands the Biblical canon to be the canon of the LXX; this is in line with the confessional tradition of which he is part. He also outlines his preference for a canonical approach to exegesis with reference to his own theological tradition, specifically to the dogmatic constitution *Dei Verbum* of the Second Vatican Council, from which Ratzinger derives, as has already been noted, "a fundamental principle of theological exegesis: If you want to understand the Scripture in the spirit in which it is written, you have to attend to the content and to the unity of Scripture as a whole."[217] Thus, canonical exegesis is also a literary and intertextual undertaking, seeking to place a single text in the context of the entire corpus of texts. The canon of Scripture, however, remains intrinsically bound up with not only the historical authors of the various texts now included into the Biblical canon, but also with the "People of God" as a collective author, as well as with God as their author at the deepest level. Given that the last two authors are still alive and well, the writing – in the sense of rereading and reinterpreting – of Scripture continues. This is of central importance to Ratzinger's understanding of the canon and also for his particular brand of canonical exegesis, in which canon and community are intrinsically connected – and the meaning and significance of Scripture continues to be developed. In fact, one could speak of a continuous process of authoring Scripture by at least two of its authors (the people of God and God). In this context, Ratzinger is willing to argue that his canonical approach does more justice to the historical subjects under investigation than a "non-canonical" historical-critical investigation of the same subject, because the meaning of a text (and of the events that it refers to), only become clear in its history of reception.

---

216   Ratzinger, *Jesus*, 71: "Psalm 91:11 now comes to fulfillment: The angels serve him, he has proven himself to be the Son, and heaven therefore stands open above him, the new Jacob, the Patriarch of a universalized Israel (cf. Jn. 1:51; Gen. 28:12)."

217   Ratzinger, *Jesus*, 10.

Second, when turning to the question of how Ratzinger applies his approach and the sort of role the canon plays in his exegesis, the following can be maintained, particularly with regard to the example of exegesis that was considered above. To begin with, Ratzinger does indeed place the one text of the temptation of Jesus in the wilderness – even if in this case the text of all three synoptic gospels seems to be Ratzinger's starting point – in the context of the broader literary whole of Scripture, a process that is guided by not in the last place by insights from patristic exegetes. This not only leads to what one might call a harmonized picture of Jesus' temptation in the wilderness, but also to an account of this event that is not primarily interested in its historical reconstruction, but rather in discovering its meaning or significance when placing it in the context of Scripture and tradition as a whole. How far Ratzinger takes all of this becomes clear when he appeals to (near-)contemporary interpreters of Scripture, such as Vladimir Soloviev and Alfred Delp, who through their lives and witnesses uncover the meaning of the historical events described in Scripture.

The last remarks lead to an answer to the third sub-question, i.e. "what effect does the canon have on the outcome of the exegesis; how is the canon appealed to in order to make decisions about interpretation and meaning?" In Ratzinger's work, his understanding of and according use of a canonical approach to Scripture has far-reaching consequences indeed. Not only does Ratzinger emphasize the unity of Scripture and the understanding of a part of Scripture in the context of the whole, but he also argues for an understanding of any part of Scripture (including the historical events that Scripture witnesses to) in relation to the unfolding faith and understanding of the people of God. The meaning of historical events, such as the temptation of Jesus in the wilderness (Ratzinger does not address the question of the historicity of this event as such) and the accounts of them are, therefore, not only found in an analysis of the sources and a reconstruction of the historical event, or by relating this event and the appertaining accounts to the historical context (including the "symbolic universe" provided by the remainder of Scripture and extra-canonical writings), but also in the continuing witness and interpretation of the people of God (presumably under God's guidance) of these accounts. This has as a consequence for the exegesis of any biblical text that the process of discovering its meaning – including the meaning of the historical event that the text refers to – is incomplete when a historical-critical construction has been provided and that it is necessary to place it in the horizon of the interpretation of the whole of Scripture by the whole people of God. As indicated earlier, Ratzinger argues that this particular kind of canonical exegesis does more justice to the historical subjects under investigation than a "non-canonical" historical-critical investigation of the same subject.

Finally, the question of what the heuristic value of a canonical approach is for the scholar studied in this section may be addressed. For Ratzinger, the answer seems to be relatively straightforward. By approaching the canonical texts as canonical texts by both acknowledging their claim to witness to God's work in Jesus Christ and by taking into account the place of Scripture in the community of interpretation that the church is, the most justice can be done to what the writings intend to communicate. This approach leads to the discovery of the meaning of texts and the meaning of the events to which they witness, e.g. the life, death, and resurrection of Jesus of Nazareth. This meaning unfolds throughout history in the life of the church and only by taking this into account can justice be done to the historical facts as well. As became clear in the analysis of the example of Ratzinger's exegesis that was presented above, the heuristic and epistemological value of this understanding of what the canonicity of the writings means for their interpretation – and for the interpretation of the historical events to which they witness – is considerable. Even the embodied interpretation of the gospel in the 20th century by a martyr can contribute to the understanding of the historical Jesus. In this way, Ratzinger's model of the historical and canonical study of the New Testament poses significant challenges to general historical-critical research; his own results differ accordingly from other reconstructions of the life of Jesus.

2.5.4   *Conclusions*

Ratzinger's canonical approach to the historical Jesus through the study of the witness of the New Testament as a canonical text, i.e. as a book that both claims to provide an authoritative witness to Jesus of Nazareth and that has its place in the community of the church, leads to an account, in which the meaning of this witness, and hence, the meaning and significance of the events that the witness refers to, unfolds further in the course of history. This combines various hermeneutical insights, many of which are shared, at least tacitly, with other canonical exegetes, in order to review what proper historical research means. That this challenges other approaches may be clear. The notion of the canon denotes for Ratzinger not merely a collection of books, but even more importantly, it describes a characteristic of these books, i.e. their relation to a particular community of interpretation, for which they are authoritative, but always as read and reread by this community. Various intertexts come into play for the interpretation of the text of the New Testament, therefore: The further canonical writings of the New Testament (a harmonizing tendency is not foreign to Ratzinger's work), the writings of the Old Testament, and beyond that, outstanding witnesses from the life of the church that give, in word and deed, a further interpretation of the texts and the events to which they witness.

2.6 The "Amsterdam School of Exegesis"

As a fifth and last approach to canonical exegesis, the so-called "Amsterdam School of Exegesis" will be considered. This approach or "school" is (or was) associated with the (former) faculty of theology at the University of Amsterdam and the Reformed divinity school that used to be affiliated with this faculty. In particular, a series of professors of Old Testament studies and/or biblical theology that taught at the Reformed Divinity School were formative for this tradition of exegesis. This series of professors included: Juda Lion Palache (1886–1944),[218] Martinus Adrianus Beek (1909–1987),[219] Karel A. Deurloo (1936-),[220] Rochus Zuurmond

---

218 See e.g. Uwe F.W. Bauer, כָּל־הַדְּבָרִים הָאֵלֶּכ *All diese Worte: Impulse zur Schriftauslegung aus Amsterdam. Expliziert an der Schilfmeererzählung in Exodus 13, 17–14, 31* (Frankfurt: Lang, 1991), 105–110. See e.g. Juda L. Palache, *Inleiding in de Talmoed* (Amstelveen: Amphora, 1922), *Het heiligdom in de voorstelling der Semietische volken* (Leiden: Brill, 1920), *Over beteekenisverandering der woorden in het Hebreeuws (Semietisch) en andere talen: een vergelijkende studie* (Amsterdam: Hertzinger, 1939), *Het karakter van het oud-testamentische verhaal* (Amsterdam: Hertzberger, 1925), *The "Ebed-Jahveh-enigma in Pseudo-Isaiah: A New Point of View* (Amsterdam: Hertzberger, 1934), *De Sabbath-idee buiten het Jodendom* (Amsterdam: Hertzberger, 1925), *Sinai en Paran: Opera minora* (Leiden: Brill, 1959), *Semantic Notes on the Hebrew Lexicon* (Leiden: Brill, 1959). The latter two titles were published posthumously.

219 See e.g. M.A. Beek, *Das Danielbuch, sein historischer Hintergrund und seine literarische Entwicklung* (Leiden: Ginsberg, 1935), *Inleiding in de joodse apocalyptiek van het Oud- en Nieuwtestamentische tijdvak* (Haarlem: Bohn, 1950), *Aan Babylons stromen* (Amsterdam: Kosmos, 1950), *Wegen en voetsporen van het Oude Testament* (Delft: Gaade, 1953), *De geschiedenis van Israël: van Abraham tot Bar-Kochba* (Zeist: De Haan, 1957), *Atlas van het Tweestromenland* (Amsterdam: Elsevier, 1960), *Wegwijzers en wegbereiders* (Baarn: Bosch Keuning, 1975), see also: M. Heerma van Voss/Ph. H.J. Houwink ten Cate/N.A. van Ugchelen, *Travels in the World of the Old Testament* (FS M.A. Beek; Assen: Van Gorcum, 1974), Lenie van Reijendam-Beek (ed.), *"Hier blijven half alle ogenblikken:" een keuze uit het werk van M.A. Beek* (Baarn: Ten Have, 1988), and Johannes Tromp, "M.A. Beek en de historische kritiek," in: R.B. ter Haar Romeny/Johannes Tromp (ed.), *Quisque suis viribus 1841– 1991. 150 jaar theologie in dertien portretten* (Leiden: Collegium Theologicum c.s. "Quisque suis viribus," 1991), 215–243.

220 On whom, see e.g. Rochus Zuurmond, "A Man of Letters: Karel Deurloo as a Theologian," in: Janet W. Dyk (ed.), *Unless some one guide me...*(FS Karel Deurloo; Maastricht: Shaker, 2001), 1–8, as well as the further contributions in this volume, and Bauer, *Worte*, 126–146. See further: Richtsje Abma (ed.), *Nog dichter bij Genesis: opstellen over het eerste bijbelboek voor Karel Deurloo* (FS Karel A. Deurloo; Baarn, Ten Have, 1995). Deurloo's work includes: K. Bouhuijs/ Karel A. Deurloo, *Dichter bij Genesis* (Baarn: Ten Have, 1967), Karel A. Deurloo, *Kain en Abel: onderzoek naar exegetische methode inzake een kleine "literaire eenheid" in de Tenakh* (Amsterdam: Ten Have, 1967), idem, "De zogenaamde 'Amsterdamse School,'" in: A.F.J. Klijn

(1930-),[221] as well as Frans Breukelman (1916–1993), an associate professor in the same field.[222] Also professors of systematic theology were influential, notably theologians such as Nico T. Bakker (1934), professor of dogmatics at the Reformed divinity school in Amsterdam, and Dick Boer (1939), associate professor of systematic theology at the faculty of theology of the University of Amsterdam,[223]

(ed.), *Inleiding tot de studie van het Nieuwe Testament* (Kampen: Kok, 1982), 165–172, idem/ Rochus Zuurmond (ed.), *De bijbel maakt school: een Amsterdamse weg in de exegese* (Baarn: Ten Have, 1984), idem/F.J. Hoogewoud (ed.), *Beginnen bij de letter Beth* (FS A.G. van Daalen; Kampen: Kok, 1984), idem/F.J. Hoogewoud, "'Communi ardore ad litteras hebraicas inflammati,' bij het vijfentwintigjarige jubileum van SHA," in: Johan de Roos/Arie Schippers/Jan Willem Wesselius (ed.), *Driehonderd jaar oosterse talen in Amsterdam: een verzameling opstellen* (Amsterdam: Juda Palache Instituut, 1986), 91–105, Karel Deurloo, "Exegese naar Amsterdamse Traditie," in: W.A.M. Beuken (ed.), *Inleiding tot de studie van het Oude Testament* (Kampen: Kok, 1986), 1988–195, idem, *De mens als raadsel en geheim: verhalende antropologie in Genesis 2–4* (Baarn, Ten Have, 1988), idem/Rochus Zuurmond, *De dagen van Noach: de verhalen rond de vloed in schrift en oudste traditie* (Baarn: Ten Have, 1991), idem/Wilken Veen (ed.), *De gezegende temidden van zijn broeders: Jozef en Juda in Genesis 37–50* (Baarn: Ten Have, 1995), idem/Bernd J. Diebner (ed.), *YHWH – KYRIOS- ANTITHEISM or THE POWER OF THE WORD* (FS R. Zuurmond; Amsterdam: DBAT, 1996), idem, *Genesis* (Kampen: Kok, ²1998). Deurloo completed a popular biblical theology in later years: Karel Deurloo, *Exodus en Exil* (Kampen: Kok, 2004), with Evert van den Berg/Piet van Midden, *Koning en Tempel* (Kampen: Kok, 2004), and *Onze lieve vrouwe baart een zoon* (Kampen: Kok, 2006).

221   On him, see e.g. the contributions in the *Festschrift*, Deurloo/Diebner (ed.), *YHWH-Kyrios-Antitheism.*

222   On whom, see e.g. the contributions in: Nico T. Bakker (ed.), *Één zo'n mannetje: Frans Breukelman en zijn invloed op tijdgenoten* (Kampen: Kok, 2004), see further also: Nico T. Bakker (ed.), *Debharim* (FS F.H. Breukelman; Kampen: Kok, 1986), Ype Bekker (ed.), *Gesprekken met Frans Breukelman* (Den Haag: Meinema, 1989). Some of his key publications, partially published posthumously, include: Frans H. Breukelman, *Debharim: der biblische Wirklichkeitsbegriff des Seins in der Tat* (Kampen: Kok, 1998), *Schriftlezing* (Kampen: Kok, 1980), "Eine Erklärung des Gleichnisses vom Schalksknecht (Matth. 18, 23–35)," in: Lother Steiger/Eberhard Busch (ed.), *Parrhesia* (FS K. Barth; Zürich: EVZ, 1966), 261–287, *De theologie van de Evangelist Mattheüs: de ouverture van het Evangelie naar Mattheüs. Het verhaal over de genesis van Jezus Christus (Mattheüs 1.1–2:23)* (Kampen: Kok, 1984), "Umschreibung des Begriffs einer 'Biblischen Theologie,'" *TuK* 31/32 (1986), 13–39, תּוֹלְדֹת: *de theologie van het boek Genesis. Het eerstelingschap van Israël temidden van de volkeren op de aarde als thema van "het boek van de verwekkingen van Adam, de mens"* (Kampen: Kok, 1992), *De theologie van de Evangelist Mattheüs: het evangelie naar Mattheüs als "Heilsbotschaft vom Königtum"* (Kampen: Kok, 1996), *Theologische opstellen* (Kampen: Kok, 1999), *De Structuur van de heilige leer in de theologie van Calvijn* (Kampen: Kok, 2003).

223   Dick Boer notably emphasized and further developed the political aspect of this tradition of exegesis, see e.g. Dick Boer, *Een fantastisch verhaal: theologie en ideologische strijd* (Voorburg: Protestantse Stichting tot Bevordering van het Bibliotheekwezen en de

while also the Dutch dogmatic theologian K.H. Miskotte (1894–1976)[224] – and behind him Karl Barth,[225] – who (both) never held a position at the University of Amsterdam, were (very) formative for this tradition of exegesis. Currently, this tradition is continued in the work of the Monshouwer chair of biblical theology at VU University Amsterdam,[226] presently held by Joep Dubbink (1958).[227] It is also practiced at the Miskotte/Breukelman-chair at the Protestant Theological University, currently held by Rinse Reeling Brouwer (1953), and in the work of Klaas Smelik (1950)[228] and René Venema (1960),[229] both from the University of Ghent. Representatives of this tradition come from a number of backgrounds, ranging from Judaism, various kinds of Protestantism, to (Old and Roman) Catholicism. This "school" or rather tradition of exegesis has developed its own pronounced way of doing canonical exegesis that has exercised a considerable

---

Lectuurvoorlichting in Nederland, 1988), idem, *Erlösung aus der Sklaverei* (Münster: ITP-Kompass, 2008), and the contributions interacting with his work in Susanne Hennecke/ Rinse Reeling Brouwer (ed.), *Afdalingen* (Gorinchem: Narratio, 1999), even if it is also present in the work of other representatives of the same tradition, see in general e.g. W. van der Spek, "Exegese en Politiek," in: Deurloo/Zuurmond (ed.), *Bijbel*, 108–114, en Bauer, *Worte*, 147–169. See also e.g.: K. Butting, *Die Buchstaben werden sich noch wundern: innerbiblische Kritik als Wegweisung feministischer Hermeneutik* (Berlin: Alektor, 1994), as well as Rinse Reeling Brouwer, *Over kerkelijke dogmatiek en marxistische filosofie: Karl Barth vergelijkenderwijs gelezen* (Den Haag: Boekencentrum, 1988).

224 See e.g. K.H. Miskotte, *Het wezen der Joodsche Religie* (Amsterdam: Paris, 1932), *Antwoord uit het onweer* (Amsterdam: Holland, 1936), *Edda en Thora* (Nijkerk: Callenbach, 1939), *Bijbelsch ABC* (Nijkerk: Callenbach, 1941), *Hoofdsom der historie* (Nijkerk: Callenbach, 1945), *Als de goden zwijgen* (Amsterdam: Holland, 1956), *Om het levende woord* (Den Haag: Daamen, 1948).

225 On whose view of Scripture in the tradition of Karl Barth, see e.g. Jan Muis, *Openbaring en interpretatie: het verstaan van de Heilige Schrift volgens K. Barth en K.H. Miskotte* (Den Haag: Boekencentrum, 1989).

226 Dirk Monshouwer (1947–2000) was a significant representative of the Amsterdam tradition of exegesis, after his premature death a foundation was established to continue his work: see for an example of his work: Dirk Monshouwer, *Markus en de Torah: een onderzoek naar de relatie tussen het evangelie en de synagogale lezingen in de eerste eeuw* (Kampen: Kok, 1987).

227 See notably *Waar is de Heer?: Dynamiek en actualiteit van het woord van JHWH bij Jeremia* (Gorinchem: Narratio, 1997).

228 See e.g.: K.A.D. Smelik, *Saul: de voorstelling van Israëls eerste koning in de Masoretische tekst van het Oude Testament* (Amsterdam: P.E.T., 1977), idem, *Hagar en Sara: de verhouding tussen Jodendom en Christendom in de eerste eeuwen* (Baarn: Ten Have, 1979), idem, *Converting the Past: Studies in Ancient Israelite and Moabite Historiography* (Leiden: Brill, 1997).

229 See e.g. G.J. Venema, *Reading Scripture in the Old Testament: Deuteronomy 9–10, 31, 2 Kings 22–23, Jeremiah 36, Nehemiah 8* (Leiden: Brill, 1998).

influence (and controversy) in the Netherlands[230] and, in part, also in Germany.[231] Its influence in the Anglophone world has remained limited.[232] Still, this tradition of exegesis makes its own critical proposal for canonical criticism, which makes it worthwhile considering here.[233] This consideration will focus first on a sketch of some key aspects of the Amsterdam approach in terms of its hermeneutics and subsequently on the analysis of a representative exegesis of a New Testament text.

2.6.1   The Canonical Approach of the "Amsterdam School of Exegesis"

The (canonical) approach of the Amsterdam school has been studied in two more encompassing studies by Oost en Bauer.[234] Here, mainly the well-documented study of Bauer will be followed. He provides an overview of the outstanding characteristics that can indeed be discerned in the work of main representatives of

---

230   On the controversial aspects, see especially the overview offered by Roel Oost, *Omstreden bijbeluitleg, aspecten en achtergronden van de hermeneutische discussie rondom de exegese van het Oude Testament in Nederland, een bijdrage tot gesprek* (Kampen: Kok, 1986).

231   A prime example is the dissertation of Bauer, *Worte*, but see also e.g. Boer, *Erlösung*, as well as Ton Veerkamp, *Die Vernichtung des Baal: Auslegung der Konigsbücher (1.17 – 2.11)* (Stuttgart: Alektor, 1983), while also the fact that Breukelman published some of his work in German (rather than in English) will have contributed to this particular kind of reception. – Analogies with a Czech tradition of exegesis have also been noted, see: Jan Heller/ Martin Prudky, "Die Prager Arbeit am Alten Testament und ihre Analogien zur sog. Amsterdamer Schule," *Summa. Blad van de theologische faculteit van de Universiteit van Amsterdam* 19 (1987), 14–18.

232   In spite of an increasing number of publications from the Amsterdam tradition in English. See e.g. M. Kessler (ed.), *Voices from Amsterdam: A Modern Tradition of Biblical Narrative* (Atlanta: Scholars, 1994), Karel A. Deurloo/G.J. Venema, "Exegesis According to Amsterdam Tradition," in: Janet W. Dyk (ed.), *The Rediscovery of the Hebrew Bible* (Maastricht: Shaker, 1999), 3–14, Dyk (ed.), *Unless*, Venema, *Reading*, Richtsje Abma, *Bonds of Love: Methodic Studies of Prophetic Texts with Marriage Imagery* (Assen: Van Gorcum, 1999), T. Walton, *Experimenting with Qohelet: A Text-Linguistic Approach to Reading Qohelet as Discourse* (Maastricht: Shaker, 2006), A.L.H.M. van Wieringen, *The Reading-Oriented Unity of the Book of Isaiah* (Maastricht: Shaker, 2006), Janet W. Dyk (ed.), *Give Ear to My Words: Psalms and other Poetry in and Around the Hebrew Bible* (FS N.A. van Ugchelen; Amsterdam: Societas Hebraica Amstelodamensis, 1996), Bert Dicou, *Edom, Israel's Brother and Antagonist: The Role of Edom in Biblical Prophecy and Story* (Sheffield: Sheffield Academic Press, 1994), J.C. Siebert-Hommes, *Let the Daughters Live!: The Literary Architecture of Exodus 1–2 as a Key for Interpretation* (Leiden: Brill, 1998).

233   See also e.g. the remarks of Reventlow, *Hauptprobleme*, 133–134.

234   See Oost, *Bijbeluitleg*, and Bauer, *Worte*; see also: idem, "Amsterdamer Schule," (www.wibilex .de) 2013, as well as Zwiep, *Tekst II*, 110–113.

this particular tradition of canonical exegesis.[235] The main points that Bauer notes can be paraphrased as follows:[236]

(1) In many ways, the "Amsterdam school" is a typically Reformed school of exegesis, with characteristic emphasis on the theology of the covenant, the prominent position of the Old Testament, and the reformed tradition of translating. This includes a particular proximity to Jewish exegesis and hermeneutics, as the exegetes of the "Amsterdam school" focus on the given text as Tenakh, are aware of its midrashic character, and of the importance of literary features of the text, such as keywords and rhythm, of the significance of the divine Name, of the Torah as Torah of liberation, and of interrelationship between religious praxis and exegesis.

(2) The "Amsterdam school" attaches high significance to the principles of "sacra scriptura sui ipsius interpres" and "sola scriptura" – the latter meaning that the divine Name uses Scripture (and only Scripture) as a means of revealing itself.

(3) The "Amsterdam school" has a particular understanding of hermeneutics: A hermeneutical approach to a text is an approach in which the reader allows the text itself to determine the criteria for its understanding. The "school" does not subscribe to any particular kind of philosophical hermeneutics.

(4) This hermeneutics is both non-idealistic, given that it has its point of departure solely in the revelation of the divine Name, as well as critical, as it goes against the authority of the autonomous subject vis-à-vis the text.

(5) Exegesis and hermeneutics appear in a particular interrelationship with one another: out of the exegesis of individual texts, the hermeneutical horizon arises within which exegesis ought to interpret the texts themselves. This type of hermeneutics is called "biblical theology" and provides the methodology necessary to make the principle "sacra scriptura sui ipsius interpres" work.

(6) Apart from enabling the principles of "sola scriptura" and "sacra scriptura sui ipsius interpres" to function again in a modern theological and scholarly setting, Amsterdam-style biblical theology also has the function of presenting Scripture as "norma normans."

---

235   See for the following Bauer, *Worte,* 190–194, see for his analysis: 26–189, see also Oost, *Bijbeluitleg.*

236   See Bauer, *Worte,* 190–194.

(7)   The unity of Scripture, consisting of the Old and New Testaments (the OT
       in the canon of the Hebrew Bible, i.e. as Tenakh) is emphasized time and
       again. This unity is provided by the unity of the (self-revelation of the)
       divine Name and the appertaining one covenant, which is reflected in a
       consistent pattern of keywords throughout both testaments. This, again,
       leads to an emphasis on the *simplex cognitio Dei* and on the *simplex rev-
       elatio Dei.*

(8)   In line with (and as a consequence of) this understanding of Scripture
       as a unity, while receiving theories about the emergence of Tenakh dur-
       ing the Babylonian exile, as well as, to a limited extent, (post)modern
       theories from the field of literary studies, the exegesis of the "Amsterdam
       School" is primarily (and often exclusively) synchronic and intends to
       safeguard and interpret the texts as they stand.

(9)   The question of the Tenakh as a historical source has been explored in
       particular by Smelik, who argued that questions about the historical
       information that may be gleaned from a text should only be asked after
       having analyzed the text as a literary product and having studied extra-
       biblical sources of historical information.

(10)   The Amsterdam school takes the (theological) primacy of the Tenakh as
       one of its starting points, accordingly, the structure and content of the
       Tenakh are the presupposition for the message of the New Testament,
       which does not so much present something new, but rather constitutes
       the goal of the Tenakh. Thus, the "Amsterdam School" reverses the com-
       mon notion of a "surplus" of the New Testament vis-à-vis the Old in favor
       of a "surplus" of the Old Testament vis-à-vis the New.

(11)   The view that the New Testament is the goal of the Tenakh also means
       that other early Jewish traditions, including the rabbinic tradition, are
       not the goal of Tenakh, as they do not agree with the deep structures of
       the Tenakh.

(12)   The notion of "pars pro toto" is of high importance of the biblical theol-
       ogy of the "Amsterdam School"; rather than attributing the particular to
       the Old Testament and the universal to the New Testament, it is argued
       that in the particularity of Israel (or Jesus), the entirety of humankind is
       at stake. In a way, one might say that the fate of Israel (and Jesus) con-
       cerns the entirety of humankind.

(13)   The use of the pars-pro-toto-principle also contains the risk of potential
       anti- Judaism, particularly when post-Jesuanic Israel is only understood
       as a witness to the wrath of God, in line with Barthian theology.

(14)   The "Amsterdam School" places emphasis on the order of the books of the
       canon of Tenakh (and also on its contents, i.e. the so-called deutero-canonical

books receive no attention), arguing that the historicizing tendency of the canon of the LXX runs the risk of turning the book into a "national history," while something else is at stake.

(15) The thesis of Karl Barth that history is a predicate of revelation is of enormous importance to the "Amsterdam School";[237] as it means that "real" or "biblical" history only takes place there, where God reveals himself or "happens," specifically as a liberating event. Human history, therefore, has no value for knowledge of the Name, and the validity of all social structures can be called into question, which is part of the political side of the "Amsterdam School."

(16) This theological thesis (i.e. as formulated above in 15) is (for some) compatible with a Marxist analysis of bourgeois-capitalist society; contemporary Marxist social analysis then serves in analogy to biblical prophetic criticism of society.

(17) The representatives of the "Amsterdam School" stand in the reformed tradition of Bible translation, which is also reflected in the Dutch *Statenvertaling*, and which is characterized by a strong idiolect translation of Scripture. Only this way of translating can safeguard the critical potential of Scripture.[238]

(18) The liturgical character of biblical texts is of high importance in the "Amsterdam School;" it is generally assumed that the liturgical use of texts led to their canonization.

This overview of the characteristics of the exegesis of the Amsterdam approach to exegesis, as provided by Bauer, also gives an indication of the place of the theological or confessional map that the main representatives of this school occupy. In spite of its Jewish roots (Palache), its liberal protestant heritage (e.g. Beek and his daughter, Lenie van Reijendam-Beek), some Old and Roman Catholic representatives, and the fact that some representatives consider the

---

237 See e.g. Nico T. Bakker, *Geschiedenis in opspraak: over de legitimatie van het concept geschiedenis: een theologische verhandeling* (Kampen: Kok, 1996), Wouter Klouwen, *Die Wirklichkeit der Geschichte: ein Vergleich zwischen K. Barth und G.W.F. Hegel* (Zoetermeer: Boekencentrum, 1998), see also the contributions in: Ype Bekker/Wouter Klouwen/Ad van Nieuwpoort (ed.), *In de ruimte van de openbaring: opstellen voor Nico T. Bakker* (Kampen: Kok, 1999), as well as the earlier doctoral dissertation of Bakker: Nico T. Bakker, *In der Krisis der Offenbarung: Karl Barths Hermeneutik, dargestellt an seiner Römerbrief-Auslegung* (Neukirchen-Vluyn: Neukirchener Verlag, 1974).

238 See e.g. Uwe F.W. Bauer, "Das sogenannte 'idiolekte' Prinzip der Bibelübersetzung – wesentliche Charakteristika und einige praktische Beispiele," in: Hans J. Barkenings/U.F.W. Bauer (ed.), *De Beproeving – over de nieuwe bijbelvertaling* (Kok: Kampen, 2005).

Amsterdam approach to be primarily literary in nature, in its most characteristic form, the theological tradition associated with the Amsterdam approach is that of Calvinism received through the lens of Barth and Miskotte.

2.6.2   *Presentation of a Representative Exegesis*

While most representatives of the "Amsterdam School" are primarily exegetes of the Old Testament/Tenakh, a number of explorations of the New Testament have also appeared, most substantially in the form of Ad van Nieuwpoort's doctoral dissertation on the Gospel of Luke (2006).[239] Van Nieuwpoort currently serves as a minister in the Protestant Church of the Netherlands and is one of the most vocal proponents of the Amsterdam tradition. In his thesis, Van Nieuwpoort offers an exegesis of a number of pericopes of Luke's gospel, one of which will be considered here. Van Nieuwpoort's exegesis leads him to a systematic-theological discussion and ditto conclusions, stating not only that "the Temple to some extent determines the structure of Luke's gospel,"[240] but also that the Gospel of Luke provides one with an "Old Testament" perspective on the Gospel and vice versa; the Gospel is thus placed in the context and (literary as well as theological) framework of Tenakh, while the Gospel also interprets Tenakh in the context of the message about the Messiah. This leads to a situation in which Tenakh and Gospel enter into a reciprocal interpretative relationship that is essential for a proper understanding of both of them.[241] In his systematic theological conclusions, including the explicit acceptance of Karl Barth's "doctrine of Scripture as Testimony,"[242] Van Nieuwpoort also makes exegetical claims, namely that "[i]n scripture we hear a great variety of voices, but they all testify about one Word and one Action,"[243]

---

239   Ad van Nieuwpoort, *Tenach opnieuw: Over het Messiaanse tegoed van het evangelie naar Lukas* (Amsterdam: Van Gennep, 2006).

240   Van Nieuwpoort, *Tenach*, 212, see for his argument and exegesis: 35–81.

241   Van Nieuwpoort, *Tenach*, 212: "Reading through the text of Luke we noticed two perspectives: An "Old Testament" perspective of the Gospel and a Gospel perspective of the Old Testament (Tenakh). In the first perspective Jesus appears within the framework of the Old Testament (Tenakh), the Old Testament elucidating the message of the Gospel. In the second perspective Tenakh appears within the framework of the message about the Anointed One, Jesus, himself opening and explaining Tenakh. Both perspectives affect each other dynamically, thus creating a mutual relationship. They cannot be separated but they may be distinguished one from the other. It is, however, remarkable that none of them ever appears in an absolute way. All through the Gospel they are heard together." For his full argument, see: 83–131.

242   Van Nieuwpoort, *Tenach*, 212.

243   Van Nieuwpoort, *Tenach*, 212.

a unity that is in the first place provided by the unity of the (divine) Name (Van Nieuwpoort acknowledges his debt to Miskotte here): the oneness (in the sense of "simplicitas") of the divine Name (YHWH ECHAD) produces the unity of Scripture.[244]

Finally, Van Nieuwpoort has developed a thesis regarding the "Messianic Credit" of the gospel (c.q. the Gospel of Luke) (capitalization in original), namely the confirmation of the unity of Scripture, which Van Nieuwpoort found in the Messiah himself, more specifically in the way in which he communicates the witness of Moses and the prophets as a true witness. For Van Nieuwpoort, this truth is precisely what Luke referred to when he wrote about the truth in his preface (Luke 1:4).[245]

Having outlined all of this, one may ask: What does the actual exegesis of a text from the Gospel of Luke look like in this context and how does it lead to these conclusions? The particular text to be considered here is the prologue of Luke's gospel (Luke 1:1–4), given its importance for Van Nieuwpoort's overall project and the observation that he already lays out the foundations for the rest of his book in his exegesis of this text.[246]

From the start, Van Nieuwpoort reads the one sentence running through Luke 1:1–4 as Luke's rendering of a theological account of what he intends with his gospel. Thus, Luke 1:1–4 contains Luke's theology *in nuce*.[247] On this basis, Van Nieuwpoort offers his own translation in the tradition of the "Amsterdam

---

244 Van Nieuwpoort, *Tenach*, 212: "This simplicity (oneness) of the Name creates the internal coherence (YHWH ECHAD); unity through simplicity! In the Gospel of Luke it is Jesus, the Anointed One, himself who by going his way shows us the way."

245 Van Nieuwpoort, *Tenach*, 212–213: "In the Anointed One himself, in the way he makes you hear and see the testimony of Moses and the Prophets as a *true* testimony. That is exactly what Luke had in mind when in the Prologue he wrote to Theophilus: 'That you may know the truth concerning the things of which you have been taught.'" (emphasis in original) – His English summary is more forceful than the Dutch main text with regard to Luke 1:4, on 210, namely, Van Nieuwpoort puts it thus: "Was dat (sc. evidencing the veracity, i.e. coherence and unity, of the witness of the Law and the Prophets) ook niet was de evangelist met zijn evangelie beoogde toen hij Theofilus schreef (1:4): '...opdat gij kennis krijgt aangaande de betrouwbaarheid van de woorden waarin gij onderwezen zijt'?"

246 For the following, see Van Nieuwpoort, *Tenach*, 23–33. – Van Nieuwpoort pays no attention whatsoever to text-critical matters; this may stand to reason for Luke 1:1–4, in which there are few serious text-critical issues, but also elsewhere, Van Nieuwpoort does not pay attention to this aspect of the biblical text – in this respect, he is representative for the Amsterdam tradition.

247 Van Nieuwpoort, *Tenach*, 23.

School,"[248] which, in itself, already contains much exegesis – as any translation would. Examples of this include Van Nieuwpoort's decision to subsume Luke's use of διήγησις in Luke 1:1 (which differs from the other gospels) under the use of εὐαγγέλιον in Acts (15:7, 20:24) and the use of the verb εὐαγγελίζομαι in Luke, so that he can say that also Luke's διήγησις is fully εὐαγγέλιον.[249] This is preparation for what Van Nieuwpoort will later do, i.e. emphasize the difference in terms of content between what Luke does and what Greek historians do. Also of interest is the note attached to ἐν ἡμῖν in the same verse, stating that this is an ecclesiological use of ἡμεῖς, namely one that is only available where the πράγματα that are also mentioned in Luke 1:1 occur – this also means that it is not the self-reference of a group with regard to Luke 1:2, the reference to "from the beginning" is suggested to be a reference to Moses and the Prophets, as well as to earlier Christians, while also an intertextual connection between the occurrence of "word" and "beginning" here and in John 1:1 is noted.[250] Concerning v. 3, Van Nieuwpoort substantiates his use of somewhat archaic Dutch ("nagevorst") in order to translate παρηκολουθηκότι with a statement that he wants to avoid the impression that Luke engaged in "journalistic research," but that what he means is a thorough study of the Tenakh.[251] Further to this, the reception of knowledge (ἐπιγινώσκω) that is referred to in v. 4 is annotated by Van Nieuwpoort, relating it to Luke 24:31, where the following is said: αὐτῶν δὲ διηνοίχθησαν οἱ ὀφθαλμοὶ καὶ ἐπέγνωσαν αὐτόν – that the use of ἐπιγινώσκω in Luke 24:31 may also have the meaning "recognize again" is not discussed by Van Nieuwpoort. Rather he claims that the knowledge referred to in Luke 1:4 is of a very special, relational kind.[252] Luke's reference to ἀσφάλεια in v. 4 is understood by Van Nieuwpoort to refer to reliability in a more existential than historical sense.[253] Equally, κατηχέω is commented upon, namely with reference to Acts 18:25, 21:21, where it appears with reference to being taught about the Scriptures, for Van Nieuwpoort, the

---

248   On which see e.g. P.J. van Midden/Karel A. Deurloo, "De Bijbel op zijn Amsterdams," in: K. Spronk (ed.), *De Bijbel vertaald: De kunst van het kiezen bij het vertalen van de bijbelse geschriften* (Zoetermeer/Kapellen: Meinema/Pelckmans, 2007), 165–179, as well as J.C. Siebert-Hommes, "De 'Amsterdamse School,'" in: P.J. Knegtmans/P. van Rooden (ed.), *Theologen in ondertal: godgeleerdheid. Godsdienstwetenschap, het Athenaeum Illustre en de Universiteit van Amsterdam* (Zoetermeer: Boekencentrum, 2003), 177–196.

249   Van Nieuwpoort, *Tenach*, 23.

250   Van Nieuwpoort, *Tenach*, 24.

251   Van Nieuwpoort, *Tenach*, 25.

252   Van Nieuwpoort, *Tenach*, 25.

253   Van Nieuwpoort, *Tenach*, 25.

Gospel of Luke is about the reliability of Tenakh, which then also determines the interpretation of v. 4.[254] That "the words," as they are mentioned in v. 4, must also refer to the Tenakh, seems to be implied. Following this translation, which as such already indicates in which direction Van Nieuwpoort is going to interpret Luke 1:1–4, an exegetical discussion follows. Here, Van Nieuwpoort restates his proposal to read Luke 1:1–4 as Luke's personal rendering of an account for what follows, for which he now finds parallels in the first and second endings of the Gospel of John (John 20:31, 21:24) and further in Rev. 1:1–3, in Van Nieuwpoort's words: "In deze proloog klinkt al helemaal dat mee, wat hij zich in de vormgeving van zijn evangelie ten doel stelt."[255] The question that Van Nieuwpoort then asks is how "the words," of which Luke wishes to assure the reliability of, are to be understood? As a first possible answer, Van Nieuwpoort refers to an interpretation in line with an understanding of Luke as a historian working along the lines of ancient historiographers, recognizing the formal parallels between Luke's prologue and that of other historians.[256] However, Van Nieuwpoort wonders whether the formal parallels between Luke and the ancient historians also mean that Luke worked indeed as an ancient historian. He doubts this, taking his point of departure in Luke 1:1, where Luke places himself in a particular tradition, consisting of πολλοί, who have already attempted to order the account (διήγησις) of the things that have taken place among "us." The question arises who these "many" are that have attempted to give an account of what has happened. Van Nieuwpoort brushes the option of "Q" aside, because so little has remained of these "many" sources ("Het zou teruggaan op Q, maar de vraag is dan waarom van die velen zo weinig materiaal is overgebleven.")[257] Van Nieuwpoort also paraphrases the position of Conzelmann, who, not unlike Bovon (according to Van Nieuwpoort), sees Luke 1:1–4 as a tool for Luke's positioning of himself with regard to the very earliest

---

254   Van Nieuwpoort, *Tenach*, 25.

255   Van Nieuwpoort, *Tenach*, 26.

256   Van Nieuwpoort, *Tenach*, 26–27, referring to the commentaries on Luke by Jakob van Bruggen, *Lucas. Het Evangelie als voorgeschiedenis* (Kampen: Kok, 1993) and François Bovon *Das Evangelium nach Lukas* 1–4 (Zürich: Benzinger, 1989–2009).– Van Nieuwpoort seems to use secondary literature sparingly, again in line with a tendency of the Amsterdam School. However, it does cause him to miss out on important works, such as Alexander's monograph on Luke 1.1-4 and Acts 1:1, see Loveday C. Alexander, *The Preface to Luke's Gospel: Literary Convention and Social Context in Luke 1:1–4 and Acts 1:1* (Cambridge: Cambridge University, 1993).

257   Van Nieuwpoort, *Tenach*, 27; Van Nieuwpoort is hard to follow here, in his main text, he refers to Q only, but in note 22 (on page 27), he notes that Craig A. Evans, *Luke* (Grand Rapids: Baker, 1990), 18, refers to Mark, Q, and other sources.

days of the nascent Christian movement.[258] Van Nieuwpoort, apparently, finds this all unconvincing and wants to explore whether it could not be the case that Luke renders a theological account of what he is about to do, theology, in this case, being distinct from history. This leads him to restating the question: Who are the "many" that Luke speaks of? In order to answer this question, Van Nieuwpoort states that it is necessary first of all to consider what Luke may have in mind when he refers to πράγματα in v. 1. The answer to this is that Luke speaks of the πράγματα of God, a thesis which Van Nieuwpoort substantiates in two ways: (a) by referring to an addition to the Hebrew text of Isa. 25:1 in the LXX;[259] and (b) by referring to Luke's combination of πράγματα with πληροφορέω, which is unusual among Greek historians. This immediately means for Van Nieuwpoort that the πράγματα here must be a way of speaking of the many דְּבָרִים that spring from the one דְּבַר of God, who spoke "in the beginning,"[260] Therefore, Luke does not talk about history here, his choice of words shows that he intends to transcend the conventions of Greek historiography, to do something completely different ("volstrekt anders").[261] That is to say: he writes not as a historian about supposedly historically verified facts ("zogenaamd historisch verifieerbaar gebeurde feiten"), but as an evangelist about that which has been given to him by the eyewitnesses and servants of the word from the beginning.[262] Based on this, Van Nieuwpoort suggests that the "many" that have already attempted to order the account of the things that have happened from the beginning, may well include Moses and the Prophets (capitalization Van Nieuwpoort) too, given that these also had their point of departure in the πράγματα that happened "among us." It is in the light of these πράγματα, that led many (i.e. apostles, Moses, prophets) to provide an orderly account, that Luke sees his task and therefore, combines, because of these πράγματα, the offices of prophet, evangelist, and apostle.[263] Subsequently, Van Nieuwpoort interprets the καὶ in v. 2 as a καὶ *epexegeticum*, by stating that the eyewitnesses

---

258   Van Nieuwpoort, *Tenach*, 27–28, see Hans Conzelmann, *Die Mitte der Zeit* (rev. ed.; Tübingen: Mohr, 1960), 203.

259   Van Nieuwpoort, *Tenach*, 28. One may debate, by the way, whether this really is an *addition* and not a translation of one word by means of two.

260   Van Nieuwpoort, *Tenach*, 28, restated on 29: "En zoals Lukas de πράγματα tilt op het niveau van de דְּבָרִים, door dit woord in de formulering te verbinden met het πληροφορέω…".

261   Van Nieuwpoort, *Tenach*, 29.

262   Van Nieuwpoort, *Tenach*, 29. This amounts to translation of "als een evangelist over datgene wat hem van 'ooggetuigen en dienaren van het woord van den beginner' is aangereikt."

263   Van Nieuwpoort, *Tenach*, 29.

are eyewitnesses as servants of the word.[264] Luke now places himself in this broad tradition, associating himself with the "ecclesiological ἡμῖν" of v. 1, not so much writing out of a feeling of deficit, because he does not belong to the first generation and had to make do with what he can achieve as an historian, but much rather, because he feels very much in touch with the πράγματα, even in a rather immediate way.[265] Having thus laid the groundwork, Van Nieuwpoort then aligns himself largely with Schürmann, who argued the following about Luke: "Führend ist bei ihm nicht...historisches Interesse, sondern ein tradiertes Schema vom 'Weg Jesu,' dem als vorgegebenem kerygmatischem Rahmen aller vorgefundene Erzählungs- und Redestoff einzufügen war" as well as "Er (Luke) schreibt nicht als 'Historiker' für Zweifelnde, die nach 'Beweisen' rufen; vielmehr muss die Übereinstimmung der katechetischen λόγοι mit der apostolischen Paradosis allen Glaubenden evident gemacht werden."[266] Schürmann seems to think of early Christian traditions regarding Jesus, though, while Van Nieuwpoort gives another interpretation, pointing to the use of κατηχέω in relation to the Scriptures (Acts 18:25, 21:21, see also Rom. 2:18). Thus, Van Nieuwpoort concludes: "In deze catechetische λόγοι gaat het in de eerste plaats om Mozes en de Profeten."[267] Therefore, the order that Luke wants to attain with his narrative is a scriptural order. In other words, it is not history, but doctrine, that counts here.[268] Van Nieuwpoort will show this in the remainder of his study, but it is already determined by his findings regarding Luke 1:1–4, as he concludes:

> "How will Theophilus, and in him all the hearers of the gospel 'gain knowledge concerning the reliability of the words?' This will happen through the proclamation of the incarnate knowledge of the Lord, through the proclamation of the Messiah Jesus. In this way, Luke is able to present his entire theological program to us in his prologue. This will

---

264 Van Nieuwpoort, *Tenach*, 29, in note 28 referring to Bovon, *Lukas*, 37: "Die Augenzeugen sind zugleich auch die Diener des Wortes." In an interesting variation on the typical Amsterdam emphasis on word order, Van Nieuwpoort adds to this "Wij zouden eerder zeggen, de bijbelse volgorde van het horen naar het zien in ogenschouw nemend: als dienaren van het Woord zijn zij ooggetuigen!" – To be sure, on p. 30, Van Nieuwpoort speaks of "ooggetuigen en dienaren van het woord" again.

265 Van Nieuwpoort, *Tenach*, 30.

266 Heinz Schürmann, *Das Lukasevangelium* 1 (Freiburg: Herder, 1984), 12.

267 Van Nieuwpoort, *Tenach*, 32: "In these catechetical λόγοι, it is in the first place about Moses and the Prophets." Whether this squares with the use of the same verb in relation to Christian teaching and proclamation in a broader sense, such as in 1 Cor. 14:16, and probably also Gal. 6:6, see further also Acts 21:24, is a question.

268 Van Nieuwpoort, *Tenach*, 32.

have to be the "order" that determines the way in which we will have to listen to his gospel in this study."[269]

2.6.3   Analysis

When turning to an analysis of this example of the canonical exegesis of the Amsterdam School, the following observations may be made.

With regard to the first sub-question, "what sort of understanding of 'canon' and 'canonical exegesis' is being used?" a fairly precise answer can be given. For Van Nieuwpoort, the biblical canon consists of the Tenakh and the twenty-seven books of the New Testament. Questions of textual criticism or questions of different canons, such as that of the LXX, do not play a role, nor does the question of the development of the canon in general. However, the way in which Van Nieuwpoort describes the canon and its functioning does imply something about this development, namely that the canonization of the Tenakh was (largely) finished by the time of the writing of the Gospel of Luke. Accordingly, the canon of the Tenakh is treated as a fixed literary unit. With regard to the development of the canon of the New Testament, Van Nieuwpoort takes a position that implies a number of things about the relationship between the two parts of the canon of the Christian Bible. Most of this has to do with his argument that the New Testament, c.q. the Gospel of Luke was written to place the Tenakh in the light of the Messiah, i.e. Jesus Christ, and to be read itself in the light of the Tenakh. With regard to the Gospel of Luke this means specifically that it is Luke's intention to present the story of Jesus in the framework of the deep structure of the canon of Tenakh, a notion fundamental to the Amsterdam School of exegesis. Luke, in other words, wrote with a certain "canonical consciousness." This deep structure, based on the *simplex revelatio* of the Word, also provides the unity both of Tenakh and of Tenakh and gospel. It also means that Luke understood the literary unity and structure of the Tenakh in the same way as Van Nieuwpoort does and patterned his own gospel after this. In other words, Van Nieuwpoort – and with him, to a large extent, the representatives of the "Amsterdam School" of exegesis – not only works with an understanding of the canon as a specific list of books, but also with a very specific understanding of the structure of these books. This structure began in the Tenakh and continued in the New Testament, and also provides for the unity of both testaments. This is, on the one hand, a literary observation

---

269   Van Nieuwpoort, *Tenach*, 33 "own translation".

and an exegetical thesis. On the other hand, this deep structure is based on a theological conviction, namely the doctrine of the *simplex revelatio* of the Word that creates unity in the diversity of literary works that the canons of both testaments also contain. To this should be added that literary and theological concerns regarding the canon and its properties cross paths in a similar manner on a related level, namely the level of history and historicity. For the Amsterdam School, at least as it is represented by Van Nieuwpoort – and certainly also by his mentors Deurloo and Bakker – the biblical books evoke and create a literary world of their own, not unlike any piece of literature does. This concept of what may be called a literary universe, governed by the structures and catchword connections already mentioned, counts at the same time as the revelatory creation of distinct "history," the history of God, or "the Name," that truly matters, unlike matters of "general history."

Concerning the second sub-question, "how is this approach applied, i.e. what sort of role does the canon play in the exegesis?" also a number of remarks may be made. It is clear from the start that Van Nieuwpoort intends to read the Gospel of Luke against the background, which turns out to mean: In light of Tenakh. Specifically, he intends to read Luke in light of a very specific understanding of Tenakh, i.e. as it is understood in the tradition of the "Amsterdam School" of exegesis, and therefore, with a clear theological framework in mind, inherent as it is to this view of the structure and unity of Tenakh. In other words, for the exegesis of New Testament texts, *in casu* the Gospel of Luke, a specific understanding of the canon of the "Old Testament," i.e. Tenakh, is of fundamental hermeneutical importance. This again means that a particular (and theologically charged) understanding of the relationship between both Testaments also guides the exegesis. The canonical vision that guides Van Nieuwpoort's exegesis provides a very clear matrix within which texts are to be read. The meaning of the text is found within the text itself, to the extent that this text is placed within the preconceived matrix of the theology of the Tenakh. What this means for the exegesis will become clear in the answer to the next sub-question.

What effect does it have on the outcome of the exegesis, i.e. how is the canon appealed to in order to make decisions about interpretation and meaning? This sub-question can be answered by pointing to the following striking aspects of Van Nieuwpoort's exegesis. First, through his exegesis runs a clear dislike of anything that reeks of reading Luke as a historian. While this is substantiated exegetically by Van Nieuwpoort, this dislike also has a basis in his understanding of the functioning of the biblical canon as a vehicle (a particular, i.e. Barthian) understanding of divine revelation that cannot be found in history, but that creates its own and normative history.

Just like the canon of the LXX is suspicious because of its – alleged – tendency to write a "national history" of the people of Israel, the possibility that Luke might be operating along the lines of Hellenistic historiography is also suspect, because it might venture into a different sort of history than it should, given the norms provided by the canonical theology of Tenakh. Second, at the level of the exegesis of particular words, the view that Van Nieuwpoort has of the biblical canon influences his interpretation to a very high extent. As may have become clear from the above presentation of parts of Van Nieuwpoort's exegesis, this approach results in a very strong tendency to read terminology that occurs in the Gospel of Luke virtually exclusively of similar language that occurs in (Greek translations of) Tenakh. More specifically: Van Nieuwpoort reads the Gospel of Luke, whenever possible – and for him, this is possible in general and especially when Luke seems to deviate a little from Greco-Roman literary conventions – in terms of the linguistic and theological deep structure of Tenakh. In fact, he argues that it is the aim of the Gospel of Luke, as outlined in the appertaining preface, to indicate that the order (or structure) of Tenakh is the order according to which the story of Christ has to be read (and written). Third, the combination of these first two points inevitably leads to theological exegesis of a particular kind. As has become clear, Van Nieuwpoort's theological and hermeneutical convictions lead him to judge the plausibility of possible meanings of words in a distinct way: Greek words are given their meaning by way of reading them – interestingly enough, often by way of the LXX – in light of their Hebrew counterpart, which in turn, receives its meaning on the basis of the canonical theology of Tenakh that is Van Nieuwpoort's starting point. Even when there is only the slightest possibility that this could be the case, Van Nieuwpoort will opt for this, without much consideration of alternatives. The reason for doing so can be found in his understanding of the canonical coherence of the Tenakh and New Testament.

Finally, one may ask what the heuristic and epistemological value of a "canonical approach?" is for the exegesis that Van Nieuwpoort presents. This value is threefold. First of all, the canonical approach enables him to relate the Gospel of Luke to the "Old Testament" in a literary and theological manner. Second, his "canonical approach" gives him an exegetical key to the Gospel of Luke on the level of the exegesis of individual words and expressions: The "canonical approach" that he uses leads him to read virtually everything Luke writes more or less exclusively in the light of similar expressions in the Tenakh. Third, on the level of theology, his canonical approach gives him a hermeneutical key to Luke's theological concept, which is none other than that of Tenakh, at least in terms of structure.

2.6.4 *Conclusions*

The "canonical approach" of the "Amsterdam school" of exegesis – both words are not used as such by those who may be seen as representatives of this tradition of exegesis, but they seem to be heuristically helpful – leads to a very pronounced kind of New Testament exegesis. Based on a very specific understanding of the canon of Tenakh in terms of a linguistic deep structure that is at the same time a theological deep structure, and reading New Testament literature, *in casu* the Gospel of Luke, along the same lines, an emphatically non-historical (in the general sense of the word) and just as emphatically theological (as understood in the Barthian tradition with which the "Amsterdam school" aligns itself in general) exegesis is reached that, in the case of the Gospel of Luke, mainly makes a theological point about the "messianic credit" of the New Testament. The canon plays a governing role in this exegesis, determining the interpretation of words and intertextual connections, and in many ways, serves as the literary container of a theology based on the deep structure of Tenakh, to which the New Testament adds, using exactly the same kind of deep structure, the story of the "Anointed One."

CHAPTER 3

Canonical Exegesis Considered: Heuristic Potential and Potential Pitfalls

Canonical approaches to Scripture, as they have been considered above, all seek to restore the relationship between biblical studies and theology or, a little broader, between biblical scholarship and the life of the church, and, a little broader yet, between the text and the community of interpretation. At the same time, all of the approaches considered above argue that by studying Scripture from a canonical perspective, they do more justice to the texts themselves than other approaches. Later authors, such as Vanhoozer, but also scholars working in the field of reception history and/or contextual hermeneutics, can be seen as having received these insights and developed them further, notably in relation to postmodern thinkers; however, the agenda has been set by those initiating the search for a canonical approach to Scripture.

In an attempt to provide an overview of the various issues addressed and questions raised by canonical critics in relation to biblical exegesis, here, the hermeneutical model of the world "behind the text," the world "of the text," and the world "in front of the text" will be used as a framework. While canonical approaches to exegesis address mainly the latter two "worlds," they also make claims about one's accessing of the first of these "worlds" and its relevance for exegesis. Therefore, all of these three "worlds" will be considered in relation to canonical criticism here. Finally, a number of potential objections to canonical approaches to Scripture will be considered. While the following section of this study does have an evaluative aspect as well, its main purpose is to probe the potential of canonical approaches to Scripture and their heuristic value through a systematization of the questions that they raise. For this reason, at times the considerations offered here will also move beyond the five canonical approaches considered above and draw attention to further points of interest – or points of contact with theological and other insights. In particular, this will be done in a subsequent chapter on ecumenical hermeneutics and canonical criticism.

3.1 Scripture and Community: The World in Front of the Text

First of all, canonical exegesis and the "world in front of the text" will be considered. All of the above canonical approaches are very much concerned with

© KONINKLIJKE BRILL NV, LEIDEN, 2015 | DOI 10.1163/9789004301016_004

the relationship between the canonical texts and the communities of interpretation that produced them and in which they continue to function. Here, attention will be given to: (1) The interrelationship between text and community; (2) the understanding of Scripture as the book of the church; (3) the relationship between (canonical) biblical criticism and theology; and (4) canonical criticism and some aspects of contemporary philosophical hermeneutics. The question of canonical criticism and ecumenical hermeneutics will be discussed in a later chapter.

3.1.1   *The Interrelationship between Text and Community*

Attention to the way in which canonical texts came into being, i.e. in communities of interpretation preceding the current canonical texts and the aim with which they came into being, were collected and handed on, serves as a basis for the canonical critics' insistence that the interrelationship between text and interpretative community is part and parcel of the canonical texts as they exist in their current form(s).[1] It is when focusing on the former, c.q. historical aspect of the relationship between text and community, that canonical approaches remain the closest to "classical" historical-critical scholarship. For example, Söding has drawn attention to this with regard to the New Testament form criticism, noting that the form critical approach to the New Testament has made clear that the writings contained in the New Testament are indeed literature intended for readers, i.e., these writings need to be understood in relation to the communities in which they came into existence; processes of canonization are not foreign to such communities.[2] Barthel has made similar observations

---

1   See with this emphasis notably also Watson, *Text*, 225–226; the same is demonstrated throughout Watson, *Gospel*. See also: Seckler, "Problematik," 31, listing new insights of canonical critics: "zum einen die Wahrnehmung der *religiösen Dimension,* der *spirituellen Eigenart* und der *ekklesiologischen bzw. Soziokulturellen Bewandtnis* eines Kanons heiliger Texte." – A certain paradox remains, of course, as Ricoeur, puts it: "To make the paradox more vivid, I will express it in the form of a circle, noting that one could see things in such a way that the Church as a textual authority, would be making a decision on a question of textual authority, basing its authority on the text itself that autorises it." (Ricoeur, "Canon," 7–8).

2   Söding, "Kanon," l-li: "Die formgeschichtliche Schule...hat...*en gros* und *en detail* deutlich herausgearbeitet, dass die biblischen Schriften in einem eminenten Sinn 'Literatur für Leser'...sind. Die Entstehung und Tradierung der alttestamentlichen Schriften setzt...die Größe Israel voraus, das sich...als Gottesvolk versteht; die neutestamentlichen Schriften sind im Prozess der Konstituierung der Ekklesia entstanden und dienen dem, was Paulus ihren 'Aufbau' genannt hat." – For considerations about "pre-canonical" aspects of the (now canonical) New Testament Becker/Scholz (ed.), *Kanon*, 623–678, 634–643.

with regard to (Old Testament) redaction criticism.[3] It is of some importance to underline this in order to avoid the impression that the relationship between canonical and non-canonical approaches to Scripture is primarily antagonistic, or that a hermetic divide exists between the two of them. Of course, it is also true that not all canonical critics are equally interested in precisely this historical relationship between text and community. While Sanders, for example, places emphasis on it (it is even part of his vantage point into canonical criticism to begin with), the Amsterdam School is only nominally interested in this question and it hardly plays a role in its exegetical praxis. Furthermore, Childs and Stuhlmacher seem to occupy positions between these two extremes represented by Sanders and the "Amsterdam School," while Ratzinger might be more interested in the relationship between the gospels and later communities of interpretation than in the original communities. By stressing the relationship between text and community in the process of the production and (earliest) reception of texts, it seems hard to deny that canonical critics have done the exegesis of the New Testament a great service by assisting in the rediscovery of the relationship between the text and the world in front of the text, and the place of the reading community in the production of texts. At the same time, it is typical of canonical approaches to Scripture to go quite substantially beyond such historical observations however important they are to appreciate early Christian texts and their readership.

3.1.2   *Scripture as the Book of the Church*

The way in which canonical approaches to Scripture go beyond the historical observations, as they were discussed in the previous section, is formulated succinctly by Luz, interacting with the work of Childs and Stuhlmacher, who states that the Bible is much more than a piece of literature, a document pertaining to the history of religious or the history of culture. Indeed, it is the book of the Church; the canonical approach to Scripture reminds the exegete of this fact.[4] This insight takes the historical relationship between "canon and community" one step further, as it indicates that the continuation of a relationship between the canonical texts and a succession of communities of interpretation is part and parcel of the way in which canonical texts function and are to be understood, i.e.: not apart from such communities. This is again based on historical observations: The process of the collecting and handing on of an ever more

---

3   See Barthel, "Debatte," 2.

4   Luz, "Exegese," 40n1: "[D]ie Bibel (ist) viel mehr als ein religionsgeschichtliches, kulturgeschichtliches oder literarisches Dokument, nämlich das Buch der Kirche. Daran erinnert der 'canonical approach.'"

developed collection of canonical books as the authoritative memory of the church(es) is a historical fact which is hard to ignore. This perspective from the field of New Testament exegesis corresponds with more philosophical and dogmatic perspectives on the canon, such as the one offered by Ricoeur and which,[5] in turn, may be regarded as widely reflected in ecumenical discussions regarding "Scripture and Tradition."[6] Another such perspective is described by Barthel:

> Die Autorität des biblischen Kanons liegt nicht im Text als solchem beschlossen, aber sie ist ebenso wenig ein reiner Akt der Zuschreibung durch die Rezeptionsgemeinschaft. Sie ergibt sich vielmehr aus dem hermeneutischen Zusammenspiel beider: auf der einen Seite steht der Text, der als Werk abgelöst von seinen Entstehungsbedingungen, der "Welt hinter dem Text," eine Welt vor sich entwirft und die Möglichkeit einer neuen Weise des In-Welt-Seins eröffnet. Auf der anderen Seite steht die Rezeptionsgemeinschaft, die jene "Welt vor dem Text" als Erschließung neuer Lebensmöglichkeiten auf ihre eigene Welt bezieht und im Verstehen des Textes zugleich ein neues Selbstverständnis entwickelt. Kanonisierung ist dabei im aktiven und prozessualen Sinne zu verstehen: Seine Autorität gewinnt der Kanon im fortschreitenden Prozess der verstehenden Aneignung, in dem die Gemeinschaft die lebenserhellende und – verändernde Kraft der kanonischen Texte erkennt und zugleich anerkennt.[7]

However, the point where canonical critics go beyond historical observations is there, where it is observed that this relationship between canonical texts and community of interpretation still exists, i.e. in the relationship between (various forms of) the Bible and (a multitude of) churches, and that exegesis of the New Testament has its place in this relationship and needs to interact with the faith of this community or these communities.[8] Or to formulate it slightly differently: Canonical critics recognize that the canonical texts of the New

---

5   See Ricoeur, "Canon," and idem, "The 'Sacred' Text and the Community," in: idem, *Figuring the Sacred, Religion, Narrative and Imagination* (Minneapolis: Fortress, 1995), 68–72.

6   See e.g. the overview offered in Peter-Ben Smit, *Tradition in Dialogue. The Concept of Tradition in International Anglican Bilateral Dialogues* (Amsterdam: VU University, 2012).

7   Barthel, "Debatte," 1.

8   To be sure, this applies to the first part of the Christian Bible as well, but that is not the topic of this study, which focuses on the New Testament, and within the New Testament on the canonical gospels.

Testament come to the present interpreter not only as historical source, but also as texts with claims upon the reader, to which they can be seen as demanding a response. Of the canonical critics considered above, particularly Stuhlmacher, Childs, and the "Amsterdam School" do not tire of emphasizing this aspect of the contemporary relationship between canonical Scriptures and their readership. Sanders, in a way that is compatible with the attention of the "Amsterdam School" for midrashic exegesis, would even argue that the *relecture* or the rewriting of the texts in the process of interpretation is part of the way in which the texts themselves wish to be interpreted. All of the canonical critics discussed above also add that such a reading of a canonical body of texts always happens with a "grammar" in mind,[9] or to put it with the terminology of the early church (received explicitly by Childs, Ratzinger, and Stuhlmacher), a "rule." While the canonical critics will generally argue that such a rule takes the shape of a confession of faith, in whichever form, it should be underlined that every community of interpretation – including a community of scholarly exegetes – has indeed such a rule. In fact, every community of interpretation, *nolens volens*, one might say, positions itself vis-à-vis the claims of the texts that it reads. In this way, canonical exegesis, which in this respect comes very close to reader-response criticism or a hermeneutics of *Rezeptionsästhetik*, is simply an accurate description of what takes place in exegesis in any case and a correction of scholarly exegesis' self-perception, rather than something really novel. What may be the most novel aspect of canonical approaches to Scripture as far as (academic) biblical scholars are concerned is the fact that they are also are seen as part of a community of interpretation that interacts with the texts that it studies, a fact that is not always readily acknowledged. Canonical approaches to Scripture, however seek to acknowledge and even emphasize this and to make it hermeneutically fruitful. The latter already implies that neither the (meaning of) canonical Scriptures, nor the identity of the interpreting community are fixed entities. In fact – and at least implicitly – canonical critics could be said to be part of a dynamic described as follows by Ricoeur in his paper "The Canon between the Text and the Community":

> ...I must immediately concur that the relationship instituted by the Canon between the community and its texts is indeed a circle. We stated as much right at the beginning: Everything revolves around the word "*between*" in the title of our paper. But what sort of circle is it? I have no hesitation in calling it hermeneutic, in the sense that it is a circle of

---

9 See, e.g., Theißen, *Religion*, 356–384

interpretation, by virtue of which a community interprets itself by interpreting its texts. In an equivalent way, we can say that through this circle
two identities are determined, in a parallel and in a mutual way: The
identity of the Bible as *this* Book, and the identity of the ecclesiastical
community as *this* community. But this mutual determination is not seen
in its result – the Canon that is already definitively closed, the Church
that is already instituted – but in its process. The mutual relationship is
between canonization and institution in the active sense of the word. It
is a relationship between processes of individualization and not between
the individualities that are constituted.[10]

3.1.3   *Is Every Critic a Theologian?*

The considerations presented in the previous section can be developed somewhat further. A starting point for this is the observation that other approaches
to biblical scholarship, not in the last so-called contextual criticism, have also
begun to emphasize the importance of the interface between a scholar's worldview and the texts he or she analyzes. For example, a scholar such as Fernando
Segovia, who subscribes to a self-description as a "cultural critic," has in recent
years put forward an argument that precisely because he reads Scripture criti-
cally – as a postcolonial and cultural critic – he ought to also consider himself
a constructive theologian, given his interaction with (the canonical) texts as
part of a community interpretation.[11] By way of example, this will be briefly
considered here, as it is of significance for what will follow about the potential
of canonical approaches to Scripture. Segovia's scholarly journey, leading to
the insight just mentioned, began in the 1960s in a Roman-Catholic seminary,
that is, with theological training in an explicitly ecclesial context.[12] From there,
Segovia moved on, especially from the agenda of historical criticism as outlined
by, for example, Stendahl,[13] to cultural studies,[14] and from there to postcolonial

---

10   Ricoeur, "Canon," 21. See also Barthel, "Debatte," 1.
11   Fernando F. Segovia, "Biblical Criticism and Postcolonial Studies: Towards a Postcolonial
      Optic," in: R.S. Sugirtharajah (ed.), *The Postcolonial Biblical Reader* (Oxford: Blackwell,
      2006), 33–44, 43.
12   See: Fernando F. Segovia, "My Personal Voice: The Making of a Postcolonial Critic," in:
      Ingrid Rosa Kitzberger (ed.), *The Personal Voice in Biblical Interpretation* (London:
      Routledge, 1999), 25–37, 35nl.
13   See Segovia, "Voice," 29, referring to Krister Stendahl, "Biblical Theology, Contemporary,"
      in: G.A. Buttrick (ed.), *The Interpreter's Dictionary of the Biblical* (Nashville: Abingdon,
      1962), 1418–1432.
14   See Segovia, "Voice," 29–32.

criticism and (again) theology. The step from "traditional" historical criticism to postcolonial criticism for Segovia involved a number of significant insights. First, he notes that he realized that a neutral and objective reader did not exist; whatever was presented as such was always a reader that had "bracketed" her or his identity.[15] Therefore, Segovia began to take the position that readers "were always inevitably positioned and interested, culturally and historically conditioned and engaged."[16] Second, there is a realization "that a text has no meaning and history without an interpreter." And finally, that there is "the profoundly political character of the interpretative task."[17] In line with this, Segovia "argued therefore, that the fundamental mode of discourse within cultural studies as a whole, and thus, within both intercultural criticism and the hermeneutics of otherness and engagement, was neither historical nor literary, but rather ideological in nature."[18] Segovia's subsequent involvement in postcolonial criticism was a specification of this cultural study's approach on a "geopolitical level."[19] The step from here to theology is not at all that large, as may be apparent from the following, longer, quotation from an essay by Segovia discussing various "grand models" in biblical criticism:

> The model of cultural studies is no less theological than any of the other models, but it does call for radical openness in this regard as well. Besides the factors of sexuality and gender (the male nature of the discipline) and socio-political status and affiliation (the Western character of the discipline), a third factor has been highly influential in biblical criticism as well: Socio-religious background and affiliation. In fact, the socio-religious matrix or ambit of the critic – his or her institutional, religious,

---

15   Segovia, "Voice," 31: "[t]here was no such thing as a neutral and disinterested reader and that the proposed de-contextualization aimed at the formation of the universal and informed reader was, but the universalization of a bracketed identity." See also e.g. Smit, "Wegweiser," it is therefore also fitting that the Louvain volume on the canon also includes a contribution that goes into precisely this direction, see: Chris Ukachukwu Manu, "Interpretations of the Bible in Africa," in: Auwers/De Jonge (ed.), *Canons*, 659–669. See also the emphasis by Scalise, *Hermeneutics*, 75, on the fact that historical-critical scholarship would be "more accurately labelled 'European Enlightenment'" scholarship, building on the work of J. Severino Croatto, *Biblical Hermeneutics: Towards a Theory of Reading as the Production of Meaning* (Maryknoll: Orbis, 1987).

16   Segovia, "Voice," 31.

17   Segovia, "Voice," 31.

18   Segovia, "Voice," 31.

19   Segovia, "Voice," 33.

and theological mooring – has been more explicit or evident than any other factor as regards the recreation of meaning from texts, the reconstruction of history behind texts, and the use of critical methodologies in relation to texts. Even when a critic pretended to the highest levels of objectivity and impartiality, his or her socio-religious identity proved inconcealable and undeniable in reading and interpretation, with the representation of ancient texts and communities bearing the unmistakable stamp of the world of that critic.[20]

Segovia also elaborates the consequences of this view, as he states a little further on in the same contribution that, given the involvement of all readers in one kind of ideology or the other, it turns them all into theologians; a consequence of a cultural studies approach to Scripture, is, therefore, a return to theology.[21] Similar insights could also be formulated with the help of more explicitly postmodern approaches, not least postmodern historiographical models, such as the work of White.[22] Segovia, however, must suffice as an

---

20   Fernando F. Segovia, "Cultural Studies and Contemporary Biblical Criticism. Ideological Criticism as Mode of Discourse," in: idem, *Decolonizing Biblical Studies. A view from the Margins* (Orbis: Maryknoll, 2000), 34–52, 48. See also the remarks of Oda Wischmeyer, *Hermeneutik des Neuen Testaments* (Tübingen: Francke, 2004), 121: "Exegeten sind im hohem Masse religiös und konfessionell geprägt. Es gibt...Möglichkeiten, diese Prägung als Vorverständnis zu erkennen und sie in den Prozess der Interpretation zu integrieren, statt sie zu einem Vorurteil im Sinne Bultmanns werden zu lassen – zu einem Vorurteil, das den Interpreten den Zugang zu den Texten verstellt, weil es die Interpretation schon zu kennen glaubt: Einmal die Reflexion auf die eigene Biographie, d.h. die autobiographische Reflexion...Diese Möglichkeit ist bisher nur zögernd wahrgenommen worden... Die Selbstreflexion der Exegeten auf ihre Verstehensvoraussetzungen ermöglichen grundsätzlich intersubjektive Interpretation. Hier liegt ein grosses Potential, das hermeneutisch ausgewertet werden muss."

21   Segovia, "Studies," 49: "For cultural studies, therefore, all readers and critics are theologians, implicitly or explicitly, by way of negation or affirmation, and all approaches to the text are theological in one respect or another. It is then, this socio-religious dimension of reading and interpretation that needs to be surfaced and examined, in terms both of belief systems and of their ramifications for ideological worldviews and stances. For cultural studies there is simply no escape from the socio-religious dimension."

22   See on this subject and – in this case – the study of the historical Jesus e.g. Moises Mayordomo/Peter-Ben Smit, "The Quest for the Historical Jesus in Postmodern Perspective: A Hypothetical Argument," in: Stanley E. Porter/Tom Holmén (ed.), *The Handbook of the Study of the Historical Jesus* 2 (Brill: Leiden, 2011), 1377–1410. See further also e.g. Jens Schröter, "Überlegungen zum Verhältnis von Historiographie und Hermeneutik in der neutestamentlichen Wissenschaft," in: Pokorný/Roskovec (ed.),

example here, chosen especially because of the scholarly journey that he has described.

3.1.4   *Points of Convergence with Contemporary Hermeneutical Thought*

When considering the canonical approaches to Scripture, it may be maintained that they have helped to place the interaction between reader and text on the exegetical agenda, not in the last place with regard to the reader's interpretative grammar and the text's claims, and the unavoidable process of interaction between the two. While this may seem detrimental to sound, objective, and scholarly exegesis, the insight that presuppositions are essential when it comes to encountering a text in any fruitful way, just as biographical and social conditioning must be regarded as an epistemological necessity, is one that has quite a substantial pedigree, especially in the interpretation of the New Testament.[23] In fact, such considerations are also compatible with the work of contemporary philosophers such as Gadamer[24] (and also Ricoeur),[25] which is indeed explicitly received by some of the canonical critics discussed here,[26]

Hermeneutics, 191–203, and Bernard C. Lategan, "History, Historiography and Hermeneutics," in: idem/idem (ed.), *o.c.*, 204.218.

23   See e.g. Rudolf Bultmann, "Is Exegesis without Presuppositions Possible," in: idem, *Existence and Faith: Shorter Writings of Rudolf Bultmann* (trans. S.M. Ogden; Cleveland: World Meridian Publishing, 1960), 289–296, the German original was published three years earlier as "Ist voraussetzunglose Exegese möglich?" *ThZ* 13 (1957), 409–417. See more recently also: Eve-Marie Becker, "Die Person des Exegeten. Überlegungen zu einem vernachlässigten Thema," in: Oda Wischmeyer (ed.), *Herkunft und Zukunft der neutestamentlichen Wissenschaft* (Tübingen: Francke, 2003), 207–243, 223, 237–238.

24   I.e.: Hans-Georg Gadamer, *Wahrheit und Methode: Grundzüge einer philosophischen Hermeneutik* (Tübingen: Mohr, ³1972).

25   See his comments on the canon: "With appropriation we touch on the very heart of the act of reading. An entire aesthetics and also a sociology of reading has been devoted to this reception of the text, which the reader, the audience, approaches with his or her own expectations. It is these expectations, in turn fulfilled, disappointed, shifted, transformed, and perhaps violated, that make the understanding of self confronted with the text the ultimate, extreme operation, with which we can complete the hermeneutics of the text." (Ricoeur, "Canon," 12).

26   See: Ratzinger, "Schriftauslegung," and the Pontifical Biblical Commission, *Interpretation*, II.A, Graf, *Unterwegs*, 129–145, as well as work of the following scholars working in the footsteps of Childs: Lyons, *Canon*, who attempts to further refine the notion of "community of interpretation" (see also the contribution of Cornelis van der Kooi, "Kirche als Lesegemeinschaft: Schrifthermeneutik und Kanon," *VuF* 51 [2006], 63–72, as well as Luz "Bibel"); Brett, *Criticism*, esp. 135–148, seeks to relate Childs' canonical approach to Gadamer's notion of a "classic," while a further attempt is represented by Noble, *Approach*;

just as it has been received, together with insights from reader-response criticism, in other parts of New Testament studies.[27] The relationship between text, community of interpretation, "grammars" of reading, as well as the embeddedness of all of this in (interpretative) traditions, as it has been emphasized by canonical critics, also offers further points of contact with contemporary hermeneutical thought. To begin with, in contemporary epistemology and hermeneutics, a certain resurfacing of the importance of tradition, and with that community, may be observed. As was already indicated, Gadamer has helped to raise awareness in this respect to a considerable extent.[28] This would also apply to, for example, the work of Alasdair MacIntyre,[29] as well as to that of Stanley Fish and his emphasis on communities of interpretation.[30]

A further step which (to my knowledge) was not taken by canonical critics-would be to delve even deeper into sociological and psychological aspects of interpretation-in-community, drawing, for example, on the work of thinkers such as Foucault, and further critics utilizing sociological and psychological tools, and hence, paying attention to the broader societal setting of interpretation

---

Driver, *Childs*, 49–60, offers a thoroughgoing critique of these latter works. See for further remarks about the (possible) compatibilities of canonical exegesis with branches of philosophical hermeneutics: Arie W. Zwiep, *Tussen tekst en lezer* I (Amsterdam: VU University, 2010), 152 (following Anthony C. Thiselton), as well as the considerations of Johannes Taschner, "Kanonische Bibelauslegung – Spiel ohne Grenzen?" in: Ballhorn/ Steins (ed.), *Bibelkanon*, 31–44. Independent of the discussion about canonical exegesis, also Prosper S. Grech, "The Regula Fidei as a Hermeneutical Principle in Patristic Exegesis," in: Jože Krašovec (ed.), *The Interpretation of the Bible* (Sheffield: Sheffield Academic Press, 1998), 589–601, 600–601, connects (Augustinian) canonical exegesis (i.e. governed by the rule of faith) with the hermeneutics of Gadamer.

27   See e.g. Moises Mayordomo-Marin, *Den Anfang hören: Leserorientierte Evangelienexegeses am Beispiel von Matthäus 1–2* (Göttingen: Vandenhoeck & Ruprecht, 1998), 11–195, 366–392.

28   See Gadamer, *Wahrheit*, see in general the studies collected in Mayordomo (ed.), *Kraft.* – For this and the following, see: Peter-Ben Smit, "The Reception of the Truth at Baptism and the Church as Epistemological Principle in the Work of Irenaeus of Lyons," *Ecclesiology* 7 (2011), 354–373, esp. 372–373.

29   See MacIntyre, *Justice*.

30   Stanley E. Fish, *Is There a Text in This Class? The Authority of Interpretative Communities* (Cambridge, MA: Harvard University, 1980). See for an overview of this question in theology e.g. Simone Sinn, "Hermeneutics and Ecclesiology," in: Gerard Mannion/Lewis S. Mudge (ed.), *Routledge Companion to the Christian Church* (London: Routledge, 2008), 576–593, and idem, *The Church as Participatory Community: On the Interrelationship of Hermeneutics, Ecclesiology and Ethics. Studies in Ecumenism, Reconciliation and Peace* (Dublin: Columba, 2002), and the literature referred to there.

and the dynamics of (for example) power involved.[31] Attention to the organization of communities, access to interpretation, and power or authority to define meaning and order participation in the interpretative process would also provide a(n even stronger) point of contact with recent ecumenical discussions about scriptural interpretation, in which the relationship between ecclesiology, interpretation, and authority has been of much importance in recent decades.[32] These issues will be addressed again when the (possible) interrelationship between canonical criticism and ecumenical hermeneutics is considered in the next chapter.

3.2   Justice to the Texts?

The next question that should be addressed here is the claim made by practically all practitioners of canonical exegesis, that their approach does more justice to the texts, rather than less; a position that is rather different from an earlier *communis opinio* in scholarly exegesis, according to which the canonical dimensions of a text were irrelevant at best and a hindrance to its proper understanding at worst. The way in which the claim is made that canonical exegesis is a more appropriate way to approach the texts of the New Testament differs somewhat among the canonical critics considered above. Therefore, it

---

31   See however, the criticism of Philipp R. Davies, *Whose Bible is it Anyway?* (Sheffield: Sheffield Academic Press, 1995), and see also the feminist critique of canonical criticism by, e.g. Bowen, "Canon," and Müllner, "Autorität;" note the comments of Childs, "Reflections," 31.

32   See above, 3.1.4.1. See also Commission on Faith and Order, *A Treasure in Earthen Vessels,* (Geneva: WCC, 1998) the work of the German project "Verbindliches Zeugnis," especially the volume Wolfhart Pannenberg/Theodor Schneider (ed.), *Verbindliches Zeugnis I. Kanon-Schrift-Tradition* (Göttingen: Vandenhoeck & Ruprecht, 1992), as well as e.g. Christoph Gestrich, "Schriftauslegung und Macht – ein unerledigtes Problem von 'sola scriptura,'" *BThZ* 22 (2005), 250–266, Walter Schmithals, "Der Kanon, die Apostolische Sukzession und die Ökumene," *BThZ* 22 (2005), 266–283; see also: Smit, *Tradition. –* Also the conditions for developing a canon mentioned by Ricoeur are hardly taken into account by the canonical critics considered here: For the establishment of authoritative texts, Ricoeur distinguishes four conditions that need to be fulfilled: The selection of texts to be preserved, the establishment of traditions of reading and interpretation, the assignment of a superior status to some texts, and "the taking charge of the entire process of interpretation and of dealing with conflicts of interpretation by a historical community, constructed on a memory, a plan, and an active arbitration in conflicts of all kinds, including conflicts of interpretation at points where various traditions of reading or interpretation meet." (Ricoeur, "Canon," 14–15, 15).

is worthwhile briefly laying out the various emphases that occur in their proposals and to see whether, and to what extent, they are compatible and even complementary. The following aspects will be considered: (1) Canonical exegesis and the "final form" of the text; (2) the canonical dimensions of the Scriptural texts themselves; (3) the role of claims that texts make themselves; (4) the role of tradition in the interpretative process; and (5) the relationship between interpretation and praxis.

3.2.1   *Canonical Exegesis and the "Final Form" of the Text*

Canonical critics, probably most emphatically Childs, the "Amsterdam School," and to some extent Stuhlmacher, emphasize that the exegesis of a text needs to consider primarily its final form, as opposed to earlier stages of text, or historical events behind the text. For the Amsterdam School this leads to a, in many cases, virtually exclusive emphasis on synchronic exegesis that hardly considers earlier stages of a text or a text's relationship to historical events.[33] In the case of Childs, the value of research into earlier stages of a text or into traditions incorporated into it exists solely in their capacity to illuminate the canonical form of the text. This emphasis on the exegesis of a text's final form and the sense it seeks to make, which began to be developed well before synchronic approaches that had their origins in the field of literary studies began to make an impact on biblical studies,[34] may certainly be seen as an important hermeneutic development, as indeed, it seeks to understand the canonical texts as they currently exist and seek to communicate. A valid question that may be raised with regard to the final form of a text stems from the field of textual criticism. Different canonical critics will answer it differently. The "Amsterdam School" largely ignores the issue, Childs proposes a "canonical approach" also to textual criticism, while Sanders builds his own approach to canonical criticism on precisely textual critical insights. In the end, the question becomes, which particular (final) form of the text is interpreted. In this context, it can also be noted that, a difference between Childs and Stuhlmacher on the one hand, and the Amsterdam School on the other, is that the former do consider earlier traditions feeding into a text's canonical form, while the latter is hardly interested in that at all and focuses on intertextual connections within the canon. However, both agree with one another and in fact with all the canonical approaches considered in this study that canonical intertextuality is of major importance. This leads to a further, closely related issue.

---

33   See e.g. the example of Van Nieuwpoort's exegesis offered above, 2.6.2–2.6.3.

34   This is, it seems, a little recognized fact, but it does speak for the hermeneutical creativity of the field of biblical studies as such.

Even if the point is not to be extensively explored, all canonical approaches discussed here take their point of departure in the bipartite canon of the Christian Bible. They do so for both historical and literary reasons. The interconnectedness of its parts is to be given attention when it comes to the interpretation of a particular section of it. Put differently: Canonical approaches to Scripture generally emphasize the character of the canon as a literary whole made up of texts that, apparently, should be understood as a corpus.[35] While the first point discussed in this paragraph, i.e. the emphasis on synchronic exegesis, should be regarded as an obvious enrichment of the exegetical repertoire, the latter should, at the very least, be regarded as a historical fact as well: The bipartite of the Christian canon has functioned – and continues to function – as a literary whole that invites interpretation as a whole, a situation that asks interesting literary questions, certainly about the "second life" of an originally decidedly non-canonical text (e.g. Paul's letter to Philemon, 3 John or Jude) as a canonical text. Such a "second life" is as much a real existence of a text as its existence in the hands, eyes, and ears of its first recipients. Ratzinger's argument of the reading community as a second author of the text has, at least, a point with regard to this dynamic.[36]

3.2.2   *The Canonical Dimension of the Texts Themselves*

Next, a point needs to be considered that is probably the most strongly emphasized by Sanders, but which can also be found back in the work of some of the other canonical critics: The canonicity of (New Testament) texts, in the sense of their being part of a canonical process, both by receiving canonical texts and by reinterpreting them, sometimes with claims to authority that come close to the authority of earlier canonical or Scriptural texts.[37] This emphasis on being part of a canonical process, with the implication that a text's (claim

---

35   This is similar to Watson's understanding of the genre of biblical texts, when he argues the following, building on the work of Barth: "If genre is a function of communal reception and usage as well as of inherent characteristics, then the genre of the biblical texts is "holy scripture:" That is to say, these texts function in a peculiar way in the life of a determinate community or set of interrelated communities." (Watson, *Text* 227; how this functions – and that this should function in this way is also laid out in idem, *Gospel*) – Watson also refers to: Werner Jeanrond, *Text and Interpretation as Categories of Theological Thinking* (Dublin: Gill and Macmillan, 1988), 118.

36   See above, 2.5.1.

37   To be sure, such claims did not automatically lead to their acknowledgement, see e.g. on the case of the Revelation of John: Konrad Huber/Martin Hasitschka, "Die Offenbarung des Johannes im Kanon der Bibel. Textinterner Geltungsanspruch und Probleme der kanonischen Rezeption," in: Auwers/De Jonge (ed.), *Canons*, 607–618.

to) canonicity is not necessarily the result of a later ecclesial decision, is shared
by Childs and Stuhlmacher[38] Various historical observations on the fact that
the New Testament texts are part of a canonical process, as underlined in particular by Sanders and Childs, have as a consequence for the exegesis of individual texts that they can be seen as rereadings of earlier (authoritative) texts
and, therefore, as steering the reception of these texts. This kind of canonicity,
i.e. providing, with a variety of claims to authority, re-readings of earlier
authoritative texts, is, as Sanders and others argue, clearly part and parcel of
the texts themselves and not a characteristic imposed upon the text at a later
stage through an ecclesial decision.[39] These observations lead, especially for
Sanders,[40] to a further hermeneutical consideration, i.e. that in order to do
justice to the texts, they need to be interpreted in line with the canonical
hermeneutics of reinterpretation and rewriting that they themselves embody,
which is, in fact, an open-ended process, even if it is governed by certain characteristics (e.g. an emphasis on obedience to the Law having to result in justice,
not in the abuse of power). This insight is also shared by others. Söding argues,
for example, on the basis of more recent research into the history and nature
of the canon, that the (New Testament) canon is best approached not by view-
ing it as a fixed literary entity, but rather as the (half-)product of an ongoing
canonical process that continues into the presence and invites the current
reader to join into a process of interpretation.[41]

---

38   See above, 2.1. and 2.3: The Amsterdam School is not particularly interested in this historical
     question; for Ratzinger, the establishment of the canon as part of developments in the life of
     the church is of much less sensitive than for the Protestant scholars, whose work he receives.
39   See on this point also e.g. Steins, "Bibelkanon." – Steins draws also on the insights of Martin
     Buber and Franz Rosenzweig, who are also of importance for the Amsterdam School.
40   Something similar could be said about Stuhlmacher, with his emphasis on understanding
     the texts as they wish to be understood themselves, Childs, with his emphasis on the rule
     of faith, and Ratzinger's emphasis on the reading of texts in the light of tradition. All
     of these would argue that their approach is, in fact, in line with the self-understanding of
     the texts and the hermeneutical principles inherent to them. Such a position also the
     Amsterdam School would take, of course, emphasizing synchronic exegesis.
41   Söding, "Kanon," lviii: "der Kanon nicht nur von seinem definierten, jedenfalls faktischen
     Endergebnis her zu erklären und verstehen ist, sondern im Zuge eines 'kanonischen
     Prozesses," der mit der Entstehung der biblischen Schriften beginnt und mit der
     Festlegung seines Umfangs nicht endet, sondern sich bis in die Gegenwart bei
     der Kommentierung und Auslegung ereignet." See also above 2.2, on Sanders; compare
     Brenneman, *Canons*, 23, and the following remarks of Taschner, "Bibelauslegung," 43: "Der
     Erwartungshorizont, auf den die biblischen Texte treffen, ist durch ihren Bezug auf die
     Glaubensgemeinschaften ausdrücklich von einem hermeneutischen Schlüssel geprägt
     (in der Alten Kirche der Kanon als Auslegungsregel), der in dieser expliziten Form der

Related to this, as previously mentioned, but not yet discussed here, is the issue of the Scriptural or canonical self-understanding of texts before they became part of an identifiable corpus of authoritative books. Most probably all New Testament writings, even when they do not necessarily claim to have canonical authority similar to what their authors saw as the Scriptures, do claim authority with regard to their witness to Christ and to "Christian" life and practice.[42] Now, a few observations may be offered with regard to what the canonical approach may have to offer to the bundle of questions that is associated with this issue.

A first station to pause at is the relationship of the New Testament (and other early Christian) to the "the Scriptures," i.e., texts that were considered authoritative,[43] in whatever precise literary form they existed at the time.[44] This is an important way in which the texts that are now found in the New Testament are oriented towards an authoritative body of texts which, depending on one's definition of "canon" and one's view of the history of the canon of the HB/LXX, could also be considered a "canonical orientation" of these texts. The interrelations between what would become the New Testament texts (and other early Christian writings) and the Scriptures (i.e. the HB/LXX) are too numerous to mention here. They can be found on the level of language and style (e.g. the stylistic orientation of some authors towards the Greek of the LXX), thought world, conceptuality and theology, but also in terms of the *relecture* of these earlier and more authoritative texts and their interpretation in light of the "Christ event", while this "Christ event" was understood in the light of the earlier

---

allgemeinen Literaturrezeption fehlt. In dem Wechselspiel von biblischem Text und so geprägten Erwartungshorizont wird nach dem verbindlichen Gotteswort und damit der relevanten Konkretisierung des Textes immer wieder neu zu fragen sein. Der in diesem Kommunikationsgeschehen immer wieder einen ein für alle Mal festgelegten Sinn ergeben, sondern den Raum für Neuinterpretationen lassen." See for considerations about this also: Johannes Nissen, "Scripture and Community in Dialogue, Hermeneutical Reflections on the Authority of the Bible," in: Auwers/De Jonge (ed.), *Canons*, 651–658, following insights from Croatto, *Hermeneutics*, 68–69, and Gerald O. West, *Biblical Hermeneutics of Liberation. Modes of Reading the Bible in the South African Context* (Pietermaritzburg: Cluster, ²1995), 154–171.

42 See e.g. Söding, "Kanon," lxx–lxxxi; this distinction became obsolete with the canonization of the New Testament writings.

43 See for a relatively succinct and illustrative overview: Richard B. Hays, "The Canonical Matrix of the Gospels," in: Barton (ed.), *Companion*, 53–75.

44 This remark pertains to both the question of a canon of the Hebrew Bible or the LXX and to the issue of the precise textual form in which the later "Old Testament" writings existed. On the latter issue, see the exemplary study of Maarten J.J. Menken, *Matthew's Bible: The Old Testament Text of the Evangelist* (Louvain: Peeters, 2004).

Scriptures at the same time. All of this applies both to the "retelling" of Israel's story in Christ's story, as it occurs in some New Testament texts,[45] and to the direct quotation of the older Scriptures in the newer texts.[46] This dimension of the "canonical orientation" of the New Testament writings, not least the gospels, has been consistently highlighted by canonical critics, be it by way of focusing on their midrashic character (Sanders, and also the "Amsterdam School"), or by placing emphasis on the unity of the two testaments of the Christian Bible (e.g. Childs, Stuhlmacher), and, in any case, by placing the interpretation of the New Testament writings squarely in the context of the "world" of the Old Testament (this applies to all considered in this study).

Furthermore, canonical criticism, to the extent that it has helped to place the question of the canon and its relevance for the exegesis of New Testament texts on the exegetical agenda, has assisted in opening the way for asking a number of broader questions, such as the following, formulated by David Sim with regard to the Gospel of Matthew:

> The evangelist certainly knew Mark and Q, and combined them along with other source material to fashion his own distinctive Gospel. What was the status of these Christian texts for the Christian Matthew? Were they authoritative and perhaps even scriptural? Did they comprise an early and formative Christian canon of scriptures for him that complemented the Jewish canon? And what of the letters of Paul? Was the evangelist aware of these texts and, if so, what importance or authority did he ascribe to them?[47]

---

45 See e.g. Dale C. Allison, Jr., *The New Moses: A Matthean Typology* (Minneapolis: Fortress, 1993).

46 The literature on this topic is too voluminous to even only begin listing it here, but see e.g. Menken, *Bible,* as well as Gregory K. Beale, *Handbook on the New Testament Use of the Old Testament: Exegesis and Interpretation* (Grand Rapids: Baker, 2012), as well as idem/D.A. Carson, *Commentary on the New Testament Use of the Old Testament* (Grand Rapids: Baker, 2007); for an older contribution, referring to ditto literature, see e.g. Prosper S. Grech, "Inner-biblical Reinterpretation and Modern Hermeneutics," in: Pokorný/Roskovec (ed.), *Hermeneutics,* 221–237.

47 David Sim, "Does the Gospel of Matthew Presuppose a Canon of Scripture?" in: Becker/Scholz (ed.), *Kanon,* 449–468, 450. – Sim himself answers these questions negatively, but expresses sympathy with the following position of Dwight Moody Smith on 465: "Matthew, given his dissatisfaction with Mark, composed his own Gospel with the intention that it would function as a Christian scripture." Hence, for Matthew, according to Sim, the canon (in the sense of a body of literature with an authoritative function for early Christian communities) included his own work.

A variety of answers can be given to these questions, and certainly even more of these questions can be asked; Sim's list only serves an illustrative purpose here, underlining the contribution that canonical criticism has made to the study of the texts of the New Testament by opening up new, or at least unfashionable, questions regarding both their relationship to earlier authoritative texts and their self-understanding as authoritative texts. To be sure, this includes the relationship between the (possible) canonical claims of some writings (and lack thereof in other cases) and their inclusion into the canon. It can be argued, for example, that the inclusion of both Matthew and Mark into the canon relativizes claims that (may well) lie behind the Gospel of Matthew (or for that matter, Luke or John) with regard to its replacement of the Gospel of Mark.[48] Other scenarios can also be imagined, e.g. when following Hengel's early dating of the gospel titles and the argument supporting it, one could also argue that precisely these titles, which, to some extent relativize the claim to present *the* gospel of Jesus Christ, allow for more than one gospel in the (canonical) memory of the church.[49] Again, the meaning of such considerations depends to a considerable extent on what one understands "canon" and "Scripture" to mean.[50]

---

48   See e.g. David Sim, "Matthew's Use of Mark: Did Matthew Intend to Supplement or to Replace His Primary Source?" *NTS* 57 (2011), 176–192. See with regard to the question of the claims to authority of the Gospel of Matthew in relation to the sources that its author used also e.g. the succinct considerations of Luz, "Exegese," 45–46. – For the Gospel of John, see e.g. the argument of Smith, *Gospel*, 181–219, with regard to the relationship between the Gospel of John, its character as canonical and scriptural text, and the need to pay attention to these aspects of the exegesis of the (literary work/historical artifact) the Gospel of John. In the Gospel of John, for example texts such as John 20:31 could be discussed in relation to other gospels (has the reference to "these things" inclusive or exclusive implications?) and John 2:21 could be discussed in relation to John's view of the Scriptures of Israel.

49   See: Martin Hengel, *Die vier Evangelien und das eine Evangelium von Jesus Christus* (Tübingen: Mohr Siebeck, 2008), 87–96, as well as Michael Wolter, "Die Vielfalt der Schrift und die Einheit des Kanons," in: John Barton/Michael Wolter (ed.), *Die Einheit der Schrift und die Vielfalt des Kanons* (Berlin: De Gruyter, 2003), 45–68, 60.

50   See, e.g., the considerations of Friedrich Wilhelm Horn, "Wollte Paulus 'kanonisch' wirken?" in: Becker/Scholz (ed.), *Kanon*, 400–422, 418: "Wollte Paulus 'kanonisch' wirken? Diese Frage kann nur aufgenommen und beantwortet werden, wenn ein allgemeiner Wortgebrauch von Kanon im Sinn von 'Norm,' nicht aber ein an ein 'Schriftenkorpus' gebundener Gebrauch von Kanon verwendet wird. Meine Untersuchung zeigt..., dass Paulus sich an einen Kanon bindet, der ein auch geographisch bestimmtes Missionskonzept beinhaltet. Gleichzeitig bindet er seine Gemeinden an einen Kanon, der auf ein Kirchenverständnis bezogen ist, in dem Juden und Heiden ohne Beachtung der sie trennenden *identity markers* verbunden sind."

While a consensus with regard to any of these questions still has to establish itself – if at all possible – these examples may be taken to indicate that the questions of the canon, canonicity, scripturality, and the claim to authority of texts, both vis-à-vis an audience and vis-à-vis other texts, have acquired a firm place on the exegetical agenda again. This, it seems, helps us to better appreciate the character of the texts themselves. Canonical approaches to Scripture have helped to achieve this.

3.2.3   *Listening to the Claims of Texts*

Besides emphasizing the need to interpret the texts "as they are," i.e. in their "final form," which leads to a focus on synchronic exegesis, and stressing the fact that the texts are part of a canonical process, canonical critics have also argued that the claims of the texts to authority are to be taken seriously in the exegetical process. While such claims may differ from text to text (compare, for example, the Gospel of John and the Apocalypse of John to Jude or 3 John), this is an important hermeneutical point nonetheless. Among the scholars studied here, Stuhlmacher stresses this aspect in a way that is compatible with the arguments of Childs and the "Amsterdam School."

In this context, of all the canonical exegetes, Stuhlmacher is particularly adamant that the exegete should strive to understand the texts as they should be understood, as they want to be understood, taking seriously their own claims about themselves. This hermeneutical premise does not only lead Stuhlmacher to his hermeneutic of "Einverständnis," but it leads one also to a broader hermeneutical issue: The extent to which the interpreter is (not) willing to interact with a text's claims to truth. For many canonical critics, such an interaction is part and parcel of an honest approach to a text, i.e. of doing it justice. Indeed, it seems that a strong argument can be put forward, without doubt in line with many emancipatory or identity-based hermeneutics and more recent developments in literary studies,[51] that to read texts in this way, i.e. by ensuring that the interpretative subject interacts with the text's claims, does more justice to a text than a – supposedly – detached and objective analysis.[52] As Schiffmann put it both eloquently and paradoxically: The canonical text is only authoritative and, in that sense, canonical *in its interpretation*; in other words, the canonical text and its meaning are a moving target, even if

---

51   See above, 3.1.3.

52   See on this point also Barthel, "Debatte," 10–11, who has (even) Childs side with postmodern thinkers in this respect.

it gives the impression of being stable.[53] The return of the interpretative subject, as was discussed in the preceding section, is also closely related to this
point; this remains, even if it may not be what Stuhlmacher and others had in
mind primarily.

3.2.4   *Interpretation through Tradition*
A point that is stressed by Ratzinger in particular, but that can be found in the
work of Childs as well, is that the meaning of texts and even of the events that
they refer to only unfolds in the process of their reception by the appertaining
community of interpretation. In the case of the texts of the New Testament, this
community is the church, and hence, the (authentic) interpretation of these
texts, i.e. the unfolding of their meaning, takes place in and through the life of
this church, that is to say: In and through ecclesial tradition. While Ratzinger's
fairly exclusive emphasis on (a particular kind of) ecclesial interpretation is
open for debate – as much for ecclesiological as for hermeneutical reasons – his
more general hermeneutical thesis that the meaning of texts (and the events
that they refer to) unfolds in the course of their interpretation seems to be a
valued one indeed. At any rate, it seems to be hard to contest the observation
that for every generation of exegetes other interpretations of a text constitute a
text's meaning. This process of taking into account the unfolding meaning of a
text throughout history is, not least with Gadamer, a hermeneutical factor that
can be argued to have to be taken into account, indeed to do justice to the texts
and their unfolding meaning themselves. As Trobisch puts it, "the history of the
Christian Bible is the history of a literary classic. Like every classic work, [it]
must be received, reconstituted, and published afresh by each generation."[54]

---

53   See, e.g., the argument of Lawrence H. Schifman, "The Reception of the Bible in Ancient
      Judaism" (paper presented at the EABS/SBL International Meeting, Vienna, 7 July 2014),
      who underlines that Holy Scripture is a moving target, given that it is factually only
      authoritative in (a continuously changing) interpretation that is always related to the
      context of the interpreters.

54   David Trobisch, *The First Edition of the New Testament* (Oxford: Oxford University, 2000),
      106; see also idem, *Die Endredaktion des Neuen Testaments* (Göttingen: Vandenhoeck &
      Ruprecht, 1996). Whereas Trobisch rightly draws the attention to early structured collec-
      tions, he does not take into account sufficiently the widely spread existence of what, from
      his perspective, must appear as "partial New Testaments," i.e. the fact that certainly not all
      would have had access to a full New Testament and that "partial New Testaments"
      remained in circulation for a very long time, which also applies to editions of the New
      Testament with additional material and the like. – See also: Ricoeur, "Canon," 12, who
      notes, with Pier Cesare Bori, a phrase attributed to Gregory the Great: "The written text
      grows with its readers."

3.2.5   *Interpretation and Praxis*

A final aspect to this discussion of canonical criticism and the world of the text, which is closely related to a central concern of all of the canonical critics above, is the issuing of the (authentic) interpretation of a text into a particular praxis or a particular walk of life.[55] This would be well in line, for example, with Ratzinger's use of the lives of saints as places where the interpretation of a text may be found. Sanders refers not only to the interpretation, but also the application of texts in line with their own hermeneutics,[56] Stuhlmacher's development of his hermeneutic of "Einverständnis,"[57] the Amsterdam School's notion of the effect of the Word, and also Childs' restoration of the interpretation of Scripture to the life of the church. While this, one would say practical theological, aspect of canonical interpretation is not explored at any length by the canonical critics studied here, and only pointed at, it seems to be an organic continuation of their thought.[58]

3.3   The World "Behind the Text?"

Canonical critics have a strong tendency to focus on the world in front of the text, i.e. the reader-text interface/the world of the text itself. However, when considering the heuristic value of canonical approaches to the New Testament, specifically to the New Testament gospels, the way in which the world "behind the text" plays a role in canonical exegesis should also be considered. A number of observations can be made, specifically on: (1) The relationship between revelation and history; (2) the relationship between witness and event; and (3) the canonical process and the world behind the text.

3.3.1   *History, Witness, and Revelation*

The question about the relationship between the witness of the Scriptural texts, history, and revelation, a topic that surfaces in virtually any canonical approach (a partial exception might be Sanders), receives a particularly

---

55   See also the remarks of Zwiep, *Tekst* II, 196–197, on Gadamer, i.e. the philosopher that is probably the most influential among canonical critics.

56   See e.g. Sanders, "Adaptable," and compare the critical comments of Childs, "Reflections," 33–34.

57   Especially in its latest phase, see e.g. Graf, *Unterwegs*, 153, Stuhlmacher, "Kanon," 190.

58   See also Hans-Joachim Eckstein, "Das Evangelium Jesu Christi. Die implizite Kanon-hermeneutik des Neuen Testaments," in: Janowski (ed.), *Kanonhermeneutik*, 47–68, 50; see further: Peter-Ben Smit, "The Meaning of 'Life.' An Essay in Ecumenical Hermeneutics," JEC 43 (2008), 320–332.

pronounced answer from many representatives of the "Amsterdam School." These scholars operate with an outspoken theology of revelation that has its origins in the theology of Karl Barth, notably in his thesis that history is a predicate of revelation. Extra-canonical historical information has, in fact, hardly any bearing on the meaning of revelation as mediated by the canonical Scriptures. Even when some (historical) information about the "world behind the text" is used, this serves mostly to better understand the literary character of texts, not to reconstruct "real history," which, in the understanding of (most representatives of) the "Amsterdam School," is found in and constituted by the witness to the revelation of the divine Name, i.e. Scripture.[59]

Furthermore, other canonical critics often have a very limited interest in the world behind the text, even if they focus less on a particular theory (or theology) of history. To begin with, Childs utilizes the category "witness" in order to conceptualize the character of the New Testament writings, and hence of the gospels, and seeks to lay out that this witness itself gives one proper access to the historical event behind the texts (notably to its meaning and significance), not historical reconstructions.[60] According to this line of thought, the story of the historical Jesus, for example, can only be understood correctly when a post-Easter perspective is applied. The relevance of the "world behind the texts" is therefore limited for Childs. Earlier stages of texts are mainly of significance to

---

59   One may also note that the idea that texts are able to construct their own world and reality has parallels in literary theory and philosophical hermeneutics as well. See e.g. the considerations of Ricoeur, "Canon," 11, who takes up the insights of Northrop Frye here, and discusses the power of the text to configure its own world, i.e. the world of the text, a notion of which he says, "I use this term to denote the product of all the re-figurations of the everyday experience of reality by the configurations of the text. I have applied this terminology to the narrative genre; but it would be possible to extrapolate it to other genres too. Northrop Frye, for example, in *The Great Code*, proceeds to a comparable generalization by taking as his starting-point not the narrative but poetry, as can indeed be done by taking the metaphor, which is an opportunity to read the world differently than using the descriptions of ordinary language. Frye's Bible is a great code in the sense that it sketches, in a different dimension of discourse that can be called poetic, the contours of a world that is called poetic, not because of any denial of reality or proclamation of unreality, or even lies or illusions, but because of verbal creations revealing aspects of being in the world that cannot be otherwise; when it is poetical, in this broader sense than poetry or narration, the literary work provides a change of scene, defamiliarises, with the strangeness clearing the way to a completely new appropriating." – See also Barthel, "Debatte," 1.

60   See also, equally in the footsteps of Barth: Watson, *Text*, 223: "Access to the reality of Jesus is textually mediated." – See also idem, *Gospel*, 604–620 (theses on the canon and the historical Jesus).

illuminate what Childs considers to be the final text.[61] When turning from Childs to Stuhlmacher, it appears that the latter would argue that the best access to the world behind the text is through the witness of the canonical texts, which are, in any event, the best sources available and also do the most justice to "what really happened" in an encompassing sense of the expression, i.e. both with regard to the event and with regard to what an event means. Accordingly, pre-Easter events can only be properly understood on the basis of their post-Easter narration as found in the New Testament, both because the New Testament texts are the best historical sources available and because they provide the most authentic witness to the meaning of the historical events. Among the canonical critics considered here, Ratzinger also offers a pronounced view of things with regard to the "world behind the text," given that his "Jesus-books" purport to present a picture of the meaning of the historical Jesus, i.e. of the Jesus of the world "behind the text." For Ratzinger, the true meaning of the historical facts that the canonical texts bear witness to is found not only in the witness of these texts, but also in their reception in the community of interpretation in which these texts are – according to Ratzinger – the most at home, i.e. in the church. This keeps together the "earthly Jesus" and the "Christ of faith." His rationale for doing so is a hermeneutic that takes into account that the significance of persons and events may be discovered and expressed most adequately only after a longer process of reflection, specifically in the church, which, as the community of interpretation within which the Scriptures came into existence, has a privileged position as an interpreter of these same Scriptures and hence of the events that they refer to. Ratzinger's

---

61 Childs would therefore, most likely disagree with the attempt of Seckler, "Problematik," 51–52, to relate the history behind the text to a "history of revelation" ("Offenbarungsgeschichte") that is of high theological importance. Still Seckler's point that there is "eine Kopräsenz des Sukzessiven im Endtext" (i.e. earlier traditions are still present in the final text) certainly rings true (Seckler, o.c., 51), although his ensuing argument might be more compatible with Sanders' than with Childs' approach: "[D]ie Stimmen, die im *framework* des Kanons und auch noch in den Schichtungen des Endtextes vernehmbar werden, [sind] nicht nur Untertöne im Text, und nicht nur Hilfsmittel der Endtextexegese, sondern – soweit rekonstruierbar – in-sich-ständige Stimmen aus jener realen Offenbarungsgeschichte, die die Referenzebene der inspirierten Texte ist. Sie sind in dieser in-sich-Ständigkeit theologisch relevant. Gott hat oftmals und auf verschiedene Weise gesprochen, zuletzt im Sohn, der der "sachliche" Ansatzpunkt des canonical approach und der hermeneutische Schlüssel für die Offenbarungsgeschichte und die ganze christliche Bibel ist. Und selbst hier, in Bezug auf ihn, kann die diachrone Dekomposition von neutestamentlichen Endtexten vom Christus des Glaubens und seinem Wort zu den ipsissima verba Jesu zurückführen, die als solche ihre eigene Würde haben."

position is, in this respect, akin to that of Stuhlmacher, whose work he also takes into account, while also paying tribute to a prominent document of the Second Vatican Council, *Dei Verbum*. Probably more than Ratzinger, however, Stuhlmacher emphasizes that an interpreter should try to identify oneself with a text in the process of interpretation in order to let the text speak (again) in the way in which a text intended to be heard originally.

Can such canonical approaches discover historical aspects of texts that remain shrouded to other historians and exegetes? That is, beyond general calls for careful historical scholarship, as e.g. Stuhlmacher issues them? In two ways they probably can, without arguing that Ratzinger and Stuhlmacher do precisely this at all times. First, by drawing attention to the "meaning" of texts, an aspect of the historical interpretation of texts that may shift to the background in "traditional" historical critical exegesis, canonical exegesis may well assist in rediscovering dimensions of the significance of the texts that are being researched that are otherwise less frequently addressed. This interpretative agenda can contribute to historical scholarship, at least by asking questions that are not always asked, but may well pertain to a more encompassing process of textual interpretation. Second, the emphasis on the history of interpretation draws attention to the historical development of meaning and interpretation, which is an aspect upon which "traditional" historical scholarship does not reflect all that frequently, with all sorts of interpretative consequences. At the same time, such an emphasis also draws attention to the fact that historical scholarship is part of the history of interpretation of a text and that it is perfectly legitimate that later approaches and interpretations highlight aspects of a text that remained hidden to an earlier generation of interpreters. At the very least, therefore, placing emphasis on the history of reception and the development of meaning leads to asking questions regarding which particular stage in a text's history of reception plays which role for which community of interpretation and which (historical) referentiality is in play (or whom) at that particular stage of a text's reception? In addition to this, the diversity as it exists in the canon, e.g., in the four canonical gospels, and the fact that this diversity is, somehow, meant to contribute to the narration of the story of Christ, or the communication of the one Gospel, studying the canonical Scriptures can also aid one to raise questions as to the necessity of the uniformity of historical narratives and their truth claims and to the possibility of allowing a multiciplicity of such narratives without necessarily losing a sense of unity. The New Testament, with its four gospels, could be seen as pointing towards a broader sense of the truth of historical events and the witness to them than a (typically modern) single historical narrative of early Christian origins would; it also brings to the fore an awareness that every history is someone's story and that access to historical phenomena and person is always textually mediated and therefore always related to the interests of those producing and reproducing these texts.[62]

3.3.2 *The Canonical Process and the World behind the Text*

Sanders is, of all the canonical critics considered here, the most interested in the world behind the text, even if it is not an interest that focuses primarily on the historical events that the texts bear witness too. This situation is a direct consequence of his approach to canonical criticism as it has developed out of the comparative study of midrash. When Sanders refers to the hermeneutical triangle comparative midrash utilizes, one of the three angles of the triangle consists of the "historical/social situation the newer [Scripture] addressed."[63] Thus, the historical context in which a text came into existence, reinterpreting and rewriting older Scripture, is of importance for Sanders. This is, indeed, part of the world behind the text, but not all of it: The world of the events that a text refers to explicitly is not necessarily addressed by this method. Cases can be adduced, in which a fictional account of an event set in history (e.g. the events recounted by the *pericopa adulterae*, of which Sanders' interpretation was discussed earlier) is not likely to have "really happened," but still there are reasons that have caused it to come into being. Sanders would be more interested in the latter than the former. Therefore, while Sanders also presents his canonical approach as an exercise in historical scholarship, he has different reasons for doing so than for example, Ratzinger and/or Stuhlmacher. For Sanders, it is an inherent characteristic of early Jewish and Christian texts that they are part of a canonical process (an observation that is to some extent analogous to Childs' emphasis on the "canonical consciousness" of texts) and for that reason, they can be interpreted in a way that takes this process into account. In other words, the canonical process of which the texts are part should be continued in order to do justice to an important characteristic of these texts. In this way, a "midrashic" and in that sense canonical interpretation of early Christian texts (and the texts of the first part of the Christian canon) becomes a hermeneutical necessity for purely textual and historical reasons. It is this necessity that sends Sanders back to the world behind the text in order to find one of the three angles of his midrashic triangle needed to interpret the texts.

---

62   See the argument of Watson, *Gospel.*
63   Sanders, "What's," 3.

3.3.3   *Concluding Observations: Canonical Approaches and History*

In sum, the canonical critics considered here are not particularly interested in reconstructing the world behind the text along the lines of "traditional" historical-critical scholarship. In fact, this is precisely what they react to. In offering an alternative, canonical critics pursue different avenues with regard to history, e.g. the "Amsterdam School" offers a theological (and philosophical) understanding of history that allows it to focus virtually exclusively and synchronically on the canonical *Letztgestalt* of the text. On the contrary, Ratzinger argues along Gadamerian lines that historical events can only be understood in and through their interpretation, which also offers a way of accessing history through the canonical writings *qua* canonical writings. Childs and Stuhlmacher focus also on the witness character of the (New Testament) texts, albeit in a somewhat milder way than the "Amsterdam School" and while holding hermeneutical positions that seem to be compatible with those of Ratzinger. Sanders is probably the most "traditional" with regard to his historiographical views. Thus, many of the canonical critics considered here do not only underline the worlds of and in front of the text, but also offer new perspectives on the way in which the world behind the text should be accessed. However one evaluates these approaches, one ought to agree that canonical criticism in its various shapes has something to offer – together with others – when it comes to questions of historiography and exegesis, at the very least simply by giving rise to new questions with regard to these topics.

3.4   Potential Pitfalls

Having considered various aspects of (possible) contributions of canonically oriented exegesis to the study of the New Testament, some (potential) pitfalls should also be noted and – to some extent – discussed. That such pitfalls exist (at least in the eyes of the many critics of canonical exegesis), need not be a surprise. To what extent they indeed detract from the contribution that canonical exegesis can make to biblical studies, more specifically the study of the New Testament, remains to be seen. The following issues will be considered here: (1) The problem of the anachronistic reading of texts; (2) the selective character of canonical criticism; (3) the artificiality of the literary context provided by the canon; (4) the appeal to later (ecclesial) traditions to interpret earlier (canonical) texts; (5) the issue of an overemphasis on the Scriptural text in relation to theological considerations; (6) the question of checks and balances on interpretation; (7) the question of control over interpretation and texts; and (8) the anachronistic character of an appeal to the canon at an early stage in the history of Christianity.

First, and somewhat in line with the view taken by earlier historical critical scholarship, canonical critics may be criticized for operating anachronistically, i.e. by interpreting texts in their canonical form and context, while they were not written as canonical writings. "Canonicity," in other words, is foreign to the texts and hence, to be disregarded when it comes to their interpretation. This kind of critique is based on the consideration that a formal biblical canon must be seen as a product of relatively late developments in the history of Christianity, in Western Christianity, specifically surrounding the Protestant and Catholic Reformations,[64] which led to the drawing up of formal lists of canonical books by entire churches.[65] Such criticism applies especially to canonical approaches that rely heavily on a fixed form of the canon, or place much emphasis on this (in this study, this applies probably most directly to Childs, Stuhlmacher and the Amsterdam School).[66] The complex historical development of the canon makes an appeal to the canon as a fixed and stable text difficult to sustain. This point can be strengthened even further when the textual history of the canonical writings is taken into account.[67] Two remarks can be made with regard to this. First of all, to a substantial extent, this kind of criticism is simply valid, given that few currently canonical books were written to be fitted into the current biblical canon. However, it ought also be acknowledged that the "canonical consciousness" of many, if not most now canonical texts is substantial; therefore, too sharp a line cannot be drawn between the original writings and their canonization, even if, say, the canonization of both Matthew and Mark might well go against the intention of their respective authors. Second, it has become more generally recognized that the notion of a fixed "canon" with a clearly defined authority in early Christianity is hard to substantiate. Of much more importance is the process of reception of authoritative writings in the life of the church(es), of which all the writings

---

64   Work such as David L. Dungan's *Constantine's Bible. Politics and the Making of the New Testament* (Minneapolis: Fortress, 2007) do not take this into account sufficiently and place too much emphasis on the influence of Constantine 1.

65   For further considerations with regard to the canon of the New Testament, see my inaugural address: *De canon – een oude katholieke kerkstructuur?* (Utrecht: Utrecht University, 2011).

66   Not surprisingly all representatives of a canonical approach with a Protestant background, see for the (conflictive) relationship between especially theology and the questioning of the stability of canon e.g. the brief remarks by Seckler, "Problematik," 34–49.

67   See e.g. the issues as they are discussed in David Parker, *The Living Text of the Gospels* (Cambridge: Cambridge University, 1997), compare also Metzger, *Canon*, 267–270, and see the proposal of Trobisch. *Edition*, who, also argues for a process of multiple editions that continues.

currently in the canon were part, both at the moment of their authoring and subsequently, when they became part of the (authoritative) collective memory of the church. Furthermore, not all kinds of canonical criticism are bound up with the notion of a fixed canon or the idea that books were written for this canon.

Second, when it comes – again – to historical research and canonical texts, another point of criticism may be highlighted: The privileging of canonical texts over others in order to reconstruct or uncover historical events, such as the life and ministry of Jesus of Nazareth. This is inadmissible, given that it privileges some sources over others for historiographically invalid reasons. Again, this criticism is valid: For rigorous historical scholarship all sources need to be considered; the "canons" of historical scholarship simply demand this. Canonical critics, therefore, need to take heed and be careful to say clearly what they do and do not do, which also applies to historical-critical scholars. For example, if one considers the New Testament gospels to be the most authentic witnesses to Jesus Christ, then one needs to be clear about this and, if necessary, distinguish this from other sources one might use in order to write the life of the historical Jesus of Nazareth. Of course, scholars such as Ratzinger, who argues that authentic access to the historical Jesus of Nazareth can only take place if one takes into account the "Christ of faith," in order to capture the historical significance of this person, or Stuhlmacher, who would argue that the best sources we have are the same as the canonical texts, represent challenging positions in this regard. In this context, it may also be noted that, with the partial exception of Ratzinger, none of the canonical critics examined here express much interest in a gospel harmony of one kind or another.[68] Rather, they focus on the witness of the gospel (pericope) at stake,[69] and beyond this, on the witness of a gospel or other text at large. Harmonization of systematization, if it takes place at all, typically only takes place at a meta-level, when interrelating the distinct witnesses of various texts. As indicated, Ratzinger is an exception to this rule, not least because he writes a book about Jesus rather than about the New Testament gospels as such, and he and his work may serve as an indication that the risk of harmonization still exists.[70]

---

68   Even if this has a long history in the interpretation of the gospels, see e.g. Dietrich Wünsch, "Evangelienharmonie," TRE 10 (1982), 626–636.

69   See also e.g. Francis Watson, "The Fourfold Gospel," in: Stephen C. Barton (ed.), *The Cambridge Companion to the Gospels* (Cambridge: Cambridge University, 2007), 34–52, 50; "truth is to be found if at all, only in and through the individual text."

70   Then again, most studies of the historical Jesus also represent a harmony of one kind or the other, given that *one* historical narrative is told.

Third, it may also be argued that canonical criticism can lead to creating unhistorical intertextual relationships, e.g. between writings which have no historical relationship, such as, according to most theories, Matthew and John, John and Luke, or Matthew and Luke. This leads to the treatment of the Bible as one coherent book with interrelated parts, rather than as a relatively random collection of (at least partially) unrelated works. As a result, all canonical writings then risk losing their own individuality. With regard to this historical objection to canonical approaches to Scripture, two remarks can be made. To begin with: Not all canonical approaches have a tendency to postulate unhistorical, i.e. "only" canonical intertextual relationships. In fact, of the scholars studied here, Stuhlmacher, Childs, and Sanders seem to be relatively reluctant to do so, even if they place much emphasis on intra-canonical intertextuality, they attempt to back up their proposals by means of historical and philological research, which also applies to – at least part of – Ratzinger's work. The "Amsterdam School" might, indeed, be the one most susceptible to this kind of criticism, given its almost exclusive reliance on a particular synchronic approach and intertextual connections between the various parts of the canonical text.[71] However, this particular kind of criticism is valid and carries considerable weight: Intra-canonical intertextual connections are often assumed and privileged over other intertextual connections, i.e. Scripture is seen as one body of texts and the individuality of the various writings that it comprises is not respected. Specifically, the risk of harmonizing (seemingly) conflicting statements and accounts in the New Testament should also be mentioned here (e.g. the four gospels among each other; the Pauline letters and Acts, etc.). While it is possible to defend such an approach based on rationales derived from the field of literary studies,[72] the question of the place of the

---

71 At the same time, it is also noticeable that in the actual exegeses of canonical critics that were considered here, with the exception of the Amsterdam School, the structure of the canon, as e.g. Niebuhr has drawn the attention to, is only of very limited importance. See Niebuhr, "Exegese." – For another account that emphasizes the structure of the New Testament canon see, however, e.g., François Bovon, "The Canonical Structure of Gospel and Apostle," in: McDonald/Sanders (ed.), *Debate*, 516–527. Certainly not all parts of the structure of the canon deserve equal weight; it would not be convincing to contribute equal weight to the sequence of the letters of Paul, the place of the Book of Revelation in the New Testament canon, and the four gospel canon in its relation to Acts. See e.g. Arie W. Zwiep, *Christ, Spirit, Community* (Tübingen: Mohr Siebeck, 2010), 117. Compare also the overview provided by Söding, *Einheit*, 232–294, on the New Testament canon especially 273–286.

72 See e.g. the considerations of Ricoeur, "Canon," 9–10: "Writing invests the discourse with a triple autonomy. Firstly in relation to the speaker, who may disappear, while the writing

pre-canonical life of the now canonical writings remains a challenge for any canonical approach to Scripture.

Fourth, more controversial than a limited view of possible intertextual connections is probably the emphasis on the connection between canonical texts and later extra-canonical ecclesial texts that most, if not all canonical critics, propose in one way or the other.[73] This also goes against the grain of much "traditional" exegetical scholarship, but in a different direction, and originates in the sense that the canonical Scriptures have their place in a specific community of interpretation that is, in a way, their author as well and continues to function as such, while the texts themselves continue to speak to this community and its theology. As this privileges one community of interpretation over others this could be seen as problematic. Should not the canonical writings be seen as equally accessible to all? In other words, the question of the ownership of texts and the authority to interpret arises: Who is allowed to read and interpret what? A related question is: How does canonical criticism, especially when it aligns itself with Gadamerian brands of hermeneutics, prevent operating with an at least implicitly apologetic agenda and with predetermined results, i.e. results that virtually automatically agree with one's interpretative tradition.[74]

---

remains. Plato was concerned by this fate of the orphaned text, unsupported by memory, at the mercy of every passer-by. One might tend to be more amazed at the second autonomy, which relates to the original situation of the discourse. Once a text is written, it potentially addresses anyone who can read. The pair of categories reader-writer takes the place of that of spoken word-written word. Augustine was astonished to be able to say of Moses: Scripsit et abiit, he wrote and went away. From now on, language can become literature. A third autonomy, this time more subtle, concerns the situation of the word that surrounds the exchange. At its oral stage, this situation is limited to local circumstances, to objects of usage that can be said to be to hand, to the spatial and temporal surroundings, to nearby interlocutors likely to enter into a relation of dialogue in short relations of question and answer; we can say, using more technical language, that the references of oral discourse are ostensible, relative to things and persons that can be indicated, pointed out. With the written word, the environment becomes swallowed up by the larger stage of the world. As Gadamer observes, Umwelt, environment, becomes Welt, the world. This is the vast space of empires where sovereigns correspond by courier with their distant provinces, the area in which circulate tablets, parchments, scrolls, and later sheets of paper bound together in books...And this space corresponds to a time that is no longer that of individual memories taken one by one, to the time of history, that of Herodotus, Thucydides and Polybius." – It is, in a way, therefore natural for the *intention auctoris* or even the original *intention operis* to give way to later interpretations and productions of meaning.

73   Even the strongly text-immanent approach of the "Amsterdam School" often seeks to relate its finding to the theologies of, notably, Karl Barth, John Calvin, and K.H. Miskotte.

74   See e.g. Zwiep, *Tekst* II, 204–221.

Fifth, it could be argued, from a more explicitly theological (rather than historical) perspective, that too strong a focus on the Scriptural canon could lead to a confusion of the word becoming flesh and the word becoming text, with the latter leading to an over-privileged position of the letter rather than of the spirit of the witness of Scripture, specifically the New Testament.[75] Again, this seems to be a valid criticism; at the same time, it might apply to some approaches more than others. For example, the "Amsterdam school," while certainly placing much emphasis on the revelatory character of the text, still points to the revelation of the divine name that is all-important. Others, such as Ratzinger and Sanders, emphasize the synergy between text and (new) context when it comes to the production of meaning.

Sixth, an issue that is both raised by canonical approaches to Scripture due to their emphasis on community and tradition and by its critics,[76] is that of power. That is to say: Who determines in what way which community, which tradition, which form of the text, is considered authoritative – and how are its interpretations judged to be legitimate or illegitimate? While much could be

---

75   See the fundamental criticism levelled against especially Stuhlmacher by Georg Strecker, "'Biblische Theologie?' Kritische Bemerkungen zu den Entwürfen von Hartmut Gese und Peter Stuhlmacher," in: Dieter Lührman/Georg Strecker (ed.), *Kirche* (Tübingen: Mohr Siebeck, 1980), 425–445, who argues that not only the presupposition and priviligisation of the (unity and normativity of the) Old and New Testaments is highly problematic, but also that the notion of "Einverständnis" or "Vernehmen" is naïve and pietistic, rather than critical and scholarly. Instead, he argues the following: "Neutestamentliche Hermeneutik hat sich...an einem Zweifachen zu orientieren, nämlich an dem im Neuen Testament bezeugten Christusgeschehen: In ihm ereignet sich das Gegenüber und Miteinander von Eschaton und Historie (Joh 1, 14); darin besteht seine absolute, Glauben begründende, soteriologische Qualität; seine fundamentale und universale Bedeutung muß das Ganze der Theologie bestimmen und läßt jede alttestamentlich-neutestamentliche Engführung scheitern; und zweitens an der anthropologischen Perspektive: Sie stellt den einzigen hermeneutisch verantwortbaren Zugang zum neutestamentlichen Christuszeugnis dar; indem sie sich von theozentrischer und anthropozentrischer Systematik freihält und die Grenzen des biblischen Vokabulars überschreitet, ist sie für den nicht einzuschränkenden Anspruch des Eschaton und ebenso für die Sprache, Vorstellungswelt und Situation der Gegenwart offen; sie macht die Antwort des Neuen Testaments auf die Frage nach dem Woher und dem Wohin des Menschen al seine für alle Menschen Mögliche Erfahrung verstehbar." (444–445) – See also Seckler, "Problematik," 52: "Nach den Grundsätzen der theologischen Prinzipienlehre hat Gott sich nicht in Texte hinein offenbart, auch nicht in den kanonischen Endtext hinein, sondern in Menschen, in sein Volk hinein. Die Bibel ist, anders als der Koran, nicht *geoffenbart,* sondern sie ist der *inspirierte* literarische Niederschlag der Offenbarung." For this, and similar criticisms, see also: Barr, "Case."

76   See e.g. Davies, *Bible.*

said about this in relation to canonical approaches to Scriptural interpretation that do not explicitly reflect on the issue of authority and power in the process of interpretation, just as much could be said about this in relation to all approaches to Scriptural interpretation that do not explicitly reflect on the issue of authority and power in the process of interpretation. Here, however, is the place for neither. It should only be pointed out that for canonical approaches to Scripture, questions of intra-ecclesial processes of discernment and decision-making,[77] the relation between academia and church policy, and the question of (non-)mainstreaming of marginalized groups in churches, might be of particular relevance.

Seventh, the open-ended nature of canonical biblical interpretation (and biblical interpretation in general) has been mentioned a number of times. Therefore, the issue of biblical interpretation that is out of control or, because it becomes strongly community-based and thus withdraws from checks and balances that are not integral to its tradition of interpretation, should also be mentioned. It seems that this is, at least in theory, a real possibility and a potential problem for canonical approaches to Scripture that also wish to be part of academia. While approaches such as that of Sanders, which is open-ended and present the process of interpretation, at least to some extent, as eing principally uncontrollable and open, or Ratzinger's approach that draws heavily on the reception of texts in an open-ended tradition, other approaches, notably those of Childs, Stuhlmacher, and in many ways also the "Amsterdam School," place much emphasis on the boundaries of interpretation. This issue, however, although it surfaces when considering the work of canonical critics, may well be one that concerns biblical studies in general, rather than canonical approaches to Scripture *per se*.

Finally, it should be considered whether the way in which the canonical critics utilize the canon is, in fact, not anachronistic in yet another way, i.e. with regard to the functioning of the Scriptural canon in the early church,[78] the

---

77   See also the discussion of aspects of this by Smit, *Tradition*, in particular in relation to the difficulties of the Anglican Communion on finding a way to communally interpret Scripture (and tradition), as well as on the relationship between ecumenical dialogues on tradition and the question of authority within the church.

78   Terminologically, the notion of a canon of Scripture only emerged in the fourth century, see e.g. Ohme, *Kanon*, 2.402-406, Christoph Markschies, *Kaiserzeitliche christliche Theologie und ihre Institutionen: Prolegomena zu einer Geschichte der antiken christlichen Theologie* (Tübingen: Mohr Siebeck, 2007), 221. The sequence in which canon and rule of faith (i.e. "grammar" of early Christianity) is presented by Theißen, *Religion* 356–384, is therefore, misleading: The development of the rule of faith chronologically precedes the canon of Scripture.

centuries during which the canon was formed and to which canonical critics
such as Ratzinger, Stuhlmacher, Childs, and the "Amsterdam School" appeal
implicitly or explicitly. In order to be able to address this topic some remarks
need to be made about the development of the canon in the early church and
its functioning.[79] First of all, it may be maintained with scholars such as
Markschies that the current view of the development of the canon has changed
considerably since, say, 1970, when Käsemann could comment that one was
very well informed about this topic indeed.[80] Specifically, this has to do with
more sensitivity to the fact that the development of "the" canon took place in
different ways in different geographical and institutional settings.[81]

Some appertaining nuances have been introduced with regard to the notion
of canonicity, e.g. by means of McDonald's differentiation between a body of
authoritative texts as such (canon 1) and a fixed list of such texts (canon 2), one
might wish to call these a *corpus* and a *codex* of texts, in analogy to, for example, the *corpus iuris canonici* and the *codex iuris canonici*.[82] The various sources
that are typically adduced to discuss the development of the canon in the early
church, e.g. the use of texts as Scripture,[83] canon lists by early theologians
and a number of local councils[84] (no council with an ecumenical claim ever

---

79   See for a more extensive argument: Smit, *Canon.*

80   See Käsemann, "Einführung," 9. – Note also the comments by Childs, "Reflections," 27, on
         this volume being somewhat of a turning point, or the conclusion of an earlier era.

81   Markschies, *Theologie*, 333–334: "Das bisherige, eher monolithische Bild der Entwicklung
         des 'Kanons' biblischer Schriften hat seine Konturen in den letzten Jahren schon erheb-
         lich durch eine starke geographische Differenzierung geändert. Unsere Beobachtungen
         zu antiken christlichen Institutionen wie den freien Lehrern mehrheitskirchlicher oder
         gnostischer Prägung, zu den monarchischen Bischöfen, Gottesdienst und Unterricht
         sowie den (gemeinde-)öffentlichen und privaten Bibliotheken zeigen, daß solche
         Institutionen jeweils einen eigenen 'Kanon' biblischer Schriften entwickelten, der sich
         zwar in Kernbereichen ebenso berührt wie die bischöflichen und synodalen Kanones
         verschiedener geographischer Regionen, aber eben auch charakteristische Unterschiede
         gegenüber dem anderer Institutionen aufweist." Zie ook: Winrich A. Löhr, "Norm und
         Kontext: Kanonslisten in der Spätantike," *BThZ* (2005), 202–229.

82   McDonald, *Canon*, 55–58, see for a terminological discussion also e.g. Barton, *Spirit*, 1–34.
         The historical backgrounds to the notion of "canon" are surveyed by Ohme, *Kanon*,
         21–337.

83   On which an extensive literature exists, see the brief overview offered by McDonald,
         Canon, 271–281.

84   This concerns (amongst others) the following texts: The Muratorian canon (on its dis-
         puted date, see e.g. Joseph Verheyden, "The Canon Muratori. A Matter of Dispute," in:
         Auwers/De Jonge [ed.], *Canons*, 487–556), the witness of Origen as recorded by Eusebius
         of Caesarea, *Hist.* 6.25:3–10, further Eusebius of Caesarea, *Hist.* 3.5, Cyril of Jerusalem,

pronounced unequivocally about the canon until the Council of Trent [1545–1563])[85] have in the past decades been restudied and led to the position quoted above. The (admittedly relatively small) differences between canons as they existed,[86] both in canon lists and the books that were actually used, were not seen as a major problem.[87] There should, therefore, be considerable reluctance to speak of the "conclusion" of the New Testament canon around, for example, 200 (Marcion),[88] or in the fourth century (Constantine I),[89] as there is indeed among many scholars.[90] The question of canonicity is further complicated when considering what are often termed the "criteria" for the canonization of writings,[91] such as apostolicity, antiquity, usage (in catechesis, but also

Cath. 4.36, Athanasius of Alexandria, *Ep.* 39.7–9, 11–12, Epiphanius of Salamis, *Adv. Haer.*, 3.76:5, the Mommsen canon, the canon lists in the codex Claromontanus and the codex Sinaiticus, the Synod of Laodicea, can. 59, and the Synod of Carthage, can. 47. See for an overview: Daniel J. Theron, *Evidence of Tradition* (Grand Rapids: Baker, 1958), 107–127, as well as Metzger, *Canon*, 305–315.

85   See the decisions made during the fourth session of the council, on 8 April 1546. – A possible exception to this rule is the Council of Trullo (692; never accepted in the West), which received a number of canon lists in its own canon two.

86   See for an overview of various canons and texts that had (only) temporary or local canonical status: Metzger, *Canon*, 143–247. See also: Rainer Berndt, "Gehören die Kirchenväter zur Heiligen Schrift? Zur Kanontheorie des Hugo von St. Viktor," *JBTh* 3 (1988), 191–199.

87   This observation gains further relief, when it is considered what *was* all regulated and decided upon by councils see: Ohme, *Kanon*, 243–337 (prior to Constantine I), 342–569 (during and after the reign of Constantine I).

88   Among modern scholars, Theißen, *Religion*, 340, places the emergence of the canon in the second century: "Es gab im Urchristentum nicht nur zwei Parteien, sondern eine Vielzahl von Strömungen, zwischen denen es Spannungen und Konflikte gab: Judenchristentum, synoptisches, paulinisches und johanneisches Christentum, dazu später der breite Strom eines gnostischen Christentums. In einem ersten Teil gebe ich einen Überblick über diese Strömungen und ihre Unterströmungen sowie die Querverbindungen zwischen ihnen. Hier sollen die Pluralität des Urchristentums herausgearbeitet werden und Indizien für seine Einheit in und hinter aller Mannigfaltigkeit gesammelt werden. Nur diese Einheit macht die Entstehung des Kanons verständlich, der sich ohne zentrale Organisationsinstanz im Urchristentum des 2. Jh. Durchsetzen konnte. Seine Entstehung ist das entscheidende Ereignis der Geschichte des 2. Jh."

89   See e.g. the argument of Dungan, *Bible*.

90   See e.g. Anton Ziegenaus, *Kanon: Von der Väterzeit bis zur Gegenwart* (Herder: Freiburg, 1990), esp. 146–162, who, although he mentions the closure of the canon, also shows that this canon was not received in the same way everywhere at all.

91   See about this, e.g. the overview of Morwenna Ludlow: "'Criteria of Canonicity' and the Early Church," in Barton/Wolter (ed.), *Einheit*, 69–93.

particularly in the ritual practice of the church), inspiration, and adaptability to new contexts.[92] Often, these criteria were only used after the fact of canonization and hence, more in the sense of ascription of particular characteristics to writings than in the sense of an evaluation of them. It is also questionable that they were indeed used in a systematic way at all.[93]

At this background, one may ask how the canon has functioned in early Christianity. Again, only an outline can be provided. First, four main aspects of the function of the New Testament canon may be identified: (1) The New Testament canon functioned to clarify the relative importance of early Christian texts (and groups associated with them). In this way, the gradual clarification of a New Testament canon also had a function in the gradual clarification of the identity of (different forms of) early Christianity;[94] (2) The New Testament canon provided a way to authorize (a certain) communal memory of Jesus and the earliest communities; (3) the New Testament canon, itself a product of the use of certain texts, also fulfilled a function in steering the usage of texts in early Christianity; and[95] (4) The New Testament canon provided, together with the earlier canonical Scriptures, the most important foundation for catechesis and preaching in early Christian communities. The reading of the canonical Scriptures was, in all of these contexts, guided by, or at least taking place in the context of, a κανών τῆς πίστεως or *regula fidei*, a rule of faith, i.e. a catechetical tool summarizing the main points of the faith.[96] It was also for this "canon" that the term "canon" was first used in early Christianity,[97] well in

---

92 McDonald, *Canon*, 401–421. See also the succinct overview of Metzger, *Canon*, 251–254.

93 See also the remarks by Ludlow, "'Criteria,'" 63–64, on this topic.

94 Especially vis-à-vis (other) Jewish groups and also within the spectrum of emerging Christian identities. See e.g. Theißen, *Religion*, 342–343.

95 See e.g. the way in which Eusebius of Caesarea and Athanasius of Alexandria write about the canonical Scriptures (as e.g., discussed by Metzger, *Canon*, 201–212, 309–310, 312–313; see also the overview provided by John Barton, *Holy Writings. Sacred Text. The Canon in Early Christianity* [London: SPCK, 1997]).

96 See e.g. Ohme, *Kanon*, 77: "das gesamte in der Taufekatechese empfangene Kerygma," and further: Richard A. Norris, Jr., "Confessional and Catechetical Formulas in First- and Early-Second-Century Christian Literature," in: Marsha L. Dutton/Patrick Terrell Gray (ed.), *One Lord, One Faith, One Baptism. Studies in Christian Ecclesiality and Ecumenism in Honor of J. Robert Wright* (Grand Rapids: Eerdmans, 2006), 14–28, 25, Klaus Wengst, "Glaubensbekenntnis(se) IV," TRE 13 (1984), 392–399, Adolf Martin Ritter, "Glaubensbekenntnis(se) V," TRE 13 (1984), 399–412, Wolfram Kinzig/Markus Vinzent, "Recent Research on the Origin of the Creed," JTS 50 (1999), 535–559, and Reinhard Meßner, *Einführung in die Liturgiewissenschaft* (Paderborn: Schönigh, 2001), 76–77.

97 See e.g. Ohme, *Kanon*, 8–19, for a succinct overview, as well as Metzger, *Canon*, 289–293.

line with classical hermeneutical insights.[98] Scriptural interpretation – even before the fixation of a formal canon – thus, becomes a dynamic interplay between the text and the "grammar" of reading provided by the rule of faith, leading to a productive dialectic between the interpretation of Scripture according to the state of the (then) exegetical and philosophical art and the development of early Christian creedal traditions.[99] The canon as a literary phenomenon, in the sense of a clearly fixed list of texts, only played a subordinate role in this context.[100] Canonical hermeneutics, if something like that can be identified in early Christianity, should be seen to exist in the interplay between authoritative texts and the faith of the community.[101]

When relating this brief overview to the canonical approaches here, it appears that especially approaches that emphasize the shape of the canon and *Letztgestalt*-exegesis (e.g. the "Amsterdam School," Childs, and to a considerable extent also Stuhlmacher), early dates of the canon (such as Stuhlmacher and Childs, to some extent also the "Amsterdam School" and Ratzinger, even if it plays a role of little importance for the latter given his emphasis on tradition as an ongoing process), might have difficulties arguing that their approach comes close to that of the early church, even if all of the approaches just mentioned do practice some form of exegesis that relates the canonical text to a rule of faith of sorts. It is probably Sanders, with his emphasis on the (eschatologically open) canonical process,[102] rather than on the canonical form, and his hermeneutical triangle that derives from his work on comparative midrash, that comes the closest to a kind of exegesis in which the canon plays a role analogous to the role it played in the exegesis of the early church.

When, by way of concluding this section, we look back at these various kinds of criticism, most of them seem to make real and substantial points with

---

98   This is not surprising, given that most early Christian authors used analogous (and partially classical) hermeneutical rules. See e.g., Frances M. Young, *Biblical Exegesis and the Formation of Christian Culture* (Cambridge: Cambridge University, 1997), *passim*, and esp. 29–45. For an overview of prominent sources, see: Michael Fiedrowicz, *Prinzipien der Schriftauslegung in der Alten Kirche* (Bern: Lang, 1998), 2–106 (also see the bibliography on xxi–xxxix).

99   See e.g. Young, *Exegesis*, 29–45.

100   See also Barton, *Writings*, 131–156. For an exemplary differing opinion, see, e.g.: John Webster, "'A Great and Meritorious Act of the Church?' The Dogmatic Location of the Canon," in: Barton/Wolter (ed.), *Einheit*, 95–126.

101   See also: Gerhard Sauter, "Kanon und Kirche," Barton/Wolter (ed.), *Einheit*, 239–259, 252.

102   See above, 2.2. – See also e.g. Christine Helmer/Christof Landmesser, "Introduction: A New Biblical-Theological Approach to the Unity of the Canon," in idem/idem (ed.), *Scripture*, 1–12.

regard to canonical approaches to Scripture. They point to pitfalls and dangers that are indeed real. None of the points raised here, however, seems to invalidate all kinds of canonical criticism. Rather, they make clearer what canonical approaches to Scripture can and cannot achieve and how indeed they do function. For example, the interpretation of a text that has become part of the canonical Scriptures of a particular church is something different to the interpretation of the same text in its earliest historical setting. Yet, both settings of such a text are real and can be studied, as can the hermeneutics involved in both of these interpretations.

CHAPTER 4

Canonical Criticism: On the Road Towards Ecumenical Hermeneutics?

4.1 Introduction

As was indicated in the beginning of this study, an attempt will be made here to explore the possible interrelationship and potential for cross-fertilization between canonical hermeneutics and ecumenical hermeneutics, understood as the approach(es) to biblical hermeneutics as developed within the context of the ecumenical movement. Such an attempt is novel, despite obvious similarities in outlook between both hermeneutical approaches, notably with regard to their emphasis on the interrelationship between text and interpretative community (mostly: The church or the churches). Before turning to a sketch of the development and current state of ecumenical hermeneutics and offering remarks connecting this kind of hermeneutics to canonical approaches to Scripture, some introductory remarks need to be made.

While on the one hand, "traditional" confessional divides in biblical scholarship (e.g. a "Protestant/Catholic" divide) have become much less pronounced,[1] other confessional divides might be on the rise (e.g. "Conservative/Liberal," "Global North/Global South," etc.); at the same time, reflection on the relationship between interpretative community, interpretation, and the organization of interpretation/knowledge in ecclesial communities is often lacking and frequently constitutes something of a blind spot in biblical studies, both in academia and in ecclesial praxis.[2] The conscious consideration of the relationship

---

1   See with regard to this and the related topic of historical Jesus research also Mayordomo/Smit, "Question." See also Smit, "Wegweiser," and idem, "Diversiteit en Nieuwe Testament. Over de productieve en heuristische inzet van biografische, levensbeschouwelijke, en culturele diversiteit bij het onderwijs in het Nieuwe Testament," *Nederlands Theologisch Tijdschrift* 68 (2014), 277–296.

2   See with regard to this also Wilckens, *Theologie* 1/1, 21: "Heute arbeitet man auf evangelischer wie katholischer Seite längst problemlos zusammen. Die konfessionelle Beheimatung eines Exegeten ist in aller Regel kaum zu bemerken. Das ist ebenso fruchtbar für die Forschung wie aber doch auch fundamentaltheologisch problematisch." See also the critical remarks of Hans-Josef Klauck, "Evangelische und katholische Exegese. Ein Erfahrungsbericht," in: Eve-Marie Becker (ed.), *Neutestamentliche Wissenschaft* (Tübingen: Francke, 2003), 337–346, 337, as well as Carolyn Osiek, "Catholic or catholic? Biblical Scholarship at the Center," JBL 125 (2006), 5–22, and Segovia, "Studies," 48.

© KONINKLIJKE BRILL NV, LEIDEN, 2015 | DOI 10.1163/9789004301016_005

between "canon and community" and the way in which the canonical texts are interpreted in relation to a community's identity and "rule of faith" might be beneficial, not only for ecumenical dialogue, but also for the understanding of the texts and their interpretation as such. This observation can be broadened in three ways. First, given that not every canon of rule of faith needs to be ecclesial and, hence, not every community of interpretation with real interpretative grammars needs to be ecclesial,[3] what was just stated also applies to other communities of interpretation, such as the one comprised of those engaged in the scholarly study of religion (see above, 3.1.3). Along these lines, canonical criticism, at least when conceptualized as has been done here, can both account for and be a tool for understanding interpretative diversity.[4] Second, one may also connect the above observations to the use of (religious) texts, (originally) belonging to a specific community of interpretation, by another community. A point in case might be the reading of religious texts of one community by another, in the context of "scriptural reasoning" or in another setting,[5] for example, Christian scholars' interpretation of Jewish texts.[6] Thus, the questions that are raised by canonical hermeneutics' reconnecting of texts and community are also relevant for ecumenical and interreligious discourses. Third, there are the issue of considerable unclarity among canonical critics when it comes to the precise definition of text, community, and rule of faith. The interaction between these three is central to canonical approaches to Scripture, leading to an interpretative process that is highly dynamic, fluid, and, for some, open-ended.[7] Not all characteristics of this

---

3   "Virtual" communities of interpretation are, in this respect, just as real as other communities of interpretation.

4   See e.g. Lieven Boeve, "Tradition, (De)Canonization, and the Challenge of Plurality," in: Van der Kooij/Van der Toorn (ed.), *Canonization*, 371–380, compare also: Ulrich Luz "Kann die Bibel heute noch Grundlage für die Kirche sein? Über die Aufgabe der Exegese in einer religiös-pluralistischen Gesellschaft," NTS 44 (1998), 317–339, and see further the considerations of Rowan Williams, "The Unity of the Church and the Unity of the Bible: An Analogy," IKZ 91 (2001), 5–21; see also Smit, "Diversiteit." – Needless to say, not all canonical critics would agree, see e.g. Childs, "Canon," 32–35.

5   On scriptural reasoning, see C.C. Pecknold/David F. Ford (ed.), *The Promise of Scriptural Reasoning* (Oxford: Blackwell, 2006).

6   See e.g. the brief remarks of Söding, *Einheit*, 80–92.

7   In line with, e.g. Sanders' approach: Other approaches will probably be more reluctant to such open process of interpretation (see e.g. the critical comments of Childs, "Reflections," 32.34, including the following comment, betraying Childs' relationship between theological anthropology and pneumatology, that for Sanders, "The role of the Holy Spirit in constantly bringing to fresh light the written scriptures as a divinely spoken Word has been replaced with the exercise of human imagination and ingenuity,"); see also e.g. Janowski, "Kanonhermeneutik," 176–180, with considerable emphasis on the limits of interpretation.

dynamic, or of its constituting components, are always equally clear in the canonical approaches studied here. This has to do with the underdefinition of precisely the three items just mentioned in the work of some of the canonical critics.[8] Childs is an interesting case in this respect; when considering his work, it becomes clear that he refrains from defining the three items just mentioned. Which church he refers to is not clear, nor is it clear how interpretation is ordered within this church, neither is the precise form of the Scriptural text (nor the shape of the canon, even if he eventually opts for the canon of the Hebrew Bible for the first part of the Christian canon), and furthermore, the rule of faith does not have a clear formulation in his work.[9] Something similar could be said about Stuhlmacher, albeit that he is somewhat clearer about the church that he presupposes, and that his rule of faith is also clearer. Sanders, by contract, is clear when considering all three aspects open and fluid, while Ratzinger does have a clear idea about the church that he addresses and presumably about the rule of faith, but outlines neither the latter nor the precise form of the text. And finally, the various representatives of the "Amsterdam School," including Van Nieuwpoort, typically do not clearly indicate what sort of church *qua* community of interpretation it presupposes, the form of the New Testament text is not a topic of major reflection in this tradition, and the rule of faith is mainly derived from the foundational works of Barth, Miskotte, and Breukelman. Of course, one might argue that it would be impossible – and even undesirable – to precisely define and thus, (attempt to) fixate the notion of "community of interpretation" (c.q. "church"), "text," and "interpretative grammar." However, further clarity than many of the authors discussed above provide would be helpful in order to further understand the process of canonical exegesis, which is, as was indicated above, factually any kind of exegesis. When looking at canonical criticism in this way, it seems that relating it to a discipline that focuses very much on precisely ecclesial interpretation and the role of communities and their traditions in the process of interpretation might be fruitful, both when it comes to investigating what canonical criticism might have to offer such a discipline, and when it comes to discovering how canonical criticism might benefit from insights and emphases from that other discipline. This will now be attempted by focusing on ecumenical hermeneutics, a discipline that is very much aware of the ecclesial aspect of interpretation, just as it is aware of the interrelationship between communities of interpretation, interpretative traditions, and the interpreted text.

---

8   See also Smit, "Wegweiser."

9   See also Smit, "Wegweiser."

4.2   Contemporary Ecumenical Hermeneutics and Canonical Criticism: An Inventarisation and Comparison

4.2.1   *Introduction*

The above considerations of the possible ecumenical or even interreligious implications of direction into which canonical criticism points, given its emphasis on the interrelationship between the identity and interpretative "grammar" of the community of interpretation and the interpretation of texts, beg the question of the relationship between canonical exegesis and ecumenical hermeneutics, or the hermeneutical reflection as it has taken place in the ecumenical movement. While this is admittedly a broad topic, a good focus and case study can be found when concentrating on the hermeneutical discussion as it has taken place in and around the World Council of Churches' Commission on Faith and Order that has had, and continues to have, a particular interest in hermeneutical questions. By way of excursus, it will be considered whether and in what ways canonical approaches to exegesis can speak to ecumenical hermeneutics, and vice versa. In order to do so, first the hermeneutical discussion in "Faith and Order" will be surveyed, after which two documents will be considered in particular: The 1998 study document *A Treasure in Earthen Vessels*[10] and the very recent document *The Church: Towards a Common Vision* (2013).[11]

In general, it is recognized that within the ecumenical movement there have been two distinct approaches to the question of hermeneutics,[12] which is here understood to refer to all discussions related to the theory and method of the interpretation of the faith and its sources, and can also be at stake where the term "hermeneutics" itself is not used. The first and oldest approach concentrates on achieving a common understanding of Scripture and tradition.[13] The central question is: How do we find a way of reading the creeds, for example, that is acceptable to all and that will bring the visible unity of our churches closer, be it in the form of reconciled diversity or in other ways? This approach is closely related to Oldham's "best and ablest minds" approach.[14] The second

---

10   Commission on Faith and Order, *Treasure.*

11   Commission on Faith and Order, *The Church: Towards a Common Vision* (Geneva: WCC, 2013).

12   See Rudolf von Sinner, *Reden vom dreieinigen Gott in Brasilien und Indien* HUT 43 (Tübingen: Mohr Siebeck, 2003), 9–28.

13   See Lukas Vischer (ed.), *A Documentary History of the Faith and Order Movement* (St. Louis, MO: Bethany Press, 1963); in the index of this work, "hermeneutics" is listed under "scripture."

14   For this and the following, see Michael G. Cartwright, "Hermeneutics", in: Nicholas Lossky/ José Míguez Bonino/John Pobee/Tom F. Stransky/Geoffrey Wainwright/Pauline Webb, *Dictionary of the Ecumenical Movement* (Geneva: WCC Publications, ²2002), 513–518.

approach reflects a later development. It does not aim at establishing a common hermeneutical framework into which all readings of scripture and tradition can fit or with which all can agree; rather, it aims to develop ways for churches to understand one another's differences. This approach is much more contextually oriented and more frequently borrows its models from the social sciences. "Understanding one another" is the best description of this approach, or one may call it, with Rudolf von Sinner, a "hermeneutics of acceptance."[15] Von Sinner refers to past World Council of Churches general secretary Konrad Raiser as a prominent spokesperson of this kind of hermeneutics, quoting him as follows: "The legitimacy of inculturation or contextualization is not a matter of debate any longer. Today's pressing question is: How can communication be achieved between theologies, confessions, and spiritualities that are all contextualized differently?"[16] In recent discussions, such as those in *A Treasure in Earthen Vessels* and responses to it, both the older approach[17] and the newer approach[18] occur; this also applies to the 2013 document *The Church: Towards a Common Vision*. Having given this broad outline, it is possible to describe the hermeneutical discussion in the ecumenical movement in somewhat more detail.

4.2.2   *Hermeneutics in the Ecumenical Movement until 1963*

The hermeneutical discussion in the ecumenical movement, especially as it is now embodied by the World Council of Churches (WCC), has its roots in the pre-1948 Faith and Order movement and was subsequently carried forward primarily in the context of the Commission on Faith and Order of the World Council of Churches, as it was founded in 1948.[19] At the first World Conference on Faith and Order (Lausanne, 1927), the topic of hermeneutics was discussed and the results of this discussion can be found in the report of this conference.[20] The topic, in the index to the conference report under the heading "Scripture," occurs thrice: Once in the context of a section on *The Nature of the*

---

15   Von Sinner, *Reden*, p. 15, "Hermeneutik der Anerkennung."

16   Konrad Raiser, *Wir stehen noch am Anfang: Ökumene in einer veränderten Welt* (Gütersloh: Gütersloher Verlagshaus, 1994), 162; quoted in Von Sinner, *Reden*, 7.

17   See *Treasure*, nos. 11–20 (pp. 11–17) and nos. 21–27 (pp. 17–21).

18   Accentuated in ibid., nos. 28–31 (pp. 21–23) and 38–48 (pp. 27–32).

19   To be sure, also the work of other commissions and parts of the WCC has hermeneutical aspects, however, the hermeneutical discussion *per se* is commonly associated with the work of Faith and Order, the commission that also received the task to study the topic of hermeneutics from the WCC at large.

20   For which, see: Vischer (ed.), *History*, 27–39; references to parts of this document are to its numbered sections.

Church (section 20), where a list is provided, some characteristics of the church are listed, which include the possession of the written Word of God, the spirited interpretation of Scripture, the preaching of the Gospel, and a ministry with that task, and twice under the heading of *The Church's Confession of Faith* (sections 28 and 31–33). Section 28 mentions the fact of the use of the Apostles' and Nicene creeds as documents that testify to "a common Christian faith." The sections 31–33 discuss variations in creeds (notably the *filioque* in 31, on which see also 129), the relationship between creeds and Scripture in different traditions (some have no creeds, some subordinate Scripture to creeds, some do the opposite; see 32), and that "competent authority in each Church" will determine how the various creeds are used.

Thus, in Lausanne, the question of hermeneutics, or, in the terminology of the day: The question of biblical interpretation and the interpretation of the faith, is primarily related to the issue of the relationship between Scripture and tradition, as well as to the role of the Church and the Spirit in the interpretation of both. This will remain characteristic for at least part of the work of the Faith and Order movement and the later WCC commission. It may also be clear that the ecumenical hermeneutical discussion as it was conducted in 1927, was still in its infancy when compared to later developments.

When turning to the next World Conference on Faith and Order (Edinburgh, 1937) and the report of this gathering,[21] it is immediately obvious that questions of interpretation receive considerably more space and attention now. Of relevance are in particular the sections 23–26 and 45–46, (part of the text under the heading *The Church of Christ and the Word of God*), the sections 65–67 (part of "*The Church of Christ: Ministry and Sacraments*"), and 128–130, 134, and 156 (part of "*The Church's Unity in Life and Worship*").

Section 23 is concerned with the nature of the written and inspired Word of God and the human character of the texts and their interpretation, some fundamental steps are taken here and the section deserves quotation in full:

> A testimony in words is by divine ordering provided for the revelation uttered by the Word. This testimony is given in Holy Scripture, which thus affords the primary norm for the Church's teaching, worship and life. We discern a parallel, though an imperfect one, between the inspiration of Holy Scripture and the incarnation of the Word in Our Lord Jesus Christ: in each there is a union, effected by the Holy Spirit, between the divine and the human, and an acceptance, for God's saving purpose, of human

---

21   For which, see: Vischer (ed.), *History*, 40–74; the references are to the document's numbered sections.

limitations. "We have this treasure in earthen vessels." We are all convinced that this conception of the revelation cannot be shaken by scientific Bible research. But if it is conscious of its true nature, such research can render the Church important services in bringing about a right interpretation of the Scripture, provided that the freedom needed for carrying out its work is not denied to it.

Thus, a theological framework is provided for the relationships between revelation, the written Word of God, and the place of scholarly biblical interpretation. In particular, the revelation through the Word is understood as being witnessed to by (human) words, in line with the divine intention, which has Scripture as its form. The report also notes an analogy between the incarnation of the divine Word in the Lord Jesus Christ and the presence of the revelation provided by this Word in the witness to it in the Scriptures. In this context, scholarly research in the field of Biblical Studies, given that it serves to further the understanding of the texts and, as a consequence, what they bear witness to, can be of service to the Church rather than a threat to it. The document, to be sure, does not outline what the "true nature" of biblical scholarship entails precisely.

Next, the report turns to the relationship between Scripture and tradition, which it identifies as "the living stream of the Church's life" (section 24), noting that there are many opinions that cannot be considered to "have the true authority of tradition" because they are in contradiction to Scripture, while other opinions that "do not rest explicitly on Scripture, though they are not in contradiction with it" are accepted as true tradition (section 24). The tension between various understandings of the authority of Scripture in relation to tradition and vice versa that is at play in this section is made even clearer in the subsequent section (and restated in section 26), given that it is noted there that the churches are one in saying that the church has been instrumental in the formation of the Bible, but differ as to the churches and the churches traditional role in the interpretation of it.[22] This tension is not resolved in the 1937

---

22 Section 25: "We are at one in recognising that the Church, enlightened by the Holy Spirit, has been instrumental in the formation of the Bible. But some of us hold that this implies that the Church under the guidance of the Spirit is entrusted with the authority to explain, interpret and complete (συμπληροῦν) the teaching of the Bible, and consider the witness of the Church as given in tradition as equally authoritative with the Bible itself. Others, however, believe that the Church, having recognised the Bible as the indispensable record of the revealed Word of God, is bound exclusively by the Bible as the only rule of faith and practice and, while accepting the relative authority of tradition, would consider it authoritative only in so far as it is founded upon the Bible itself."

report – in fact, it will continue to be a matter of attention in the work of "Faith and Order" for the decades to come.

A next instance of the discussion of hermeneutics occurs when the report of the Edinburgh conference turns to the topic of "The Gift of Prophecy and the Ministry of the Church." Here, the document states that "we are agreed that the presence and inspiration of the Holy Spirit are granted to His chosen instruments today, and especially to those called to be minsters of the Word of God." (section 45) As the report continues to emphasize, all members of the church have received the Spirit and the work of interpretation and preaching is necessary for the life of the church. This also leads to a position in which the work of the Spirit and the prophetic voice of church members is emphasized, while underlining that all prophecies must also be tested.[23] While this emphasis addresses one ecclesiological and pneumatological issue that is related to the interpretation of Scripture and tradition and solves it at least partially, i.e. the place of the interpretation of Scripture by the "laity" in the Church, it also introduces another one: The testing of prophecies and discerning what is good and what is not.

A further instance of a discussion of hermeneutical topics occurs under the heading *The Church of Christ: Ministry and Sacraments*. Here, hermeneutics, or, more specifically: The relationship between Scripture and other parts of the church's tradition and life, is addressed in particular in the sections 65–67, where it is underlined that the sacraments are not instruments of power of the church, but Christ's gift to the Church, which itself is guided towards the truth (65). In addition, the Spirit is described as enabling the Church to exercise stewardship with regard to the "tradition concerning the sacraments." (66) Furthermore, a remark occurs that identifies Scripture as the *norma normans* vis-à-vis the sacraments: The latter need to be evaluated on the basis of Scripture. Finally, under the heading of "The Church's Unity in Life and Worship" and the subheading "Likeness in Faith or Confession as a Basis for

---

23   Section 46: "In Christ all the truth of God's redemptive purpose for men is fully and suffi-
       ciently contained, but every age has its own problems and its own difficulties, and it is the
       work of the Spirit in every age to apply the one truth revealed in Christ to the circum-
       stances of the time. Moreover, as past experience shows, these new applications bring to
       the Church a new understanding of the truth on which they rest. The Spirit may speak by
       whomsoever He wills. The call to bear witness to the Gospel and to declare God's will does
       not come to the ordained ministry alone; the Church greatly needs, and should both
       expect and welcome, the exercise of gifts of prophecy and teaching by laity, both men and
       women. When prophetic gifts appear it is for the Church not to quench the spirit or
       despise prophesyings but to test these prophesyings by their accordance with the abiding
       truth entrusted to it, and to hold fast that which is good."

Unity" (i.e., 127–129), the relationship between the creed and Scripture is again, in many ways, repeating what had been said in 23–26. It is fitting, therefore, when "the problem of the authority of Scripture and the modes of its interpretation" is identified as "the most classical instance" of disagreement among churches (154).

When, in 1948, the World Council of Churches was founded as a merger of the Faith and Order and Life and Work movements, the report of the first assembly of the WCC mentions questions of hermeneutics in three instances. Even though this document is not, *sensu stricto*, a document of the Commission on Faith and Order, it is of high significance for tracing the development of the discussion about hermeneutics in (this part of) the ecumenical movement. In its section 14, under the heading *Common Beliefs and Common Problems*, the document identifies the relationship between Scripture and tradition as one of the three key problems of ecumenical dialogue, next to the relationship between church and Israel (first problem) and the place of ordained ministry and the sacraments in the church (third problem). Then, under the heading *The Unity in Our Difference*, section 24 of the document addresses the tension between the single revelation and its many interpretations, which has resulted in many differences between the churches. At the same time, the report addresses the fundamental unity underlying all of this diversity, which can be found in the unity of God's revelation. In the subsequent section, 25, which has the heading *The Glory of the Church and the Shame of the Churches*, questions of hermeneutics are very briefly mentioned when the document notes that, in the last years, many Christians have learned to understand Scripture anew in a church that was indeed living "under the cross." This reference to a contextual interpretation of Scripture is noticeable at this stage of the ecumenical discussion about questions of interpretation and hermeneutics.

Following the founding of the World Council of Churches, a next world conference on Faith and Order took place in Lund in 1952. In its report, five sections address questions of hermeneutics, at least according to the index of the *Documentary History* of Faith and Order.[24] Section 20 mentions questions of interpretation very briefly, as it registers that there is a common acceptance of the "Holy Scripture" and that this is a basis for ecumenical theology. Furthermore, this section states that ecumenism is not a "scissors and paste" exercise that combines various traditions in the smartest way possible, but that there is much rather a common calling and duty to conform to Christ, the head of the church. These remarks also reflect a methodological shift from "comparative ecclesiology" to a more constructive approach based on a joint,

---

24   See for the report: Vischer (ed.), *History*, 85–130.

ecumenical discernment of the faith.[25] Section 50, with as title *Consensus in Doctrine*, contains a, in comparison to earlier documents, more extensive listing of various possibilities to envisage the relationship between Scripture, tradition, and the role of the Spirit. Thus, it addresses all those aspects of Scriptural interpretation that are debated amongst the various churches; church authority remains somewhat hidden in the list, but it is implied by all appeals to sources of authority other than Scripture itself.[26] The situation regarding these topics has, it seems, become even more complicated than was indicated by earlier sections of the document so far (see also 51–52), given that at least four (partially overlapping) groups are identified: (1) Those that "accept the Holy Scriptures as either the sole authority for doctrine or the primary and decisive part of those authorities to which they would appeal" (which applies to "all" – even though it seems that this formulation refers to two different positions regarding the authority of the Scriptures); (2) Those that, in addition, "assign a special importance to the creedal documents of the early Ecumenical Councils" (held by "some"); (3) Those that reject position (2) and consider it to mean that one attempts "to found unity on…something human, namely, our understanding of the Gospel and our theological work in formulating its meaning"; and (4) Those that "judge in accordance with the Inner Light and the leadings of the Spirit" and are therefore critical of the use of creeds (position [2]) – this group does not have to be identical with (3). This diversity is left unresolved, even if the basic position under (1) can be understood as an attempt to indicate a fundamental consensus on at least one aspect of the question at hand.

Next, section 136 underlines the place of Scripture in the ecumenical process: It is of importance that all ecumenism has its basis in Scripture and not in non-theological motivations. The sections 181–182 of the 1952 document

---

25   See e.g. the overview in Peter-Ben Smit, *Old Catholic and Philippine Independent Ecclesiologies in History. The Catholic Church in Every Place* Brill's Series in Church History 52 (Leiden: Brill, 2011), 24–29.

26   Section 50: "Most accept the Ecumenical Creeds as an interpretation of the truth of the Bible or as marking a distinctive stage in the working-out of the orthodox faith. Some assign a special importance to the creedal documents of the early Ecumenical Councils. Some would say that to found unity on any creeds is to found it on something human, namely, our understanding of the Gospel and our theological work in formulating its meaning. Some judge in accordance with the Inner Light and the leadings of the Spirit and are therefore concerned to witness against the use of outward creeds when these are held to be necessary or sufficient."

are much more extensive. There, it is first of all retained that God's self-revelation took place at a particular time and place in history, which also applies to the subsequent proclamation of the faith. This means that God's truth cannot be expressed fully at any moment in time, which, however, does not mean that the message of the church is subjected to the vicissitudes of history. The reason for this is that the revelation in Jesus Christ is unique and normative and can, therefore, not be "subordinate to the relativities of history." The whole of section 181 is dedicated to this tension, i.e. between historical contextuality and universal validity. A dominant perspective found in this section is that of a given content (i.e. the content of the Gospel) that needs to be recontextualized in new historical circumstances in order to be communicated effectively. In section 182, the special role of Scripture for ecumenical dialogue is emphasized. Specifically, it is remarked, while referring to the reformers, that "our" understanding of Scripture (with its transcendent image of God, etc.) has much improved, which also applies to issues such as biblical hermeneutics and biblical ways of communication; as biblical scholarship is interconfessional, precisely this field of studies can make an important contribution to the ecumenical debate.

Two years after the Lund conference, the second assembly of the WCC took place (Evanston, 1954). The report of that meeting addresses issues of interpretation and hence of hermeneutics in three instances.[27] In the first relevant section (6), the gift of interpretation (i.e., proclamation) is mentioned as one of the gifts that God has bestowed upon the church. Also in section 12, where the document sums up what the churches have in common and what they do and can do together: Reading Scripture and interpreting it (again in terms of its proclamation) is part of this list. Section 24 acknowledges that the latter is not an easy task, as it refers to the "struggle" that is necessary in order to learn to understand the message of Scripture. For this process, faithfulness to the message of Scripture, as it emerges from joint study of Scripture, is of importance, just as the study of the liturgy and of tradition.

Seven years on, the third assembly of the WCC (New Delhi, 1961) also mentioned issues of interpretation and hermeneutics in its final report.[28] Interestingly, the first issue of interpretation that is mentioned here is related to the interpretation of the ecumenical movement itself (and not to other issues, such as the relationship between Scripture and tradition), given that many of its aspects are interpreted differently in different contexts. For example, the notion

27   For the text, see: Vischer (ed.), *History*, 131–143.
28   For the text, see: Vischer (ed.), *History*, 144–163.

of unity is not understood in the same way everywhere – the document makes a point of emphasizing that there is, for the WCC, a difference between unity and uniformity. Section 12 (see also 13) again addresses the relationship between Scripture and tradition. It does so in a way that foreshadows the influential formulations of the 1963 World Conference on Faith and Order that will be discussed next. It does so by underlining that, while the Scriptures of the Old and New Testaments bear witness to the apostolic faith, itself the "events which constitute God's call of a people to be his people," Jesus Christ himself is the heart of the Gospel as such. Also the creeds of the Church are witnesses to this faith.[29]

Subsequently, it points to the work being undertaken by "Faith and Order's Theological Commission on Tradition and Traditions." Also section 33, which discusses the topic of "doctrinal agreement," addresses the question of Scripture and tradition, drawing attention to the historical contextuality of various witnesses to the faith, and recommending that as a next step towards unity, "a fresh consideration of our various doctrinal bases, in the light of the primacy of Scripture and its safeguarding in the Church by the Holy Spirit" (33) would be called for.

4.2.3 *Hermeneutics at the World Conference on Faith and Order in Montreal (1963)*

A next milestone in the ecumenical movement as such is the fourth World Conference on Faith and Order of 1963 that took place in Montreal. This meeting would prove to be of central importance to the ecumenical discussion on hermeneutics. It produced a document entitled *Scripture, Tradition and Traditions*. In it, an attempt is made to address the question of the relationship between Scripture and tradition, a classical point of controversy since the protestant and catholic Reformations. In particular, the following, influential statements were made, which deserve quotation in full here:

> By the Tradition is meant the Gospel itself, transmitted from generation to generation in and by the Church, Christ Himself present in the life of the Church. By tradition is meant the traditionary process. The term traditions is used...to indicate both the diversity of forms of expression and also what we call confessional traditions, for instance the Lutheran tradition or

---

29   Section 12: "The Holy Scriptures of the Old and New Testament witness to the apostolic faith. This is nothing else than those events which constitute God's call of a people to be his people. The heart of the Gospel (Kerygma) is Jesus Christ himself, his life and teaching, his death, resurrection, coming (parousia) and the justification and sanctification which he brings and offers to all men. The creeds of the Church witness to this apostolic faith."

the Reformed tradition...the word appears in a further sense, when we speak of cultural traditions. (section 39)

Our starting point is that we as Christians are all living in a tradition which goes back to our Lord and has its roots in the Old Testament and are all indebted to that tradition inasmuch as we have received the revealed truth, the Gospel, through its being transmitted from one generation to another. Thus we can say that we exist as Christians by the Tradition of the Gospel (the *paradosis* of the *kerygma*) testified in Scripture, transmitted in and by the Church, through the power of the Holy Spirit. (section 45)

The traditions in Christian history are distinct from, and yet connected with, the Tradition. They are the expressions and manifestations in diverse historical terms of the one truth and reality which is Christ. This evaluation of the traditions poses serious problems... How can we distinguish between traditions embodying the true Tradition and merely human traditions? (sections 47–48)[30]

Thus, the document makes a distinction between Tradition with a capital "T" which is understood to indicate "Christ Himself present in the life of the Church," next tradition with a lower case "t" with which the process of traditioning is meant, and finally the document introduces the category of traditions (lower case "t" plural), with which the various particular ecclesial traditions are meant, in which the one Tradition has become and still is embodied. Sections 46–47 of the 1963 document state this eloquently, as they note that what is being handed on in the process of tradition is the Christian faith, understood as a living reality. In this living tradition, the life of the church (embodied in various traditions with a lower case "t"), "Tradition" ("God's revelation and self-giving in Christ") is present.[31]

Thus, the question of "Scripture or tradition" becomes a different one: Which traditions can be seen as authentic expressions of Tradition? The question

---

30   See for the text: Günther Gassmann (ed.) *Documentary History of Faith and Order 1963–1993* (Geneva: WCC Publications, 1993), 10–18, 10.

31   Sections 46–47: "What is transmitted in the process of tradition is the Christian faith, not only as a sum of tenets, but as a living reality transmitted through the operation of the Holy Spirit. We can speak of the Christian Tradition (with a capital T), whose content is God's revelation and self-giving in Christ, present in the life of the Church. But this tradition which is the work of the Holy Spirit is embodied in traditions (in the two senses of the word, both as referring to diversity in forms of expression, and in the sense of separate communions). The traditions in Christian history are distinct from, and yet connected with, the Tradition. They are the expressions and manifestations in diverse historical forms of the one truth and reality which is Christ."

concerning the relationship between these two, i.e. the one Tradition and the many traditions is as old as the church itself, as is the search for criteria (for this, see sections 48–49). In the course of the history of the church, various attempts have been made to develop criteria (e.g. the biblical canon) in order to be able to better identify Tradition in the traditions and hence to evaluate the latter. However, besides the canon of Scripture, further criteria are necessary according to this document, given that Scripture can be both liberating Spirit and killing letter. (sections 49–52) The search for hermeneutical criteria has led to different choices in different churches; the ecumenical movement is now looking for convergence in this matter. This, of course, is again closely related to the various confessional views of the importance and character of ecclesial tradition (see sections 51–55 and 56–63). It also was a question that the 1963 conference did not answer, as the 1998 document *A Treasure in Earthen Vessels* noted: "It must be recognized that Montreal left open the vital question of how churches can discern the one Tradition. Therefore there is a danger that churches identify the one Tradition exclusively with their own tradition." (18) In spite of this, however, the Montreal conference did point in some practical directions (joint study of Scripture, the Fathers of the church and the reevaluation of the own confessional traditions, see 55) and offered further theoretical considerations. Some of these pertain in particular to the Orthodox churches, that had recently joined the WCC, and, as section 57 seems to indicate, saw much more identity between the Tradition and their traditions than other churches did. Furthermore, the document calls for a more ecumenical approach to history, which can aid the rapprochement between churches (e.g. section 60). Finally, the 1963 report offers a consideration of contextuality and catholicity (64–73), which provides another field of tension for the interpretation of tradition. Still, in the context of the discussion of these topics, emphasizing both the universal character of the faith and the church and the need for contextualization, one criterion for the discernment of true tradition is formulated. This criterion to distinguish the Spirit from other spirits is that the authentic proclamation of the Gospel is never characterized by oppression, but is always a "joyful, liberating and reconciling power." (68) Furthermore, the authentic interpretation leads to a fuller experience of community, given that only in communion with all, the fullness of Christ can be known.[32] With all of

---

32   Section 70: "The traditionary process involves the dialectic, both of relating the Tradition as completely as possible to every separate cultural situation in which men live, and at the same time of demonstrating its transcendence of all that divides men from one another. From this comes the truth that the more the Tradition is expressed in the varying terms of particular cultures, the more will its universal character be fully revealed. It is only "with all the saints" that we come to know the fullness of Christ's love and glory (Eph. 3.18-19)."

this in mind and given the strongly mondialized character of society, the church faces a double challenge: The Tradition has to be passed on in new forms both in relation to modern culture and in relation to contemporary critical thought (72).

At the conference in Montreal, much emphasis was placed on the correct interpretation of Scripture and on the discernment of true and authentic tradition. However, these calls were as much to the point as they were problematic, given that each tradition had different criteria to do both. Therefore, "Montreal" was followed by a number of meetings at which this issue was studies more thoroughly. The results of this process were collected in the volume *The Bible: Its Authority and Interpretation in the Ecumenical Movement*.[33] This work is concerned with biblical hermeneutics, especially with regard – again – to the relationship between Scripture and tradition. It would go too far to discuss it extensively here, though, given that the main lines of thought that it contains have also found a place in the later document *A Treasure in Earthen Vessels*, which will be discussed at somewhat greater length subsequently.

4.2.4   *From "Montreal" to a Treasure in Earthen Vessels* (1998)

As the Faith and Order Paper 182, *A Treasure in Earthen Vessels*, itself outlines, hermeneutical discussion continued with some intensity following the Montreal conference. A good summary of this can be found in *A Treasure in Earthen Vessels*:

> After Montreal, Faith and Order undertook important studies on the hermeneutical significance of the Council of the Early Church Several reports on the Authority of the Bible were assembled as a contribution to the hermeneutical discussions of that period. The Odessa consultation (1977) on "How does the Church teach authoritatively today?" addressed aspects of the hermeneutical problem, especially the question of continuity and change in the doctrinal tradition of the Church. Also, after Accra (1974), Faith and Order began to collect newer expressions of faith and hope from around the world. These were published in a series, and also summarized at Bangalore (1978) in "A Common Account of Hope". This work, which found continuation in the Faith and Order study on the Apostolic Faith, produced an awareness of the contextual aspects of confessions of faith, both in the sense of the original contexts in which they were made and of the effect on their use produced by the changing contexts of Christian discipleship. (section 1)

---

33   Ellen Flesseman-Van Leer, *The Bible: Its Authority and Interpretation in the Ecumenical Movement* (Geneva: WCC Publications, 1980).

Thus, *A Treasure in Earthen Vessels* is clearly aware of the tradition of ecumenical, not least hermeneutical, reflection of which it is part. It also identifies, however, the specific development within the ecumenical movement that gave rise to a further study of hermeneutics: The process of reception of Faith and Order's 1982 report on *Baptism, Eucharist, and Ministry*, i.e. the BEM-report,[34] a report that was itself also keenly aware of the hermeneutical issues involved, not only in the common discernment of authentic traditions, but also of the interrelationship between the life of the church in the broader sense of the word and discernment.[35] However, the reception of the document itself also gave reason for further hermeneutical considerations, as *A Treasure in Earthen Vessels* underlines.[36]

A further historical contextualization of the document is offered in section 1 of the document, where under the heading "Past exploration of the theme" various developments that occurred after Montreal 1963 are highlighted, a description of which was quoted at the beginning of this section. In particular, this concerns the document that was produced by the fifth World Conference on Faith and Order of 1993 in Santiago di Compostella, where the various responses to BEM and the dynamics of this report's reception were discussed. This conference subsequently identified the three main issues for future work: Overcoming and reconciling criteriological differences pertaining to the faithful interpretation of the Gospel; communicating the Gospel across various

---

34   Commission on Faith and Order, *Baptism, Eucharist and Ministry 1982–1990: Report on the Process and the Responses* Faith and Order Paper 149 (Geneva: WCC Publications, 1990).

35   See section 34 of the report: "Apostolic tradition in the Church means continuity in the permanent characteristics of the Church of the apostles: witness to the apostolic faith, proclamation and fresh interpretation of the Gospel, celebration of baptism and the eucharist, the transmission of ministerial responsibilities, communion in prayer, love, joy and suffering, service to the sick and the needy, unity among the local Churches and sharing the gifts which the Lord has given to each."

36   As *A Treasure in Earthen Vessels* puts it itself: "the churches' response to the Baptism, Eucharist and Ministry text made it especially clear that Faith and Order needed to reflect on what is involved when authors, readers and interpreters of ecumenical documents come from many different contexts and confessions." (Preface) See also from section 11: "In particular, the texts *Baptism, Eucharist and Ministry; Confessing the One Faith* and *Church and World* have raised hermeneutical questions for the life of the churches. The process of officially responding to BEM has revealed many unexamined hermeneutical assumptions underlying not only the churches' responses but also the very question concerning the extent to which they can recognize in the BEM-text the faith of the Church through the ages. The fresh urgency to reflect together about hermeneutics is further heightened as new challenges of Christian living in today's world threaten to create new schisms within as well as among churches."

(socio-cultural) contexts; and working towards mutual accountability, discernment, teaching, and credibility in common witness vis-à-vis the world.[37] As *A Treasure in Earthen Vessels* goes on to note, it will address these issues in the following way:

· In the first section (B. Common Understanding of the One Tradition), an explicitly hermeneutical framework will be applied to the important themes raised by the Montreal study "Scripture, Tradition and traditions." This reflection may take us beyond Montreal, as it considers the interpretation of Scripture and tradition in a more hermeneutically conscious way, especially with greater sensitivity to the conditions involved in interpretation.
· In the second section (C. One Gospel in Many Contexts), the text explores the hermeneutical and theological significance of the fact that the ecumenical movement includes the participation of communities from many differing cultures and contexts, and offers reflections which can lead to a more successful inter-contextual dialogue.
· The third section (D. The Church as a Hermeneutical Community) explores three dimensions of the process of interpretation: The activity of discernment, the exercise of authority and the task of reception. (section 13)

In the second section of the document, the tension of the hermeneutical problem is illustrated by means of 2 Cor. 4:7, where Paul makes a point regarding a treasure in earthen vessels: God's revelation has been delivered to fragile human interpretation in all its diversity and with varying results.[38] This issue is

---

37   Section 12: "* to overcome and to reconcile the criteriological differences with regard to a faithful interpretation of the one Gospel, recognizing the multiform richness and diversity of the Canon of the Scriptures, as it is read, explicated and applied in the life of the churches, but at the same time strengthening the awareness of the one Tradition within the many traditions; * to express and communicate the one Gospel in and across various, sometimes even conflicting contexts, cultures and locations; * to work toward mutual accountability, discernment and authoritative teaching and towards credibility in common witness before the world, and finally towards the eschatological fullness of the truth in the power of the Holy Spirit."

38   The first four sections of the document as a whole make this same point, using the same metaphor, at greater length as well: "1. The unsearchable mystery of God's love was made manifest,through the power of the Holy Spirit, in the covenant with Israel and fully revealed in the life, death and resurrection of Jesus Christ. This mystery has been proclaimed in the Scriptures of the Old and New Testaments. Christian faith is the saving gift from God, which enables believers to receive the good news of God's love for all human beings and to become children of God and members of Christ's body the Church. Faith in

of much importance for the wcc, because there is still much diversity regarding the interpretation of the faith, which is one of the reasons why the *koinonia* between the churches is still incomplete, even though "unity in confessing the faith is among the essential ways in which the *koinonia* of the Church is made visible" (3). Section 4 underlines that the current time is one of many and quick changes, to which a robust response is needed.

The topic of the paper is formulated clearly when "the task of ecumenical hermeneutics" is addressed.[39] In the first place, hermeneutics is described here as "[B]oth the art of interpretation and application of texts, symbols and practices in the present and from the past, and the theory about the methods of such interpretation and application."[40] Thus, hermeneutics is not only concerned with the interpretation of texts, but also of "symbols and practices." Theological hermeneutics, as the document states,[41] is concerned in particular

---

Christ gives life to the communion (*koinonia*) of the Church. This faith has been handed on and received since apostolic times, from one generation to the next and from culture to culture. 2. This transmission takes place within the ambiguities of human history and the challenges of daily Christian life. So Paul can speak of us as having "this treasure in earthen vessels" (2 Cor 4:7). Thus faith also relies upon human forms of expression and interpretation, dialogue and communication, all of which are fragile and all too often fragmented embodiments, none of which is completely adequate, of the mystery which has been revealed. These manifold human forms of expression include not only texts but also symbols and rites, stories and practices. Only at the end of time will the Church's contemplation of God's revealed mystery go beyond a partial knowledge and arrive at that "knowing even as we are known" of which Paul writes in 1 Cor 13: 9–12. 3. Unity in confessing the faith is among the essential ways in which the *koinonia* of the Church is made visible. The ecumenical movement has helped divided Christian communities to realize that even now they are united in a "growing, real though still imperfect *koinonia*" (Santiago de Compostela, 1993). This realization, however, cannot obscure the fact that significant differences in interpreting the faith still remain. In order to fulfil their vocation to grow in communion, the churches need to reflect together about the various ways in which the faith is expressed and interpreted. 4. The unprecedented changes occurring in our times because of the developments in mass media and in the means of communication make Christians more acutely aware of the religious, cultural, political and economic diversities which characterize the human family. The community of believers must formulate its faith anew within such contexts. In this sense, the mission to proclaim the Gospel in terms meaningful to people of today is essentially a hermeneutical task. All churches share the challenge of proclaiming God's Word in credible ways within the diversity of contemporary cultures and by means of the oral and visual instruments of communication, be they traditional or those made available by contemporary technology."

39   *Vessels*, sections 5–10.
40   *Vessels*, section 5.
41   *Vessels*, section 5.

with the theory and practice of interpretation of texts, symbols, and practices, in the context of a tradition and community of faith. Ecumenical hermeneutics, as part of theological hermeneutics, then, is understood as serving the particular task of concentrating on the way in which texts, symbols, and practices are interpreted and (eventually) received in the context of church dialogue(s).[42] As a hermeneutics that seeks to serve the unity of the church, ecumenical hermeneutics should should lead to three things:[43] (1) More coherence in the interpretation of the faith; (2) a mutually recognizable and acceptable usage of the sources of the Christian faith; and (3) roads towards confessing and worshipping together. This kind of hermeneutics, is, therefore, interested in unity and coherence, therefore it is called a "hermeneutics of coherence."[44] Because this emphasis on coherence might seem to obscure the (self-)critical task of hermeneutics, the authors of *A Treasure in Earthen Vessels* emphasize the need for a "hermeneutics of suspicion": "In a constantly ongoing process, a responsible ecumenical hermeneutics will try to serve the truth, alerted by suspicion but always aiming at coherence."[45] Another aspect of ecumenical hermeneutics is that it is always related to the community of the church (and to the community of churches) and that any ecumenical hermeneutics is always a hermeneutical approach that is community-based. Another aspect of ecumenical hermeneutics that is mentioned is that of confidence, specifically confidence in the sincerity of the one with whom a dialogue is conducted and also in the hermeneutical process itself.[46] Having outlined this, and also given an overview of previous explorations of the topic (sections 11–20, here discussed somewhat more extensively on the preceding pages), *A Treasure in Earthen Vessels* turns to a number of specific hermeneutical topics.

First, the interpretation of Scripture itself is addressed.[47] A topic that is considered immediately is that of the academic study of Scripture, which has been considered as accepted in the context of Faith and Order since a consultation on the subject in 1967, especially because it has contributed in a significant way to the ecumenical understanding of Scripture. The results of ancient, historical-critical (21) and more post-modern (22) research have demonstrated

---

42   *Vessels*, section 5: "[It] serves the specific task of focusing on how texts, symbols and practices in the various churches may be interpreted, communicated and mutually received as the churches engage in dialogue. In this sense it is a hermeneutics for the unity of the Church."

43   *Vessels*, section 5.

44   *Vessels*, section 6.

45   *Vessels*, section 6.

46   *Vessels*, section 8.

47   *Vessels*, sections 21–27.

the contextuality of biblical stories and the importance and influence of interpretations through the centuries. For the current consideration of canonical and ecumenical hermeneutics this is of some importance, given that the way in which *A Treasure in Earthen Vessels* speaks about the emergence of biblical texts seems to echo some concerns of canonical critics, especially to the extent that they emphasize a canonical process and the claims to authority that are inherent to the texts. Furthermore, the way in which the document discusses other approaches sheds light on the interface between text and (ecclesial) context, which is also dear to canonical critics. Sections 21 and 22, therefore, deserve quotation in full:

> 21. The primary authority of Scripture within hermeneutical work is not weakened by our understanding of the way in which the text has been handed down within the Church through the process of transmission. The texts of Scripture thus received offer their revelatory character after a handing on through oral transmission. The written texts subsequently have been interpreted by means of diverse exegetical and scholarly methods. Wrestling with the principles and practice of interpretation, Faith and Order affirmed (Bristol, 1967/68) that the tools of modern exegetical scholarship are important if the biblical message is to speak with power and meaning today. These tools have contributed in vital ways to the present ecumenical convergence and growth in koinonia. The exegetical exploration of the process of tradition within the Bible itself, together with the recognition of multiple interpretations of God's saving actions in history within the unity of the early apostolic church, points to ways the Word of God is expressed in human language and by human witness. This is to say, the Word of God is expressed in language and by witnesses shaped amid diverse situations of human life, which are historically, culturally and socially conceived. This is also to say: "The very nature of biblical texts means that interpreting them will require continued use of the historical-critical method... [since] the Bible does not present itself as a direct revelation of timeless truths, but as the written testimony to a series of interventions in which God reveals himself in human history." Though some churches and individual Christians reject historical-critical interpretation, common study of the Scriptures of the Old and New Testaments now has a long history of achieved agreement. Ecumenical hermeneutics can use the historical-critical method to establish, e.g., the background of the texts, the intentions of the authors, and the inter-relationship of the different books.

22. Interpretation should not, however, depend only on this method, now shared by those of different traditions and theologies. Many other approaches to the text, both of long standing and of modern development, help in the recognition of the meaning of Scripture for the churches today and for the many different situations of the world Church. In particular the historical-critical method needs to be combined with a reading in critical interaction with experience, the experience both of individuals and of communities. Other methods are those inherent in traditional biblical interpretation including patristic, liturgical, homiletic, dogmatic and allegorical approaches to the text. Contemporary methods include those that focus on the original social setting of the texts (e.g. sociological methods); those that focus on the literary form of texts and the internal relationships within a text and between texts (e.g. semiotic and canonical methods); and those that focus on the potential of the text for readings generated by the encounter of the text with human reality (e.g. reader-response method). All these methods can also be used to deal with extra-biblical sources. Some methods help to open up neglected dimensions of the past from the perspective of marginalized groups. Examples of the latter are feminist or liberationist analyses of systems of power and patronage.

In its next section (23), the document stresses the actual practice of a community in which texts have their place and from which their interpretation emerges; this elaborates on aspects of section 22, while underlining that interpretation also takes place without the (conscious) application of a scholarly method. That Scripture is, in the end, the *norma normans* again is mentioned in section 24. The way in which this is done, however, is of significance as it refers to canonical texts in ways that seem to be compatible with, for example, Ricoeur's view of them, as it is stated that canonical texts transcend the limitations of the context in which they were uttered originally and become a universal message.[48] Thus, the tension that is typical for canonical texts and that

---

48   Section 4: "Because the biblical texts originated in concrete historical situations, they witness to the salvific presence of the Triune God in those particular circumstances. However, the texts also transcend this particularity and become part of the world of the readers in each generation, of the witnessing community through the ages into the present. Although embedded in the life and times in which it was given written form, Scripture, as inspired testimony, provides a measure for the truth and meaning of human stories today. In this sense, hermeneutical priority belongs to the Word of God, which has critical authority over all traditions."

plays a role of much importance in canonical exegesis, i.e. the fact that canonical texts, in the way in which they are used and received, function beyond their original contexts, is also identified as part of ecumenical hermeneutics. Next, in section 25, *A Treasure in Earthen Vessels* discusses the eschatological dimension of the ecclesial interpretation of Scripture: "Just as Scripture constantly looks forward in hope to God's future, the interpreting activity of the Church is also an anticipatory projection of the reality of the reign of God, which is both already present and yet to come" (section 25). For this reason, all aspects of the Church's life as a hermeneutical community that is eschatologically oriented, are also part of this eschatologically oriented process of interpretation, which includes the interpretation of Scripture through and in "the struggle for peace, justice, and the integrity of creation, the renewed sense of mission in witness and service, [and] the liturgy in which the Church proclaims and celebrates the promise of God's reign and its coming in the praxis of the faith" (section 25). Subsequently, the document attempts to restate the interrelationship between Scripture and tradition in various churches and how this relationship should be conceptualized in order to further an ecumenical approach to Scripture. It argues in particular that the study of Scripture as the normative texts of the church is essential and that, if it is done properly, that is to say: In a way that respects the texts' authority, that is dialogical in character, and that issues into communion, it leads to a discovery and shared experience of the one Tradition and communion within it.[49]

---

49   Section 27: "Common study of Scripture has achieved ecumenical advance. However, it has not by itself led to the visible unity of the Church. Interpreters from different churches and traditions have not been able to reach sufficient agreement for that. All Christians agree that Scripture holds a unique place in the shaping of Christian faith and practice. Most agree that the expression of apostolic faith is not confined to the formulation of that faith expressed in Scripture but that norms of faith have also been expressed in the life of the churches throughout the ages. The Church receives the texts of Scripture as part of the *paradosis* of the Gospel. The texts are to be respected as coming from outside to the interpreter to be engaged dialogically. In the process of interpretation, which involves the particular experiences of the reader, Scripture is the primary norm and criterion. Particular traditions need to be referred continuously to this norm by which they find their authenticity and validity. This response to Scripture takes shape communally and ecclesially in worship, in the sacramental life where hearing, touch and sight come together, in the *anamnesis* of the lives of biblical witnesses and in the lives of those who live the biblical message, inspired by the Holy Spirit. Scripture itself refers to the one Tradition, lived under the guidance of the Holy Spirit. The one Tradition, therefore, is the setting for the interpretation of Scripture."

Having addressed the interpretation of Scripture, the interpretation of the interpreters is addressed.[50] This primarily concerns a certain awareness of contextuality, both because "amid this hermeneutical task, Christians are to be conscious that interpretations come out of special historical circumstances and that new issues may come out of various contexts" (28), and because the document addresses the following four items: (1) Paying attention to the point of view ("location") from which a text is interpreted; (2) reflecting on the choice of a particular text for interpretation; (3) considering the influence of structures of power on the interpretative process; and (4) paying attention to presuppositions and prejudices that influence the process of interpretation. When considering this, the document also clarifies how the hermeneutics of suspicion can be made useful for the development of a hermeneutics of coherence that aims at discovering the complementarity and compatibility of various differing traditions.[51] This happens through an awareness that a hermeneutics of suspicion "does not mean the adoption of an attitude of mistrust but the application to oneself and one's dialogue partners of an approach which perceives how self-interest, power, national or ethnic or class or gender perspectives can affect the reading of texts and the understanding of symbols and practices" (28). Thus, mutual understanding can be furthered and a hermeneutics of coherence and unity can begin to function. As the document goes on to emphasize, presuppositions for this whole process of the development of a hermeneutics of unity are, in the first place, the good will of the participants, and in the second place, the necessity and possibility of *metanoia* that makes *koinonia* a real possibility. Finally, it is also of importance to learn to understand each other's method of interpretation (including the way in which authority functions and is structured in different churches) and to learn to value it (31).

Having discussed the interpretation of Scripture, the focus of *A Treasure in Earthen Vessels* turns to the issue of the Tradition and the traditions.[52] This part of the document begins with a new definition of Tradition and the traditions: "The 'one Tradition' signifies the redeeming presence of the resurrected Christ from generation to generation abiding in the community of faith, while the 'many traditions' are particular modes and manifestations of that presence."[53] Tradition itself, is, therefore, also signifying, given that God also transcends God's own revelation. Ecumenical dialogue and study has helped churches to

---

50   *Vessels*, sections 28–31.

51   *Vessels*, sections 28–29.

52   *Vessels*, sections 32–37.

53   *Vessels*, section 32.

grow closer together and to discern together the Tradition. Much has happened in this field already, as it is evidenced by many ecumenical theological projects, and therefore, the churches are now challenged to move from "mutual understanding" to "mutual recognition" and to the establishment of visible unity (34). Towards the end of this section, two further relevant items are mentioned: The notion that hermeneutics needs to be able to engage the full range of interpretative practices, including rituals and the like, and on the other hand the receptive character of interpretation (i.e. the church receives revelation) and its eschatological orientation.[54]

The next part of *A Treasure in Earthen Vessels* is entitled "One Gospel in Many Contexts" and focuses on the issue of hermeneutics and contextuality in more detail. It first outlines how particular texts can exercise a life-giving influence in particular contexts (38; with examples). Next, the condition of mutual openness and a willingness for *metanoia* is formulated for a constructive conversation across contextual differences (39), while it is stressed how, in the past, cross-cultural encounters have also gone wrong, e.g. through the close association of imperial power and mission, and how complex such encounters are in general (40–42). In this context, a criterion for the authentic interpretation of the Gospel is also formulated: "Wherever the Gospel is authentically engaged by diverse cultures, its interpretation and proclamation will be life-giving for men and women, young and old, sick and healthy, rich and poor, uneducated and educated."[55] Having stated this, the document continues by discussing the relationship between catholicity and contextuality.[56] The point of departure is the fundamental unity of all Christians through their relationship with God through Jesus Christ. In this way, they constitute the one universal (catholic) church. Both this unity and the diversity of the various Christian communities are gifts of the Spirit. Catholicity and contextuality are good concepts to capture these two aspects: Contextuality, because it indicates that the faith only reaches people when if it permeates their context like salt and leaven and thus enlivens it, and catholicity, because this concept indicates that the faith is oriented towards community and fullness. An expression of this all is the celebration of the Eucharist that expresses both the unity of the local community and the connectedness of that community with the universal church.[57] The interpretation of the Gospel has to have its place in this setting, in which catholicity and contextuality provide the poles of a hermeneutical

---

54   *Vessels*, sections 35–37.

55   *Vessels*, section 40.

56   *Vessels*, sections 43–48.

57   *Vessels*, section 46.

ellipse, so to speak.[58] This is possible, as long it happens while recognizing that no single interpretation is absolute, but always contextually determined. In this way, an appreciation for different interpretations in different contexts can also emerge.

In the next part of the document, which is entitled "[T]he Church as a Hermeneutical Community," what has been said so far is elaborated further. This happens, in the first place, from the perspective of "Ecclesial discernment and the truth of the Gospel."[59] The document adopts this perspective, because hermeneutics is related to the dynamics that is given with the interrelationship between contextuality and catholicity, and because the hermeneutical task belongs to the apostolic duty of the church. Because it is about the church, interpretation is not the task of specialists, but of the entire people of God.[60] This also means that the faithful need to be taught to interpret and to be aware of influences that might prevent a life-giving interpretation (sections 51–52). In this context, and in order to achieve a fruitful dialogue among the churches, especially concerning the interpretation of texts and practices, the document formulates three conditions for such dialogue: (1) For a genuine dialogue, dialogue partners need to regard each other as equal partners; (2) they need to speak to each other rooted in and from the perspective of their respective (traditional) interpretations of the faith; and (3) they need to engage in a dialogue with a willingness to consider (and reconsider) their own interpretations from the point of view of their dialogue partners.[61]

Having summed up these conditions, the document continues to discuss the topic "[A]uthority, apostolicity and mutual accountability."[62] The starting point of this discussion is that although various communities of faith have developed different structures of ministry and authority, there still is agreement among them "that ministerial structures must serve the purpose of the

---

58   *Vessels*, sections, 47–48.

59   *Vessels*, sections 49–53.

60   *Vessels*, section 49.

61   *Vessels*, section 53:

"- For dialogue to be genuine, these representatives need to see each other as equal partners.

- They must, on the one hand, speak to each other from the perspective of their traditional interpretations of the apostolic faith as articulated in their confessional documents, their liturgies and their experience.

- But they must do so with a willingness to view their own interpretations from the vantage point of those with whom they are in dialogue. This involves being attentive to the insights provided by the dialogue partner, taking care to take into account one's own unwitting prejudices and limited perspectives." (section 53)

62   *Vessels*, sections, 54–62.

Church, to lead all into unity with God by the power of the Holy Spirit."[63] Thus, the document stresses that ministries are for the service of the community and do not exist on their own. Naturally, this also applies to those exercising the ministry of *epikope* as they in particular are called to lead the church in discerning what the Spirit is saying and to what it calls the church (55–56). The unity of the church and its collegial structure is emphasized and expressed when multiple persons that exercise a ministry of *episkope* come together, consult with one another and make joint decisions and statements (57).[64] Such a collegial *modus operandi* of the churches and their ministers is already a reality in many ways and is also facilitated by the WCC itself; as a form, it has its origins in the early church (59–61).[65]

Finally, before reaching its conclusion, *A Treasure in Earthen Vessels* addresses "reception as a hermeneutical process" (63–66). "Reception" means both that churches need to listen to one another receptively and to receive each other's points of view charitably, and that there is a process of reception of ecumenical documents and statements themselves, about which it is noted that they are too often only read by a small group of specialists and enthusiasts. This is a problem and the ecumenical movement should take care not only to produce documents, but also to ensure their broader reception within the churches.[66]

The conclusion of the document also offers a summary of the document itself, therefore, it is appropriate to quote it in full:

> 67. Under the power of the Holy Spirit the Church is intended to be God's special instrument for bringing about the encounter between the Word of Life and human beings. When this Word is received, it nourishes as the living bread, which "gives life to the world," for which Jesus' listeners asked: "Lord, give us this bread always" (Jn 6:33–34).
>
> 68. In and through diverse historical and contemporary forms of inculturation and contextualization the bread of life, which is to be broken and distributed, remains one bread. Although the Word enters history, this historicity does not limit it to any single historical form or formulation. Yet this insight leads neither to limitless diversity nor to ecumenical complacency. Rather, as a hermeneutical community, the Church is called to grow into full *koinonia* by Spirit-guided discernment of the living Tradition. The Church should not be imprisoned by holding on to

---

63   *Vessels*, section 54.
64   *Vessels*, section 57.
65   *Vessels*, sections 59–61.
66   *Vessels*, section 66.

inadequate answers form the past, nor should it silence the Word of God by endlessly putting off a clear recognition of the way this Word continues to impart meaning and orientation for human life. Under the guidance of the Holy Spirit, in faithfulness to the living Tradition, and though genuine ecumenical forms of conciliar deliberation and reception, the Church is called to "interpret the signs of the times" (Mt 16:3) by looking to the One who is both in and beyond time, to the One "who is the same, yesterday, today and forever" (Heb 13:8).[67]

4.2.5 *Hermeneutics in the Church. Towards a Common Vision* (2013)

A final major document stemming from the ecumenical movement that needs to be considered here is the 2013 position paper of the WCC's Commission on Faith and Order that is often regarded as the (intended) successor to the BEM-report. Given this situation, it is worthwhile considering what this document has to say on the subject of hermeneutics. The following observations can be made.

First, in section 11, the document retains that all Christians consider Scripture to be normative and to constitute an indispensable source for growth in unity, in spite of the New Testament's ecclesiological diversity, which has been received through various interpretative traditions in the course of the history of the church. Such interpretation can be regarded as being led by the Spirit, which makes it a "living tradition" in which the churches participate.[68] The formulations used in this section seek to tie together the authority of both the Scriptures and subsequent tradition by having the same Spirit guide the process of the production of Scripture and of its faithful interpretation. This faithful

---

67   See also Smit, "Meaning."

68   *Church*, section 11: "All Christians share the conviction that Scripture is normative, therefore the biblical witness provides an irreplaceable source for acquiring greater agreement about the Church. Although the New Testament provides no systematic ecclesiology, it does offer accounts of the faith of the early communities, of their worship and practice of discipleship, of various roles of service and leadership, as well as images and metaphors used to express the identity of the Church. Subsequent interpretation within the Church, seeking always to be faithful to biblical teaching, has produced an additional wealth of ecclesiological insights over the course of history. The same Holy Spirit who guided the earliest communities in producing the inspired biblical text continues, from generation to generation, to guide later followers of Jesus as they strive to be faithful to the Gospel. This is what is understood by the "living Tradition" of the Church. The great importance of Tradition has been acknowledged by most communities, but they vary in assessing how its authority relates to that of Scripture."

interpretation is called "living Tradition" and it can be noticed that its importance is acknowledged by most communities, even though its relation to
Scripture is conceptualized in a variety of ways. A somewhat similar statement
is found later on in the document, when it discusses the "essential elements of
communion," which are: "Faith, sacraments, ministry," noting that, while all are
agreed regarding the importance of faith, there is an important tension between
the (necessary) contextual interpretation of the faith and the equally necessary continuity of the faith in all times and places with the original apostolic
faith.[69] Thus, again the tension between faithfulness to the original faith and
its reinterpretation in the context of "changing times and places" is noted. Also,
A Treasure in Earthen Vessels is acknowledged, albeit that it is made clear that
much work still remains at the same time.[70] In line with the latter sentiment,
the issue of hermeneutics and interpretation returns in this document when
the question of authority in the church is addressed. There, the current ecumenical situation is described as follows:

> Significant steps towards convergence on authority and its exercise have
> been recorded in various bilateral dialogues. Differences continue to
> exist between churches, however, as to the relative weight to be accorded

---

69   *Church*, section 38: "Regarding the first of these elements, there is widespread agreement
      that the Church is called to proclaim, in each generation, the faith 'once for all entrusted
      to the saints' (Jude v. 3) and to remain steadfast in the teaching first handed on by the
      apostles. Faith is evoked by the Word of God, inspired by the grace of the Holy Spirit,
      attested in Scripture and transmitted through the living tradition of the Church. It is con-
      fessed in worship, life, service and mission. While it must be interpreted in the context of
      changing times and places, these interpretations must remain in continuity with the
      original witness and with its faithful explication throughout the ages. Faith has to be lived
      out in active response to the challenges of every age and place. It speaks to personal and
      social situations, including situations of injustice, of the violation of human dignity
      and of the degradation of creation."

70   *Church*, section 39: "In 1998, *A Treasure in Earthen Vessels* explored the ongoing interpreta-
      tion of Scripture and Tradition in handing on the faith, noting: 'The Holy Spirit inspires
      and leads the churches each to rethink and reinterpret their tradition in conversation
      with each other, always aiming to embody the one Tradition in the unity of God's Church.'
      While the churches generally agree as to the importance of Tradition in the generation
      and subsequent interpretation of scripture, more recent dialogue has tried to understand
      how the Christian community engages in such interpretation. Many bilateral dialogues
      have acknowledged that ecclesial interpretation of the contemporary meaning of the
      Word of God involves the faith experience of the whole people, the insights of theolo-
      gians, and the discernment of the ordained ministry. The challenge today is for churches
      to agree on how these factors work together."

to the different sources of authority, as to how far and in what ways the Church has the means to arrive at a normative expression of its faith, and as to the role of ordained ministers in providing an authoritative interpretation of revelation. Yet all churches share the urgent concern that the Gospel be preached, interpreted and lived out in the world humbly, but with compelling authority. May not the seeking of ecumenical convergence on the way in which authority is recognized and exercised play a creative role in this missionary endeavour of the churches?[71]

The kind of ministry that is the most directly addressed when it comes to the interface interpretation – authority, is that of *episkope*, given that the document states that a main task of this ministry is the safeguarding and faithfully handing on of the faith.[72]

Having thus outlined the discussion on ecumenical hermeneutics in, especially, the Faith and Order movement and commission, noting the continuous occurrence of the question of the relationship between Scripture, ecclesial traditions, ecclesial authorities, context, hermeneutical criteria and method, and ecclesial unity, it is now possible to turn to a consideration of this in light of what has been said previously about the canonical approaches considered in this study.

4.3   Ecumenical and Canonical Hermeneutics: Compatibilities and Challenges

When considering this sketch of the discussion about hermeneutics in the context of the ecumenical movement, especially as it is embodied by "Faith and Order,"[73] a number of observations may be made in relation to the canonical approach(es) to exegesis as they have been discussed previously. First, a number of compatibilities will be noted, affirming what was said before about

---

71   Introductory text, preceding section 52 of *Church*.

72   *Church*, section 52: "In addition to preaching the Word and celebrating the Sacraments, a principal purpose of this ministry is faithfully to safeguard and hand on revealed truth, to hold the local congregations in communion, to give mutual support and to lead in witnessing to the Gospel."

73   In this context, it may also be noted that the view of canonical approaches to Scripture that is mentioned in *A Treasure in Earthen Vessels* 22 is somewhat limited, as there canonical approaches are mentioned in the same breath as approaches focusing on intertextuality, which, it seems, does not do full justice to the interrelationship between Scripture and community that is so strongly emphasized by canonical approaches to Scripture.

the ecumenical direction into which canonical approaches to Scripture point (see 3.1.4.). Next, a number of aspects of ecumenical hermeneutics will be identified that might challenge canonical approaches to Scripture, in order to advance underdeveloped aspects of this approach – in all its diversity – and indeed to develop it into an approach to exegesis that would be both ecumenically oriented and in line with insights achieved in the ecumenical discussion on hermeneutics. Some remarks will also be made about the way in which canonical criticism could enrich ecumenical hermeneutics.

First, the discussion about hermeneutics in relation to Scripture, ecclesial tradition, and the process of ecumenical dialogue can well be seen to have a counterpart in the exegetical discourse that canonical approaches are part of, i.e. they also deal with the interpretation of Scripture, in relation to ecclesial teaching, and in relation to diverging interpretations and approaches. The kind of hermeneutical ideas that are outlined in the ecumenical movement are particularly close to those of canonical critics such as Childs, Stuhlmacher, and Ratzinger, by whom the place of Scripture in the life of the church is largely taken for granted. The questions that ecumenical hermeneutics raises, then, have not so much to do with the issue of whether the church is the hermeneutical community that undertakes the interpretation of Scripture. This is not questioned (as it would be by many of those that reject canonical approaches to Scripture) at all.[74] Rather, just like most canonical approaches to Scripture, an ecumenical approach to Scriptures recognizes the inherent communal and tradition-bound character of all interpretation and values it, drawing attention to the necessary contextuality of all interpretation. Instead, the questions that are raised by ecumenical hermeneutics have to do with the role of ecclesial traditions in relation to Scripture, with the relation of both Scripture and ecclesial traditions to Tradition as understood by the 1963 Montreal conference, with the role of structures of authority, and with the contextuality of interpretations beyond matters of ecclesial tradition and questions of authority.[75] As will have become clear above, the question of structures of authority hardly receives any attention among canonical critics, nor does the question of contextuality as such, while the use of ecclesial traditions and the reflection on their role differs strongly from author to author. Ratzinger, for example, reflects explicitly on the

---

74   In fact, canonical approaches to Scripture, typically undertaken by biblical scholars (Ratzinger is an exception) may well be seen as providing the exegetical and historical underpinning for something that is, generally speaking, simply assumed by those involved in ecumenical hermeneutics (and who are, often, systematic theologians rather than biblical scholars).

75   On the discussion about tradition in the ecumenical movement, see also Smit, *Tradition*.

role of tradition and makes heavy use of it, certainly when compared to a critic like Childs, who does draw on ecclesial traditions strongly (e.g. on the work of Irenaeus), but does so in a rather opaque way. The same applies to the "Amsterdam School" (e.g. in relation to Calvin and Barth), while Sanders and Stuhlmacher occupy positions in between of these two extremes. It seems that more awareness both of the significance of structures of authority and power, and of concrete contextuality and its heuristic significance (see also *A Treasure in Earthen Vessels* 22) might be beneficial to canonical approaches to Scripture.

Second, the notion of "traditions" (with a lower case "t") as it was introduced by the 1963 World Conference on Faith and Order (Montreal)[76] comes close to the notion of the "rule of faith" as it figures (explicitly or implicitly) in canonical approaches to Scripture. that is to say: The "traditions" are seen as the lenses through which Tradition is interpreted, just as a rule of faith guides the interpretation of Scripture. It is of significance that both canonical approaches to Scripture and ecumenical hermeneutics underline the significance of this aspect of interpretation. In this context, it may also be remarked that the discussion surrounding the particular lens through which Scripture is read, and which traditions of interpretation guide the reading of Scripture as a whole, has surfaced in the Faith and Order discussion on the subject. This is the criterion of life-givingness, i.e. an interpretation is authentic when it makes life possible.[77] At least explicitly, this criterion does not occur among the canonical critics studied here, although it does come close to the Amsterdam School's understanding of the Torah as a Torah of liberation and to Sanders' view of the content of the canonical hermeneutics that he has identified.

Third, the eschatological dimension of biblical interpretation, as it is, e.g., acknowledged explicitly by Sanders (and at least implied by Ratzinger and some strands of the "Amsterdam School") is also prominent in later stages of the ecumenical discussion about hermeneutics. *A Treasure in Earthen Vessels* is a good example of this, as becomes clear at the very start of the document, where it is noted that all human interpretations of the faith will remain partial until their fulfillment in the eschaton.[78]

---

76   This also applies to the ecumenical discussion about hermeneutics preceding the Fourth World Conference on Faith and Order of 1963 given that the various ways of looking at Scripture and tradition that were thematized there, also addressed different ecclesial traditions' ways of approaching the *depositum fidei*, so to speak, and thus their rules of faith.

77   See for a more extensive argument, Smit, "Meaning."

78   *Vessels*, section: "[F]aith also relies upon human forms of expression and interpretation, dialogue and communication, all of which are fragile and all too often fragmented embodiments, none of which is completely adequate, of the mystery which has been revealed. These manifold human forms of expression include not only texts but also symbols and

Fourth, a further point of convergence between canonical approaches to exegesis and ecumenical hermeneutics can be found in the emphasis on coherence that both have in common. While this may be clear from the consideration of the five different canonical approaches above, *A Treasure in Earthen Vessels* also notes that an ecumenical hermeneutics "aims at greater coherence in the interpretation of the faith" (6).

Fifth, ecumenical hermeneutics aims at a particular praxis resulting from the joint interpretation of the faith, i.e. realized *koinonia* among the churches and a way of life that makes life possible and that struggles against all life-denying forces. Agreement can be noted with most of the canonical critics considered here, who also identify a praxis as the destination of all interpretation.[79]

Having identified these points of convergence, now a number of points may be noted that constitute challenges posed by ecumenical hermeneutics to canonical approaches to Scripture. It seems, namely, that while canonical approaches to Scripture provide the historical and exegetical underpinning for things that are simply assumed by ecumenical hermeneutics, specifically the intricate relationship between the scriptural texts and community and its hermeneutical significance, ecumenical hermeneutics draws attention to a number of aspects of this relationship that are not often underlined in canonical approaches to Scripture.

First, an important aspect of ecumenical hermeneutics is that it seeks to be a critical hermeneutics as well, i.e. apart from a search for coherence and unity, suspicion (in the sense of a hermeneutics of suspicion) also has its place. In particular, this is part of the "interpretation of the interpreters," in the context of which also "the application to oneself and one's dialogue partners of an approach which perceives how self-interest, power, national or ethnic or class or gender perspectives can affect the reading of texts and the understanding of symbols and practices" (*A Treasure in Earthen Vessels* 28, see also 6) takes place. While suspicion as such, especially of earlier and/or non-canonical approaches to Scripture, certainly has its place in canonical approaches to Scripture, suspicion vis-à-vis the influence of the factors that *A Treasure in Earthen Vessels* identifies is mostly lacking. It would seem plausible, however, to argue that such suspicion should have a place in a hermeneutics that is so strongly bound to a (particular) community of interpretation as a canonical approach to Scripture is in most cases, as well. To this may be added that attention to contextuality, cultural, social, and ecclesial, also receives much more explicit

---

rites, stories and practices. Only at the end of time will the Church's contemplation of God's revealed mystery go beyond a partial knowledge and arrive at that "knowing even as we are known" of which Paul writes in 1 Cor 13: 9–12."

79   See above, 3.2.5.

attention in ecumenical hermeneutics than in canonical approaches to Scripture. Such attention, however, would be fitting, as various aspects of the context of a community of interpretation and its rule of faith could well be determined by precisely such contextual factors.[80]

Second, an aspect that receives a lot of attention in ecumenical hermeneutics, but that is virtually ignored by canonical approaches to Scripture – even when they emphasize the place of Scripture in the church[81] – concerns the role of structures of authority and power in the church, which have as at least one of their tasks the interpretation of the faith, including the interpretation of Scripture. Especially in the case of Ratzinger, the relevance of this issue for canonical approaches to Scripture may be obvious, but also when it comes to other representatives of canonical approaches to Scripture and their use of texts and traditions that have been molded by ecclesial authorities (and other factors), the claims to authority of their own interpretation, and their relationship to the church at large and to their particular church. In fact, the question of power and authority is a blind spot among canonical critics who could, in this respect, learn from ecumenical hermeneutics.

Third, given the emphasis that canonical approaches to Scripture place on the position of Scripture in the church and the role of the church as a community of interpretation with its own tradition of interpretation, and the fact that these churches/communities of interpretation are not always the same, brings to the fore the question of the relationship between these communities, traditions, and interpretations. It is not typically raised by canonical critics, however.[82] Again, it seems that ecumenical hermeneutics, concerned as it is with precisely the encounter between different communities of interpretation, might be able to point in a helpful direction. In particular, the following remark from *A Treasure in Earthen Vessels* could be made fruitful for canonical approaches to Scripture, as it seeks to point out what happens when different communities of interpretation, i.e. churches, and their interpretations of the faith encounter one another:

> As the churches engage in dialogue in the growing communion of churches in the ecumenical movement, a further and wider hermeneutical community

---

80 See also Smit, "Wegweiser," and the considerations offered below in the outlook of this study.

81 See, however, Brenneman, *Canons*.

82 In all likelihood, this has to do with the phenomenon of the underdefinition of terms such as "church" in the work of many canonical critics; as long as the impression is given that it is simply "the" church that is the community of interpretation and not a more particular community or confessional tradition, the problem of different and competing communities of interpretation simply remains invisible.

is created. As it engages in ecumenical dialogue each church and tradition opens itself to being interpreted by other churches and traditions. To listen to the other does not necessarily mean to accept what other churches say, but to reckon with the possibility *"hermeneutics of confidence"*. A hermeneutics for unity should entail an ecumenical method whereby Christians from various cultures and contexts, as well as different confessions, may encounter one another respectfully, always open to a *metanoia* which is a true "change of mind" and heart. (8, see also section 9)

Also, the emphasis that is placed on the reception of dialogue partners of one another in ecumenical hermeneutics might speak to the issue of conflicting traditions and their encounter.[83] Thus, the interface between ecumenical hermeneutics and canonical approaches to Scripture might, in fact, lead to something like an intra-Christian variant of "scriptural reasoning," or at least to a process with similar characteristics.

---

83   See e.g. sections 49–53 from *A Treasure in Earthen Vessels*, as discussed above.

CHAPTER 5

General Conclusions and Outlook: Perspectives for Canonically Inspired Exegesis

When looking back at the above discussion and analysis of outstanding canonical approaches to the New Testament gospels, a number of concluding observations may be offered in response to the research question of this study ("What are the advantages and disadvantages of the 'canonical approach' in the scholarly discussion about it, and how are they reflected in the actual use of this approach in the exegesis of the four New Testament gospels?"), which provide perspectives for the canonical exegesis of the New Testament gospels and biblical hermeneutics that wish to make constructive use of their canonical character at the same time. These concluding observations have their basis in the entire discussion presented above, while some aspects of them are more closely related to some approaches than to others, given the differences between them.

First, canonical approaches to the New Testament and to the gospels in particular have drawn attention forcefully to both the importance of the world "of the text" and the world "in front of the text." This is a consequence of the emphasis that (many) canonical approaches place on the integrity of the canonical text (in whatever form) and its claims (see notably Childs, Stuhlmacher, and the Amsterdam School). Together with an emphasis on the synchronic analysis of the text stemming from, e.g., literary approaches, this has helped to give synchronic exegesis a much more prominent place on the exegetical agenda in the course of the past forty years. Although originating out of different concerns than literary approaches, canonical approaches have at the very least contributed to raising the awareness of these dimensions of exegesis. For the New Testament gospels, this means that their character as both works of literature with their own "story world" and their own aims at communicating a particular message to a particular audience, rather than – to overstate it somewhat – being sources for the "world behind the text" (be it the historical Jesus or the history of early Christianity), has received a firmer place on the exegetical agenda. As canonical approaches also served to reestablish the relationship between text and community in the scholarly mind, both with regard to the historical situations in which the texts came into existence, and to the current functioning of texts in communities of interpretation, they also contributed to renewed attention for the question of how texts that have become

© KONINKLIJKE BRILL NV, LEIDEN, 2015 | DOI 10.1163/9789004301016_006

canonical texts came into existence as such and functioned in communities of interpretation, and how they continue to function. Such questions, arising from canonical criticism, are of course related to the study of the historical emergence of canons and can even be argued to have influenced this particular branch of scholarship,[1] just as the study of canons and their functioning in other parts of ancient society (and beyond) has informed biblical scholarship concerned with the same.[2]

Second, the attention drawn to the topic of the canon by canonical critics and by those involved in related research on the emergence and functioning of canonical texts has also helped to raise awareness of the embeddedness of texts in a canonical process. That is to say: The awareness that these texts (often) have a "canonical consciousness" and that they (or at least some of them) make "canonical claims." In other words, the notion of canonicity, at least in a qualified way, cannot be regarded any longer as a concept completely foreign to all New Testament texts *per se*. For the New Testament gospels this leads to an intriguing situation about which the last word certainly has not yet been said: While all four canonical gospels can be seen to make claims to (canonical?) authority, they also seem to make these at the expense of one another.

Third, canonical approaches, with their attention for the interaction between text, reader, and the community and tradition of interpretation that a reader is part of, as well as for a reader's "rule of faith" (or "interpretative grammar"), strongly draw attention to the insight that *all* interpretations of (any) Scripture have to do with the elements just listed and are, therefore, contextual. This observation, however, does not mean a complete relativization of all interpretations *per se*, but a clearer understanding of what they are and how and under which conditions interpretations function. Acknowledging this does serve to level the playing field somewhat between different kinds of exegesis; e.g. not only so-called "contextual" interpretations of Scripture are contextual, but also "theological" or "academic" interpretations are, given that they are caught up in an analogous interplay between text, reader, community, tradition, and interpretative grammar. In other words, canonical exegesis as it has been studied here draws attention to the significance of a reader's theological outlook, or, in a broader sense: Worldview, for the process of interpretation, especially

---

1 See Von Lips, "Kanondebatten," 123, on canonical debates and the study of the canon: Certainly Markschies' own study of the development and the role of the scriptural canon in early Christianity is informed by his reception of (virtually always theologically flavored) debates about the significance, relevance, and function of the canon in exegesis (see also his remarks in "Epochen," 578–589).

2 See e.g. the literature surveyed above, in section 1.

in the sense that precisely the interaction between the reader and his or her worldview and the text leads to a productive reading of the text (while acknowledging the dangers of a "dogmatic" reading of texts in the negative sense of the word).[3] Above, this was explored in relation to ecumenical hermeneutics, where the contextuality of readings – and also their relationship to structures of power and authority – is much more explicitly thematized. It seems that a dialogue between canonical approaches and ecumenical hermeneutics, the former providing exegetical and historical insights as to the relationship between text, context, and community, and the latter providing insights into this interplay today, may well prove to be mutually beneficial. Similar interfaces may well be imagined with the fields of missiology, intercultural theology, and even interreligious dialogue (e.g. through "scriptural reasoning").[4]

Awareness of the interrelationship between worldview, group identity, and interpretation, as is also emphasized by various other critical and/or emancipatory approaches, not least by ecumenical and/or intercultural readings of Scripture, can be hermeneutically beneficial, especially when attention is also given, as is not commonly done in canonical criticism, to structures of power and authority that govern interpretative processes. To put it somewhat succinctly: Canonical approaches to Scripture can make one aware that *all* approaches to Scripture are canonical (in the sense just discussed, i.e. "contextual"), and even theological or ideological, while they are certainly bound up in power struggles related to competing interpretations. It was argued above that canonical approaches to Scripture have something to learn in this respect from more contextually aware ecumenical hermeneutics. This awareness can have consequences for the way in which one's own interpretation and that of others are viewed and how communities of interpretation relate to one another.[5] While this might read as subsuming biblical interpretation to the dictates of interpreting communities, there is more to it than just this. The conscious

---

3   See on this also my earlier study: Peter-Ben Smit, "Biblische Hermeneutik im Spannungsfeld persönlicher und kirchlicher Identität," *Internationale Kirchliche Zeitschrift* 96 (2006), 135–151.

4   See for the latter the remarks of Söding, *Einheit*, 92–102, and the work of such scholars as J.H. de Wit, *My God, She Said. "Ships Make Me so Crazy," Reflections on Empirical Hermeneutics, Interculturality and Holy Scripture* (Amsterdam: VU University, 2008), and idem/Louis Jonker/ Marleen Kook/Daniel S. Schipani (ed.), *Through the Eyes of Another: Intercultural Reading of the Bible* (Amsterdam: VU University, 2004), idem/Gerald O. West (ed.), *African and European Readers of the Bible in Dialogue. In Quest of a Shared Meaning* (Brill: Leiden, 2008), and Segovia, "Voice," and idem, *Decolonizing*.

5   See also the remarks of Markschies, "Epochen," 578–579, and esp. Söding, *Einheit*, 68–80.

interaction between communities of interpretation with different "grammars" may also lead to a certain cross-fertilization. As a result of posing new questions to old texts, in (and because of) new contexts of interpretation, new interpretations are produced with regard to the texts involved. Examples of this abound, one need only point to the awareness of gender in texts, of issues of power, etc., as they have become part of ever more broadly shared exegetical (mainstream) agendas, on which they have found a place after having been developed in smaller interpretative communities. Even for the most "traditional" historical-critical scholar, this must mean that the interaction between various communities of interpretation also helps to do more justice to the texts by asking new and heuristically helpful questions. Furthermore, such insights, derived from canonical exegesis, might also help to bridge the (ever-increasing?) gap between biblical studies and systematic theology.[6] A reason to think this is that canonical approaches, on the one hand, draw attention to the claims that emerge from texts (e.g. to authority, truth, etc.), and on the other hand, interpret these texts also by relating them to a community of interpretation and a grammar of reading,[7] which, therefore, necessarily involves a critical interplay between philological, historical, hermeneutical, philosophical, and theological disciplines. Notably, the interface between canonical approaches to Scripture and ecumenical hermeneutics may be productive in this regard.

Before moving on to a consideration of the canonical gospels and their interpretation from a canonical point of view, one further point may now be made. When looking back at the canonical approaches as they have been considered in this study, it seems that one of their most important achievements is to contribute to raising new questions. These questions notably concerns the following:

(1)   Canonical approaches, with their attention to the canonical process and the reception of canonical texts, make one ask certain questions more

---

6   See e.g. the call for more dialogue between these disciplines in a Dutch context by Ed Noort, "Het Oude Testament en zijn levers: Van toen naar de toekomst," in: Wessel Stoker/Henk C. van der Sar (ed.), *Heroriëntatie in de Theologie* (Kampen: Kok, 2003), 56–63, esp. 61–62. – From the perspective of kind of canonical criticism considered in this study, a dialogue with approaches to systematic theology that underlines the significance of a "grammar" of faith, or indeed, a rule of faith, might be fruitful. See with regard to this, for example, the work of George Lindbeck, *The Nature of Doctrine: Religions and Theology in a Post-liberal Age* (Philadelphia: Westminster John Knox, 1984). On Lindbeck, see the brief overview offered by Zwiep, *Tekst* II, 107–109.

7   See also the considerations of Söding, "Kanon," li.

precisely. For example, when interpreting a canonical gospel, the following question may be asked: Which gospel (e.g. earlier stages of traditions, the final text, or the final text in its canonical context), written by whom (a single author, the canonizing community, etc.) is interpreted by whom (of which interpretative community is the reader part, what position does he or she occupy in it) and for whom (original audience, a later audience, etc.)? Surely, reader-response criticism, various kinds of emancipatory (or identity-based) approaches, ecumenical and intercultural approaches, and approaches that take into consideration postmodern historiography might lead to asking this and similar questions, but clearly canonical criticism has also raised the awareness for the importance of asking these questions, even if the perspective of canonical critics can be developed further through dialogue with other hermeneutical disciplines (e.g., ecumenical hermeneutics, as was explored above).

(2) Canonical approaches to Scripture have played a key role in raising the question of the notion of the canon as a literary and cultural phenomenon again, as part of the community's collective (and cultural) memory, and how texts relate to this. Questions concerning the meaning-making based on texts, about the kind of access provided by texts to historical events and regarding the relationship between the history of reception of a (canonical) text and its meaning, are also relevant here. Therefore, when surveying the above considerations, Seckler's point, that both new insights from the (historical) study of the canon and a new sensitivity to the theological and philosophical dimensions of canonical texts mutually reinforce each other, seems to be well taken.[8]

As was explored above and is hinted at by Seckler's reference to ecclesiology, the relationship between canonical approaches and ecumenical hermeneutics is one particular example of the cross-fertilization mentioned in this quotation.

---

8 Seckler, "Problematik," 32: "Die außerordentliche Lebendigkeit und Brisanz der heutigen Kanondebatte erklärt sich somit insgesamt aus dem Zusammenwirken und der wechselseitigen Befruchtung zweier Komponenten: Einerseits einer Intensivierung der empirischen Kanonforschung, die zu neuen Einsichten in die historische und sachliche Komplexität des Kanonproblems führt, andererseits einer veränderten Empfänglichkeit für die theologischen, d.h. die religiösen, spirituellen, ekklesiologischen und wissenschaftstheoretischen Bewandtnisse eines Kanons heiliger Schriften." – A good example of this can be found in the following essay by Bernd Janowski: "The Contrastive Unity of Scripture: On the Hermeneutics of the Biblical Canon," in: Seitz/Richards (ed.), *Bible*, 37–62, esp. 62–62.

Finally, then, by way of outlook, some of the bearing of all of this on the exegesis of the New Testament gospels and their understanding as canonical documents needs to be considered, as they have served as test cases in this study, but also represent, on a smaller scale, issues that also affect the issue of the canon and of canonical exegesis as a whole. Given the rivers of ink spilled over this question, it cannot be addressed in full here. This is also not the point of this study. Much rather, the shape of canonical exegesis in the sense of exegesis that takes into account the interrelationship between text and reading community with its "rule of faith," as it has emerged from this study, needs to be related to the question of unity and diversity within the canon. This should be done using the example of the four canonical gospels that are not only diverse, but of which some (Matthew, Luke, and John) may well have been meant to replace another (Mark, but also Q and other sources/earlier versions of gospels). The question that needs to be addressed here, therefore, is not the historical question of the emergence of the four-gospel-canon, but the question of what the canonization of a text that is conflictuous and contradictory in itself means for the interpretative process in terms of canonical exegesis.

To begin with, one aspect of the canonization of the four canonical gospels is the fact that with their canonization part of the canonical process has been canonized as well,[9] given that the canonization of both Mark *and* Luke, Matthew, and John represents (at least) two stages of this process. When considering this from the perspective of Sanders' concept of canonical criticism in particular, which leaves the most room for both the canonical process and for principled diversity in the canonical witness, it seems,[10] the question could be asked as to whether this canonization of part of the canonical process should have any consequences for the way in which the canonical text is seen as normative. In other words, would the canonization of the four gospels also imply a canonical hermeneutic that is, so to speak, written into the canon *qua* normative collective memory of the church (or churches), through the

---

9   On which, see e.g. the extensive study of Theo K. Heckel, *Vom Evangelium zum vierge-staltigen Evangelium* (Tübingen: Mohr Siebeck, 1999), as well as the thought-provoking essays in: Richard Bauckham (ed.), *The Gospels for All Christians: Rethinking the Gospel Audiences* (Grand Rapids: Eerdmans, 1998).

10   This probably also has to do with Sanders' eschatological view of the process of interpretation: In the work of Stuhlmacher, by contrast, the meaning is much more fixed to Scripture itself as interpreted by means of historical tools and taking into account the "canon within the canon," in the cases of Ratzinger and Childs, the "faith of the church" can be seen to smooth over all differences, while the "catchword" – approach of the "Amsterdam School" might also be seen as having a very strong tendency to systematize things and leave little room for real diversity.

canonization of parts of the canonical process, resulting in a self-contradictory canon?[11] It seems indeed inviting to pursue this route. A first reason to think so can be found in Sanders' thought, while further reasons can be found in recent work by Gruber,[12] who, in turn, takes her cue from Wolter. Wolter argued that the tension between unity and diversity is part and parcel of Christian identity and existence as such and cannot be solved, neither in relationship to the canon, nor in relationship to Christian identity as such.[13] The encounter with the Christian other and the non-Christian other is, in other words, constitutive for Christian identity, as is also emphasized by missiologists, or postmodern (and postliberal) theologians such as Vanhoozer.[14]

The canonized Scriptures, including the four gospels, therefore, reflect and pass on not so much one stable Christian identity, but they rather bear witness to the (conflictuous) search for it, as evidenced by the disagreements between the various texts.[15] While this certainly sounds relativistic vis-à-vis views of early Christianity as possessing a stable identity, it is anything but that, given that this view of canonical diversity does, in fact, not so much relativize as change the notion of the identity of early Christianity and its unity; unity and

---

11 To be sure, an analogous question may well be asked about the relationship between the relationship of the New Testament writings to those of the Old Testament/Scriptures of Israel.

12 See Judith Gruber, *Theologie nach dem Cultural Turn. Interkulturalität als theologische Ressource* (Stuttgart: Kohlhammer, 2013). – See for compatible considerations also: Janneke Stegeman, "'Reading Jeremiah Makes Me Angry!' the Role of Jeremiah 32 [39] in Transformation within the "Jeremianic" Tradition,' in: Wido Th. van Peursen/Janet Dyk (ed.), *Tradition and Innovation in Biblical Interpretation* (Leiden: Brill, 2011), 45–67.

13 Wolter, "Vielfalt," 52–53: "Die intensive Suche nach einer sprachlich wie existentiell aus-differenzierbaren und einheitsstiftenden Mitte der christlichen Identität und die Unmöglichkeit, sie eindeutig...zu bestimmen, [war] bereits von Anfang an integraler Bestandteil der geschichtlichen Existenz der christlichen Gemeinden...Die Spannung zwischen Einheit und Vielfalt wäre demnach nicht ein erst mit dem Kanon gegebenes Problem, sondern eine fundamentale und damit unaufhebbare Gegebenheit der geschichtlichen Existenz des Christentums überhaupt." See also Barthel, "Debatte," 1, who notes that also the identification with a pluralistic and "broken" canon of Scriptures can be constitutive for the identity of a community, which, therefore, also becomes plural and "broken."

14 See Kevin J. VanHoozer, "Theology and the Condition of Postmodernity: a report on knowledge of God," in: idem (ed.), *Cambridge Companion to Postmodern Theology* (Cambridge: Cambridge University, 2003), 3–25, esp. 22–25, with reference to the work of Andrew Walls and Lammin Sanneh.

15 See Gruber, *Theologie*.

identity become more fluid, more processes than fixed forms.[16] For the canonized New Testament, this means that not so much a hopelessly diverse collection of texts has been assembled, nor that their messages really can or even
should be harmonized in the end, but rather that (canonical and hence normative!) room for the negotiation of identity appears.[17] The kind of identity that
is presented as normative by the canon of the New Testament, notably by the
conflicting claims and witnesses of the four gospels, is therefore, an identity
that in itself contains dialogue, struggle, and even conflict with regard to this
very identity.[18] When maintaining a dialogue with Wolter's considerations
here, this also has leads to a further consequence for the canonicity of texts:
When a text is considered "canonical," this does not only mean that it is normative, but also that a text does not stand on its own anymore, but is "canonical"
only as part of an ensemble of texts and, therefore, in dialogue with other texts.
The individual text is not canonical, but the dialogue (or conflict) between
them is canonical – and therefore also productive.[19] All of this, it seems, can be

---

16   Wolter, "Vielfalt," 55: "Die Ausdifferenzierung des einen Bekenntnisses in unterschiedli-
       che und miteinander konkurrierende Heilskonzepte einschließlich ihrer lebensweltli-
       chen Implikationen [darf] nicht als Verlust einer ursprünglichen Einheit verstanden
       werden, sondern [ist] ein integraler Bestandteil der Plausibilität des Bekenntnisses selbst
       gewesen, ohne die die Rezeption der christlichen Heilsbotschaft nicht möglich gewesen
       wäre. Was das Zeugnis vom Christusereignis konkret bedeutet (d.h. mit welchen Zeichen
       diesem Zeugnis welche Bedeutung zugeschrieben wird) steht nicht von vornherein fest,
       sondern wird in kontextabhängigen Bedeutungsprozessen ausverhandelt; das wird im
       Kanon dokumentiert." – Compare also Childs' emphasis on the fourfold witness of the
       four canonical gospels (Childs, *Biblical Theology*, 262).
17   See: Gruber, *Theologie*, 19: "Die Differenzen, die ein genealogischer Blick im Kanon offen-
       legt, lassen ihn als eine Kompilation von partikularen Theologien erscheinen von
       Theologien, die vom Christusereignis im Rückgriff auf die Bedeutungsstrukturen ihres
       kulturellen Kontextes Zeugnis ablegen. Die Differenzen werden nicht ausgeblendet,
       sondern innerhalb des Kanons zusammengestellt. In den Differenzen konstituiert sich –
       so wurde oben aufgezeigt – ein Raum der Interkulturalität. Indem der Kanon Differenzen
       sichtbar macht, schafft er einen Raum der Interkulturalität, in dem christliche Identität
       verhandelt wird; Als normativ gesetztes Dokument normiert er sie damit als disparates
       Produkt interkultureller Übersetzungs- und Transformationsvorgänge zwischen partiku-
       laren Theologien." – See also the feminist plea for "Dialogizität" by Müller, "Autorität."
18   See Gruber, *Theologie*, 20: "Christliche Identität geschieht hier performativ im Konflikt –
       gerade weil über unterschiedliche Interpretationen verhandelt wird, zerfällt christliche
       Identität nicht. Die im Kanon normative gesetzte konfliktive Interkulturalität weist so
       einen Weg zwischen einem Verständnis von christlicher Indentität, das Differenzen aus-
       blendet, und ihrer Zersplitterung entlang der im Kanon dokumentierten Bruchlinien."
19   See Wolter, "Vielfalt," 65, Gruber, *Theologie*, 20.25-26; see further also Judith M. Lieu,
       Neither Jew nor Greek? Constructing Early Christianity (London: T. & T. Clark, 2002), 2–3:

brought into dialogue again rather productively with insights gained from the study of the canon as a literary phenomenon, i.e. as a collection of texts that productively interact with one another in a double new context: That of the canon as a body of texts and that of a (new) interpretative community,[20] which in interaction with one another, guided by certain interpretative rules, seek to reformulate and reconstitute the identity of this group.

These latter considerations, it may be underlined, have much in common with contemporary ecumenical hermeneutics, where also the notion of the joint search for a common Christian identity has been foregrounded, with emphasis on 1) the joint and dialogic interpretation of the shared sources of the faith; 2) the acknowledgement of the particular traditions of which the various interpreters of Scripture are part and their heuristic value and relativity vis-à-vis Christ to whom they seek to witness; 3) probably most significantly, on the reception of the interpreters and churches of one another, as part of the process through which Christian faith and identity is discerned and rediscovered.

Canonical approaches to Scripture, specifically to the New Testament gospels, therefore, as they have been considered in this study, have, at the very least, helped to pave the way for new methodological insights concerning the interpretation of Scripture. This concerns new insights regarding the significance of the world of the text and of the latter in relation to the worlds behind and in front of the texts. Furthermore, the notion of "canonicity," it may safely be said, can no longer be used in a pejorative sense or be considered irrelevant, given that it can be shown to be bound up with the texts themselves. Furthermore, precisely canonical exegesis can assist in bridging a number of interdisciplinary gaps and, finally, the renewed consideration of precisely the

---

Texts do not simply reflect a "history" going on independently of them, they are themselves part of the process by which...Christianity came into being. For it was through literature that...a self-understanding was shaped and articulated, and then mediated to and appropriated by others, and through literature that people and ideas were included or excluded. What the texts were doing is sometimes as, if not more, important than what they were saying.

20 See e.g. Egbert Ballhorn, "Das historische und das kanonische Paradigma in der Exegese. Ein Essay," in: idem/Steins (ed.), *Bibelkanon*, 9–30, 13, even if one must be critical of the sharp distinction he makes between the "unhistorical" scholarship of the early church that relied more on the rule of faith and modern day historical scholarship that does not do so. Rather, both kinds of exegesis included elements of both historical information (and curiosity) and, *nolens volens*, elements of a "rule of faith." See on the latter also Tobias Nicklas, 'Leitfragen leserorientierte Exegese. Methodische Gedanken zu einer "biblischen Auslegung,"' in: Ballhorn/Steins (ed.), *o.c.*, 45–61, 48. – The definition of "canon" offered by Theißen, *Religion*, 341–342, suits this well.

canon in its relationship to early Christian identity can, as was just shown, point the way for an understanding of the canon and canonicity as a very productive, rather than restrictive aspect of the process of the construction of early Christian memory and its reconstruction in new contexts (especially in relation to ecumenical hermeneutics).[21] A price for the latter, it may be argued, may well be that the process of the interpretation becomes even more dynamic and open-ended (and according to both some canonical critics and to some models for ecumenical hermeneutics: Eschatologically oriented).[22] It seems, however, that this price is not only unavoidable, but also a small one considering the interpretative horizons and challenges that canonical approaches have yet to offer. These horizons and challenges look particularly interesting when the interface between canonical criticism with its attention of text, community, and tradition and ecumenical hermeneutics is taken into account. In fact, in many ways canonical criticism is ecumenical hermeneutics *in nuce*. Acknowledging this can help to develop canonical criticism further as a hermeneutical approach to Scripture, specifically by drawing even more attention to questions of contextuality, power, and dialogue.

---

21   See along similar lines also: Michael Wolter, "Probleme und Möglichkeiten einer Theologie des Neuen Testaments," in: Rieuwerd Buitenwerf/Harm W. Hollander/Johannes Tromp (ed.), *Jesus, Paul, and Early Christianity* (Brill: Leiden, 2008), 417–436, esp. 435–436.

22   See on this both VanHoozer's emphasis (e.g., in *Meaning*) as well as the line of thought of various Faith and Order documents, such as *A Treasure in Earthen Vessels.*

Bibliography

Abma, Richtsje (ed.), *Nog dichter bij Genesis: opstellen over het eerste bijbelboek voor Karel Deurloo* (FS Karel A. Deurloo; Baarn, Ten Have, 1995).

Abma, Richtsje, *Bonds of Love: Methodic Studies of Prophetic Texts with Marriage Imagery* (Assen: Van Gorcum, 1999).

Abraham, William J., *Canon and Criterion in Christian Theology. From the Fathers of Feminism* (Oxford: Clarendon, 1998).

Ådna, Jostein/Scott J. Hafemann/Otfried Hofius (eds.), *Evangelium – Schriftauslegung – Kirche* (FS Peter Stuhlmacher, Göttingen: Vandenhoeck & Ruprecht, 1997).

Agouridis, Savas, "The *regula fidei* as Hermeneutical Principle Past and Present," in: *L'Interpretazione della Bibbia nella Chiesa, Atti del Simposio promosso dalla Congregazione per la Dottrina della Fede* (Vatican: Libreria editrice Vaticana, 2001), 225–231.

Alexander, Loveday C., *The Preface to Luke's Gospel: Literary Convention and Social Context in Luke 1:1–4 and Acts 1:1* (Cambridge: Cambridge University, 1993).

Allison, Dale C. Jr., *The New Moses: A Matthean Typology* (Minneapolis: Fortress, 1993).

Assmann, Aleida, "Kanonforschung als Provokation der Literaturwissenschaft," in: Von Heydebrand (ed.), *Kanon* (1998), 47–59.

Assmann, Aleida, *Einführung in die Kulturwissenschaft: Grundbergriffe Themen, Fragestellungen* (Berlin: Schmidt, ²2008).

Assmann, Aleida/Jan Assmann (ed.), *Kanon und Zensur* (München: Fink, 1987).

Assmann, Jan, *Das kulturelle Gedächtnis. Schrift, Erinnerung und politische Identität in frühen Hochkulturen* (München: Beck, 1992).

Assmann, Jan, *Fünf Stufen auf dem Wege zum Kanon: Tradition und Schriftkultur im frühen Judentum und seiner Umwelt* (Münster: LIT, 1999).

Auwers, Jean-Marie/Henk Jan de Jonge (eds.), *The Biblical Canons* (Louvain: Peeters, 2003).

Bakker, Nico T., *In der Krisis der Offenbarung: Karl Barths Hermeneutik, dargestellt an seiner Römerbrief-Auslegung* (Neukirchen-Vluyn: Neukirchener Verlag, 1974).

Bakker, Nico T. (ed.), *Debharim* (FS F.H. Breukelman; Kampen: Kok, 1986).

Bakker, Nico T., *Geschiedenis in opspraak: over de legitimatie van het concept geschiedenis: een theologische verhandeling* (Kampen: Kok, 1996).

Bakker, Nico T. (ed.), *Één zo'n mannetje: Frans Breukelman en zijn invloed op tijdgenoten* (Kampen: Kok, 2004).

Ballhorn, Egbert, "Das historische und das kanonische Paradigma in der Exegese. Ein Essay," in: Steins/Idem (eds.), *Bibelkanon* (2007), 9–30.

Barr, James, *Holy Scripture: Canon, Authority, Criticism* (Westminster John Knox, 1983).

Barr, James, "The Theological Case against Biblical Theology," in: Gene M. Tucker/ David L. Petersen/Robert R. Wilson (eds.), *Canon, Theology and Old Testament*

Interpretation. Essays in Honor of Brevard S. Childs (Philadelphia: Fortress, 1988), 3–19.

Barr, James, *The Concept of Biblical Theology: An Old Testament Perspective* (Minneapolis: Fortress, 1999).

Barthel, Jörg, "Die kanonhermeneutische Debatte seit Gerhard von Rad: Anmerkungen zu neueren Entwürfen," in: Janowski (ed.). *Kanonhermeneutik*, 1–26.

Barton, John, "Canonical Approaches Ancient and Modern," in: Auwers/De Jonge (eds.), *Canons* (2003), 199–209.

Barton, John, *Reading the Old Testament: Method in Biblical Study* (London: Darton, Longman and Todd, 1984).

Barton, John, *Holy Writings. Sacred Text. The Canon in Early Christianity* (London: SPCK, 1997a).

Barton, John, *The Spirit and the Letter* (London: SPCK, 1997b).

Barton, John/Michael Wolter (eds.), *Die Einheit der Schrift und die Vielfalt des Kanons* (Berlin: De Gruyter, 2003).

Bauckham, Richard (ed.), *The Gospels for All Christians: Rethinking the Gospel Audiences* (Grand Rapids: Eerdmans, 1998).

Bauer, Uwe F.W., כָּל־הַדְּבָרִים הָאֵלֶּה *All diese Worte: Impulse zur Schriftauslegung aus Amsterdam. Expliziert an der Schilfmeererzählung in Exodus 13, 17–14, 31* (Frankfurt: Lang, 1991).

Bauer, Uwe F.W., "Das sogenannte 'idiolekte' Prinzip der Bibelübersetzung – wesentliche Charakteristika und einige praktische Beispiele," in: Hans J. Barkenings/Uwe F.W. Bauer (eds.), *De Beproeving – over de nieuwe bijbelvertaling* (Kok: Kampen, 2005).

Beale, Gregory K., *Handbook on the New Testament Use of the Old Testament: Exegesis and Interpretation* (Grand Rapids: Baker, 2012).

Beale, Gregory K./D.A. Carson, *Commentary on the New Testament Use of the Old Testament* (Grand Rapids: Baker, 2007).

Becker, Eve-Marie, "Die Person des Exegeten. Überlegungen zu einem vernachlässigten Thema," in: Oda Wischmeyer (ed.), *Herkunft und Zukunft der neutestamentlichen Wissenschaft* (Tübingen: Francke, 2003), 207–243.

Becker, Eve-Marie/Stefan Scholz (eds.), *Kanon in Konstruktion und Dekonstruktion. Kanonisierungsprozesse religiöser Texte von der Antike bis zur Gegenwart. Ein Handbuch* (Berlin: De Gruyter, 2012).

Beek, M.A., *Das Danielbuch, sein historischer Hintergrund und seine literarische Entwicklung* (Leiden: Ginsberg, 1935).

Beek, M.A., *Aan Babylons stromen* (Amsterdam: Kosmos, 1950a).

Beek, M.A., *Inleiding in de joodse apocalyptiek van het Oud- en Nieuwtestamentische tijdvak* (Haarlem: Bohn, 1950b).

Beek, M.A., *Wegen en voetsporen van het Oude Testament* (Delft: Gaade, 1953).

Beek, M.A., *De geschiedenis van Israël: van Abraham tot Bar-Kochba* (Zeist: De Haan, 1957).

Beek, M.A., *Atlas van het Tweestromenland* (Amsterdam: Elsevier, 1960).

Beek, M.A., *Wegwijzers en wegbereiders* (Baarn: Bosch Keuning, 1975).

Bekker, Ype (ed.), *Gesprekken met Frans Breukelman* (Den Haag: Meinema, 1989).

Bekker, Ype/Wouter Klouwen/Ad van Nieuwpoort (eds.), *In de ruimte van de openbaring: opstellen voor Nico T. Bakker* (Kampen: Kok, 1999).

Benedict XVI/Joseph Ratzinger, *Jesus of Nazareth. The Illustrated Edition* (New York: Rizzoli, 2009; first edition: 2007).

Benedict XVI/Joseph Ratzinger, *Jesus of Nazareth: Holy Week: From the Entrance into Jerusalem to the Resurrection* (San Francisco: Ignatius, 2011).

Benedict XVI/Joseph Ratzinger, *Jesus of Nazareth. The Infancy Narratives* (New York: Image, 2012).

Berndt, Rainer, "Gehören die Kirchenväter zur Heiligen Schrift? Zur Kanontheorie des Hugo von St. Viktor," *JBTh* 3 (1988), 191–199.

Bird, Michael/Michael Pahl (eds.), *The Sacred Text: Excavating the Texts, Exploring the Interpretations, and Engaging the Theologies of the Christian Scriptures* (Piscataway: Gorgias, 2010).

Bockmuehl, Markus, *Seeing the World: Refocusing New Testament Study* (Grand Rapids: Baker, 2006).

Boer, Dick, *Een fantastisch verhaal: theologie en ideologische strijd* (Voorburg: Protestantse Stichting tot Bevordering van het Bibliotheekwezen en de Lectuurvoorlichting in Nederland, 1988).

Boer, Dick, *Erlösung aus der Sklaverei* (Münster: ITP-Kompass, 2008).

Boeve, Lieven, "Tradition, (De)Canonization, and the Challenge of Plurality," in: Van der Kooij/Van der Toorn (eds.), *Canonization* (1998), 371–380.

Böhler, Dieter, "Der Kanon als hermeneutische Vorgabe biblischer Theologie. Über aktuelle Methodendiskussionen in der Bibelwissenschaft," *ThPh* 77 (2002), 161–178.

Bouhuijs, K./Karel A. Deurloo, *Dichter bij Genesis* (Baarn: Ten Have, 1967).

Bovon, François, "The Canonical Structure of Gospel and Apostle," in: McDonald/Sanders (eds.), *Debate* (2002), 516–527.

Bovon, François, *Das Evangelium nach Lukas* 1–4 (Zürich: Benzinger, 1989–2009).

Bowen, Nancy R., "Canon and the Community of Women: A Feminist Response to Canonical Criticism," in: Weiss/Carr (eds.), *Gift* (1996), 237–252.

Braaten, Carl E./Robert W Jenson (eds.), *Reclaiming the Bible for the Church* (Grand Rapids: Eerdmans, 1995).

Breck, John, *Scripture in Tradition: The Bible and Its Interpretation in the Orthodox Church* (Crestwood, NY: SVS Press, 2001).

Brenneman, James E., *Canons in Conflict: Negotiating Texts in True and False Prophecy* (Oxford: Oxford University, 1997).

Brett, Mark G., *Biblical Criticism in Crisis? The Impact of the Canonical Approach on Old Testament Studies* (Cambridge: Cambridge University, 1991).

Breukelman, Frans H., *Schriftlezing* (Kampen: Kok, 1980).

Breukelman, Frans H., *De theologie van de Evangelist Mattheüs: de ouverture van het Evangelie naar Mattheüs. Het verhaal over de genesis van Jezus Christus* (*Mattheüs 1:1–2:23*) (Kampen: Kok, 1984).

Breukelman, Frans H., "Umschreibung des Begriffs einer 'Biblischen Theologie'," *TuK* 31/32 (1986), 13–39.

Breukelman, Frans H., תּוֹלְדֹת: *de theologie van het boek Genesis. Het eerstelingschap van Israël temidden von de volkeren op de aarde als thema van "het boek van de verwekkingen van Adam, de mens"* (Kampen: Kok, 1992).

Breukelman, Frans H., "Eine Erklärung des Gleichnisses vom Schalksknecht (Matth. 18, 23–35)," in: Lother Steiger/Eberhard Busch (eds.), *Parrhesia* (FS K. Barth; Zürich: EVZ, 1966a), 261–287.

Breukelman, Frans H., *De theologie van de Evangelist Mattheüs: het evangelie naar Mattheüs als "Heilsbotschaft vom Königtum"* (Kampen: Kok, 1996b).

Breukelman, Frans H., *Debharim: der biblische Wirklichkeitsbegriff des Seins in der Tat* (Kampen: Kok, 1998).

Breukelman, Frans H., *Theologische opstellen* (Kampen: Kok, 1999), *De Structuur van de heilige leer in de theologie van Calvijn* (Kampen: Kok, 2003).

Bruce, F.F., *The Canon of Scripture* (Downers Grove: InterVarsity, 1988).

Bruggen, Jakob van, *Lucas. Het Evangelie als voorgeschiedenis* (Kampen: Kok, 1993).

Bultmann, Rudolf, "Ist voraussetzunglose Exegese möglich?" *ThZ* 13 (1957), 409–417.

Bultmann, Rudolf, "Is Exegesis without Presuppositions Possible," in: Idem, *Existence and Faith: Shorter Writings of Rudolf Bultmann* (trans. S.M. Ogden; Cleveland: World Meridian Publishing, 1960), 289–296.

Butting, Klara, *Die Buchstaben werden sich noch wundern: innerbiblische Kritik als Wegweisung feministischer Hermeneutik* (Berlin: Alektor, 1994).

Callaway, Mary C., "Canonical Criticism," in: Stephen Haynes/Steven McKenzie (eds.), *To Each Its Own Meaning* (Louisville: Westminster/John Knox, 1993), 142–155.

Callaway, Mary, *Sing, O Barren One* (Atlanta: Scholars, 1986), Peter Pettit, *Shene'emar: The Place of Scripture Citation in the Mishna* (PhD dissertation: Claremont Graduate School, 1993).

Campenhausen, Hans Freiherr von *The Formation of the Christian Bible* (Philadelphia: Fortress, 1972).

Carson, D.A./John D. Woodbridge (eds.), *Hermeneutics and Canon* (Grand Rapids: Baker, 1995).

Cartwright, Michael G., "Hermeneutics," in: Nicholas Lossky/José Míguez Bonino/John Pobee/Tom F. Stransky/Geoffrey Wainwright/Pauline Webb (eds.), *Dictionary of the Ecumenical Movement* (Geneva: WCC Publications, ²2002), 513–518.

Childs, Brevard S., "Interpretation in Faith: The Theological Responsibility of an Old Testament Commentary," *Interpretation* 18 (1964), 432–449.

Childs, Brevard S., *Biblical Theology in Crisis* (Philadelphia: Westminster Press, 1970).

Childs, Brevard S., *The Book of Exodus. A Critical Theological Commentary* (Philadelphia: Westminster Press, 1974).

Childs, Brevard S., *Introduction to the Old Testament as Scripture* (London: SCM, 1979).

Childs, Brevard S., *The New Testament as Canon. An Introduction* (Valley Forge: Trinity International Press, 1984).

Childs, Brevard S., *Biblical Theology of the Old and New Testaments. Theological Reflection on the Christian Bible* (Minneapolis: Fortress, 1992).

Childs, Brevard S., "Towards Recovering Theological Exegesis," *Pro Ecclesia* 6 (1997), 16–26.

Childs, Brevard S., *Isaiah* (Louisville: Westminster John Knox, 2001).

Childs, Brevard S., *The Struggle to Understand Isaiah as Christian Scripture* (Grand Rapids: Eerdmans, 2004).

Childs, Brevard S., "The Canon in Recent Biblical Studies. Reflections on an Era," *Pro Ecclesia* 14 (2005), 26–46.

Childs, Brevard S., *The Church's Guide for Reading Paul: The Canonical Shaping of the Pauline Corpus* (Grand Rapids: Eerdmans, 2008).

Commission on Faith and Order, *Baptism, Eucharist and Ministry 1982–1990: Report on the Process and the Responses*, Faith and Order Paper 149 (Geneva: WCC Publications, 1990).

Commission on Faith and Order, *A Treasure in Earthen Vessels, an Instrument for an Ecumenical Reflection on Hermeneutics* (Geneva: WCC Publications, 1998).

Commission on Faith and Order, *The Church. Towards a Common Vision* (Geneva: WCC, 2013).

Conzelmann, Hans, *Die Mitte der Zeit* (rev. ed.; Tübingen: Mohr, 1960).

Croatto, J. Severino, *Biblical Hermeneutics: Towards a Theory of Reading as the Production of Meaning* (Maryknoll: Orbis, 1987).

Davies, Philipp R., *Whose Bible is It Anyway?* (Sheffield: Sheffield Academic Press, 1995).

Davis, Ellen F./Richard B. Hays (eds.), *The Art of Reading Scripture* (Grand Rapids: Eerdmans, 2003).

Deurloo, Karel A., *Kain en Abel: onderzoek naar exegetische methode inzake een kleine 'literaire eenheid' in de Tenakh* (Amsterdam: Ten Have, 1967).

Deurloo, Karel A., "De zogenaamde 'Amsterdamse School'," in: A.F.J. Klijn (ed.), *Inleiding tot de studie van het Nieuwe Testament* (Kampen: Kok, 1982), 165–172.

Deurloo, Karel A., "Exegese naar Amsterdamse Traditie," in: W.A.M. Beuken (ed.), *Inleiding tot de studie van het Oude Testament* (Kampen: Kok, 1986), 1988–195.

Deurloo, Karel A., *De mens als raadsel en geheim: verhalende antropologie in Genesis 2–4* (Baarn, Ten Have, 1988a).

Deurloo, Karel A., *Genesis* (Kampen: Kok, 1998b).

Deurloo, Karel A., *Exodus en Exil* (Kampen: Kok, 2004).

Deurloo, Karel A., *Onze lieve vrouwe baart een zoon* (Kampen: Kok, 2006).

Deurloo, Karel A./Wilken Veen (eds.), *De gezegende temidden van zijn broeders: Jozef en Juda in Genesis 37–50* (Baarn: Ten Have, 1995).

Deurloo, Karel A./Bernd J. Diebner (eds.), *YHWH – Kyrios – Antitheism or The Power of the Word* (FSR. Zuurmond; Amsterdam: DBAT, 1996).

Deurloo, Karel A./F.J. Hoogewoud (eds.), *Beginnen bij de letter Beth* (FS A.G. van Daalen; Kampen: Kok, 1984a).

Deurloo, Karel A./Rochus Zuurmond (eds.), *De bijbel maakt school: een Amsterdamse weg in de exegese* (Baarn: Ten Have, 1984b).

Deurloo, Karel A./F.J. Hoogewoud, "'Communi ardore ad litteras hebraicas inflammati', bij het vijfentwintigjarige jubileum van SHA," in: Johan de Roos/Arie Schippers/Jan Willem Wesselius (eds.), *Driehonderd jaar oosterse talen in Amsterdam: een verzameling opstellen* (Amsterdam: Juda Palache Instituut, 1986), 91–105.

Deurloo, Karel A./Rochus Zuurmond, *De dagen van Noach: de verhalen rond de vloed in schrift en oudste traditie* (Baarn: Ten Have, 1991).

Deurloo, Karel A./G.J. Venema, "Exegesis According to Amsterdam Tradition," in: Janet W. Dyk (ed.), *The Rediscovery of the Hebrew Bible* (Maastricht: Shaker, 1999), 3–14.

Deurloo, Karel A./Evert van den Berg/Piet van Midden, *Koning en Tempel* (Kampen: Kok, 2004).

Dicou, Bert, *Edom, Israel's Brother and Antagonist: The Role of Edom in Biblical Prophecy and Story* (Sheffield: Sheffield Academic Press, 1994).

Dohmen, Christoph, "Der Biblische Kanon in der Diskussion," *ThRv* 91 (1995a), 451–460.

Dohmen, Christoph, "Probleme und Chancen Biblischer Theologie aus alttestamentlicher Sicht," in: Thomas Söding/Christoph Dohmen (eds.), *Eine Bibel – Zwei Testamente. Positionen biblischer Theologie* (Paderborn: Schönigh, 1995b), 9–17.

Dohmen, Christoph/Manfred Oeming, *Biblischer Kanon warum und wozu?* (Friedberg: Herder, 1992).

Donne, Anthony Le, "Theological Memory Distortion in the Jesus Tradition: A Studying Social Memory Theory," in: Stuckenbruck/Barton/Wold (eds.), *Memory*, 163–177.

Driver, Daniel R., *Brevard Childs, Biblical Theologian: For the Church's One Bible* (Tübingen: Mohr Siebeck, 2010).

Dubbink, Joep, *Waar is de Heer? Dynamiek en actualiteit van het woord van JHWH bij Jeremia* (Gorinchem: Narratio, 1997).

Dungan, David L., *Constantine's Bible. Politics and the Making of the New Testament* (Minneapolis: Fortress, 2007).

Dunn, James D.G., "Social Memory and Oral Jesus Tradition," in: Stuckenbruck/Barton/Wold (eds.), *Memory*, 179–194.

Dyk, Janet W. (ed.), *Give Ear to My Words: Psalms and other Poetry in and around the Hebrew Bible* (FS N.A. van Uchelen; Amsterdam: Societas Hebraica Amstelodamensis, 1996).

Ebner, Martin, "Der christliche Kanon," in: Idem/Stefan Schreiber (eds.) *Einleitung in das Neue Testament* (Stuttgart: Kohlhammer, 2008), 9–52.

Eckstein, Hans-Joachim, "Das Evangelium Jesu Christi. Die implizite Kanonhermeneutik des Neuen Testaments," in: Janowski (ed.), *Kanonhermeneutik*, 47–68.

Evans, Craig A., *Luke* (Grand Rapids: Baker, 1990).

Evans, Craig A./H. Daniel Zacharias (eds.), *Jewish and Christian Scripture as Artifact and Canon* (London: Bloomsbury, 2011).

Farmer, William R./Denis Farkasfalvy, *The Formation of the New Testament Canon* (New York: Paulist, 1983).

Fiedrowicz, Michael, *Prinzipien der Schriftauslegung in der Alten Kirche* (Bern: Lang, 1998).

Finkelberg, Margalit/Guy G. Stroumsa (eds.), *Homer, the Bible, and Beyond. Literary and Religious Canons in the Ancient World* (Leiden: Brill, 2003).

Finn, Leonard G., "Reflections on the Rule of Faith," in: Seitz/Richards (eds.), *Bible*, 221–242.

Fish, Stanley E., *Is There a Text in This Class? The Authority of Interpretative Communities* (Cambridge, MA: Harvard University, 1980).

Flesseman-Van Leer, Ellen, *The Bible: Its Authority and Interpretation in the Ecumenical Movement* (Geneva: WCC, 1980).

Florovsky, Georges, *Bible, Church, Tradition: An Easter Orthodox View* (Belmont: Nordland, 1972).

Focant, Camille, "La canonicité de la finale longue (Mc 16,9-20) vers la reconnaissance d'un double texte canonique?" in: Auwers/De Jonge (eds.), *Canons* (2003), 587–297.

Ford, David F./Graham Stanton (eds.), *Reading Texts. Seeking Wisdom: Scripture and Theology* (Grand Rapids: Eerdmans, 2004).

Fowl, Stephen E. (ed.), *The Theological Interpretation of Scripture: Classic and Contemporary Readings* (Oxford: Blackwell, 1997).

Fowl, Stephen E., *Engaging Scripture. A Model for Theological Interpretation* (Oxford: Blackwell, 1998).

Frey, Jörg, "Historisch-kanonisch-kirchlich: Zum Jesusbild Joseph Ratzingers," in: Söding (ed.), *Jesus-Buch*, 43–53.

Gadamer, Hans-Georg, *Wahrheit und Methode: Grundzüge einer philosophischen Hermeneutik* (Tübingen: Mohr, ³1972).

Gamble, H.Y., *The New Testament Canon: Its Meaning and Making* (Philadephia: Fortress, 1985).

Gassmann, Günther (ed.) *Documentary History of Faith and Order 1963–1993* (Geneva: WCC, 1993).

Gestrich, Christoph, "Schriftauslegung und Macht – ein unerledigtes Problem von 'sola scriptura'," *BThZ* 22 (2005), 250–266.

Gorak, Jan, *The Making of the Modern Canon. Genesis and Crisis of a Literary Idea* (London: Athlone, 1991).

Gorak, Jan (ed.), *Canon vs. Culture: Reflections on the Current Debate* (London: Routledge, 2001).

Graf, Daniel, *Unterwegs zu einer Biblischen Theologie: Perspektiven der Konzeption von Peter Stuhlmacher* (Göttingen: Vandenhoeck & Ruprecht, 2011).

Grech, Prosper S., "Inner-biblical Reinterpretation and Modern Hermeneutics," in: Pokorný/Roskovec (eds.), *Hermeneutics* (2002), 221–237.

Grech, Prosper S., "The Regula Fidei as a Hermeneutical Principle in Patristic Exegesis," in: Jože Krašovec (ed.), *The Interpretation of the Bible* (Sheffield: Sheffield Academic Press, 1998), 589–601.

Greschat, Katharina, "Die Entstehung des neutestamentlichen Kanons: Fragestellungen und Themen der neueren Forschung," *VuF* 51 (2006), 56–63.

Grube, Christoph, "Die Entstehung des Literaturkanons aus dem Zeitgeist der Nationalliteratur-Geschichtsschreibung," in: Becker/Scholz (eds.), *Kanon* (2012), 71–108.

Gruber, Judith, *Theologie nach dem Cultural Turn. Interkulturalität als theologische Ressource* (Stuttgart: Kohlhammer, 2013).

Hägglund, Bengt, "Die Bedeutung der Regula fidei als Grundlage theologischer Aussagen," *STh* 12 (1958), 1–44.

Hahn, Ferdinand, *Theologie des Neuen Testaments* I-III (Göttingen: Vandenhoeck & Ruprecht, 1990–1995).

Hahn, Scott, *Letter and Spirit: From Written Text to Living Word in the Liturgy* (New York: Doubleday, 2005).

Halbertal, Moshe, *People of the Book, Canon, Meaning, and Authority* (Cambridge, MA: Harvard University, 1997).

Hays, Richard B., "The Canonical Matrix of the Gospels," in: Barton (ed.), *Companion*, 53–75.

Heckel, Theo K., *Vom Evangelium zum viergestaltigen Evangelium* (Tübingen: Mohr Siebeck, 1999).

Heckel, Theo K., "Neuere Arbeiten zum neutestamentlichen Kanon I-II," *ThR* 68 (2003), 286–312, 441–459.

Heller, Jan/Martin Prudky, M., "Die Prager Arbeit am Alten Testament und ihre Analogien zur sog. Amsterdamer Schule," *Summa. Blad van de theologische faculteit van de Universiteit van Amsterdam* 19 (1987), 14–18.

Helmer, Christine/Christof Landmesser (eds.), *One Scripture or Many? Canon from Biblical, Theological, and Philosophical Perspectives* (Oxford: Oxford University, 2004).

Helmer, Christine/Christof Landmesser, "Introduction: A New Biblical-Theological Approach to the Unity of the Canon," in Idem/Idem (eds.), *Scripture* (2004), 1–12.

Hengel, Martin, *Die vier Evangelien und das eine Evangelium von Jesus Christus* (Tübingen: Mohr Siebeck, 2008), 87–96.

Hennecke, Susanne/Rinse Reeling Brouwer (eds.), *Afdalingen* (Gorinchem: Narratio, 1999).

Heydebrand, Renate von (ed.), *Kanon, Macht, Kultur. Theoretische, historische und soziale Aspekte ästhetischer Kanonbildungen* (Stuttgart: Metzler, 1998).

Hoedemaker, Bert, Houtepen, Anton, Witvliet, Theo *Oecumene als leerproces, Inleiding in de Oecumenica* (Zoetermeer: Meinema, 1995[2]).

Horn, Friedrich Wilhelm, "Wollte Paulus 'kanonisch' wirken?" in: Becker/Scholz (eds.), *Kanon* (2012), 400–422.

Hübenthal, Sandra, "Social and Cultural Memory in Biblical Exegesis," in: Kåre Berge/Pernille Carstens (eds.), *Cultural Memory in Biblical Exegesis* (Piscataway: Gorgias, 2012).

Huber, Konrad/Martin Hasitschka, "Die Offenbarung des Johannes im Kanon der Bibel. Textinterner Geltungsanspruch und Probleme der kanonischen Rezeption," in: Auwers/De Jonge (eds.), *Canons* (2003), 607–618.

Janowski, Bernd, "Kanonhermeneutik: eine problemgeschichtliche Skizze," *BThZ* 22 (2005), 161–180.

Janowski, Bernd (ed.). *Kanonhermeneutik: Vom Lesen und Verstehen der christlichen Bibel* (Neukirchen-Vluyn: Neukirchener Verlag, 2007).

Janowski, Bernd, "Die kontrastive Einheit der Schrift. Zur Hermeneutik des biblischen Kanons," in: Idem (ed.), *Kanonhermeneutik* (2007), 27–46.

Janowski, Bernd, "The Contrastive Unity of Scripture: On the Hermeneutics of the Biblical Canon," in: Seitz/Richards (eds.), *Bible* (2013), 37–62.

Janssen, Claudia/Ute Ochtendung/Beate Wehn/Luise Schottroff (eds.), *Grenzgänger-Innen: Unterwegs zu einer anderen biblischen Theologie* (Mainz: Grünewald, 1999).

Jeanrond, Werner, *Text and Interpretation as Categories of Theological Thinking* (Dublin: Gill and Macmillan, 1988), 118.

Jonge, Henk Jan de, "The New Testament Canon," in: Auwers/De Jonge (eds.), *Canons* (2003), 309–319.

Käsemann, Ernst, "Einführung," in: Idem (ed.), *Testament* (1970), 9–12.

Käsemann, Ernst (ed.), *Das Neue Testament als Kanon* (Göttingen: Vandenhoeck & Ruprecht, 1970).

Kessler, M. (ed.), *Voices from Amsterdam: A Modern Tradition of Biblical Narrative* (Atlanta: Scholars, 1994).

Kinzig, Wolfram/Markus Vinzent, "Recent Research on the Origin of the Creed," *JTS* 50 (1999), 535–559.

Kirk, Alan, "Social and Cultural Memory," in: Idem/Tom Thatcher (eds.), *Memory, Tradition and Text* (Atlanta: SBL, 2005), 1–24.

Klauck, Hans-Josef, "Evangelische und katholische Exegese. Ein Erfahrungsbericht," in: Eve-Marie Becker (ed.), *Neutestamentliche Wissenschaft* (Tübingen: Francke, 2003), 337–346.

Klouwen, Wouter, *Die Wirklichkeit der Geschichte: ein Vergleich zwischen K. Barth und G.W.F. Hegel* (Zoetermeer: Boekencentrum, 1998).

Kooi, Cornelis van der, "Kirche als Lesegemeinschaft: Schrifthermeneutik und Kanon," *VuF* 51 [2006], 63–72.

Kooij, Arie van der/Karel van der Toorn (eds.), *Canonization & Decanonization* (Leiden: Brill, 1998).

Krauter, Stefan, "Brevard S. Childs' Programm einer Biblischen Theologie," *ZThK* 96 (1999), 22–48.

Kugel, James/Rowan Greer, *Early Biblical Interpretation* (Philadelphia: Westminster, 1986).

Kuhn, Peter (ed.), *Gespräch über Jesus. Papst Benedikt XVI. im Dialog mit Martin Hengel und Peter Stuhlmacher* (Tübingen: Mohr Siebeck, 2010).

Lategan, Bernard C., "History, Historiography and Hermeneutics," in: Pokorný/Roskovec (eds.), *Hermeneutics* (2002), 204–218.

Lehmann, Karl (ed.), *"Jesus von Nazareth" kontrovers* (Münster: LIT, 2007).

Lieu, Judith M., *Neither Jew nor Greek? Constructing Early Christianity* (London: T.&T. Clark, 2002).

Lindbeck, George, *The Nature of Doctrine: Religions and Theology in a Post-liberal Age* (Philadelphia: Westminster John Knox, 1984).

Lips, Hermann von, "Kanondebatten im 20. Jahrhundert," in: Becker/Scholz (eds.), *Kanon* (2012), 109–126.

Lips, Hermann von, "Was bedeutet uns der Kanon? Neuere Diskussion zu theologischen Bedeutung des Kanons," *VuF* 51 (2006), 51–56.

Lips, Hermann von, *Der neutestamentliche Kanon. Seine Geschichte und Bedeutung* (Zürich: TVZ, 2004).

Löhr, Winrich A., "Norm und Kontext: Kanonslisten in der Spätantike," *BThZ* (2005) 202–229.

Ludlow, Morwenna, "'Criteria of Canonicity' and the Early Church," in: Barton/Wolter (eds.), *Einheit*, 69–93.

Luz, Ulrich, "Kann die Bibel heute noch Grundlage für die Kirche sein? Über die Aufgabe der Exegese in einer religiös-pluralistischen Gesellschaft," *NTS* 44 (1998) 317–339.

Luz, Ulrich, "Kanonische Exegese und Hermeneutik der Wirkungsgeschichte," in: Hans Gerny/Harald Rein/Maja Weyermann (eds.), *Die Wurzel aller Theologie: Sentire cum Ecclesia* (FS Urs von Arx; Bern: Stämpfli, 2003), 40–57.

Luz, Ulrich *Theologische Hermeneutik des Neuen Testaments* (Göttingen: Vandenhoeck & Ruprecht, 2014).

Lyons, William John, *Canon and Exegesis. Canonical Praxis and the Sodom Narrative* JSOT 352 (Sheffield: Sheffield Academic Press, 2002).

Maier, Gerhard (ed.), *Der Kanon der Bibel* (Giessen: Brunnen, 1990).

Markschies, Christoph, "Epochen der Erforschung des neutestamentlichen Kanons in Deutschland. Einige vorläufige Bemerkungen," in: Becker/Scholz (eds.), *Kanon* (2012), 578–604.

Markschies, Christoph, *Kaiserzeitliche christliche Theologie und ihre Institutionen: Prolegomena zu einer Geschichte der antiken christlichen Theologie* (Tübingen: Mohr Siebeck, 2007).

Mayordomo, Moisés (ed.). *Die prägende Kraft der Texte. Hermeneutik und Wirkungsgeschichte des Neuen Testaments* (Stuttgart: Katholisches Bibelwerk, 2005).

Mayordomo, Moises/Peter-Ben Smit, "The Quest for the Historical Jesus in Postmodern Perspective: A Hypothetical Argument," in: Stanley E. Porter/Tom Holmén (eds.), *The Handbook of the Study of the Historical Jesus* 2 (Brill: Leiden, 2011), 1377–1410.

Mayordomo-Marin, Moises, *Den Anfang hören: Leserorientierte Evangelienexegeses am Beispiel von Matthäus 1–2* (Göttingen: Vandenhoeck & Ruprecht, 1998).

McDonald, Lee M., *The Biblical Canon: Its Origin, Transmission, and Authority* (Peabody, MA: Hendrickson, [3]2007), 55–58.

McDonald, Lee M./James A. Sanders (eds.), *The Canon Debate* (Peabody, MA: Hendrickson, 2002).

Melugin, Roy F., "Canon and Exegetical Method," in: Tucker/Peterson/Wilson (eds.), *Canon*, 48–61.

Mendels, Doron, "Societies of Memory in the Graeco-Roman World," in: Stuckenbruck/Barton/Wold (eds.), *Memory* (2007), 143–162.

Mendels, Doron, *Memory in Jewish, Pagan and Christian Societies of the Graeco-Roman World* (London: T&T Clark, 2004).

Menken, Maarten J.J., *Matthew's Bible: The Old Testament Text of the Evangelist* (Louvain: Peeters, 2004).

Metzger, Bruce M., *The Canon of the New Testament: Its Origin, Development and Significance* (Oxford: Clarendon, 1987).

Meßner, Reinhard, *Einführung in die Liturgiewissenschaft* (Paderborn: Schöningh, 2001).

Midden, P.J. van/Karel A. Deurloo, "De Bijbel op zijn Amsterdams," in: K. Spronk (ed.), *De Bijbel vertaald: De kunst van het kiezen bij het vertalen van de bijbelse geschriften* (Zoetermeer/Kapellen: Meinema/Pelckmans, 2007), 165–179.

Mihoc, Vasile, "Basic Principles of Orthodox Hermeneutics," in: Mayordomo (ed.), *Kraft* (2005), 38–64.

Miller, P.D., "Der Kanon in der gegenwärtigen Diskussion," *JBTh* 3 (1988), 217–239.

Miskotte, K.H., *Het wezen der Joodsche Religie* (Amsterdam: Paris, 1932), *Antwoord uit het onweer* (Amsterdam: Holland, 1936).

Miskotte, K.H., *Edda en Thora* (Nijkerk: Callenbach, 1939).

Miskotte, K.H., *Bijbelsch ABC* (Nijkerk: Callenbach, 1941).

Miskotte, K.H., *Hoofdsom der historie* (Nijkerk: Callenbach, 1945).

Miskotte, K.H., *Om het levende woord* (Den Haag: Daamen, 1948).

Miskotte, K.H., *Als de goden zwijgen* (Amsterdam: Holland, 1956).

Monshouwer, Dirk, *Markus en de Torah: een onderzoek naar de relatie tussen het evangelie en de synagogale lezingen in de eerste eeuw* (Kampen: Kok, 1987).

Moos-Grünewald, Maria (ed.), *Kanon und Theorie* (Heidelberg: Winter, 1997).

Muis, Jan, *Openbaring en interpretatie: het verstaan van de Heilige Schrift volgens K. Barth en K.H. Miskotte* (Den Haag: Boekencentrum, 1989).

Müllner, Ilse, "Dialogische Autorität. Feministisch-theologische Überlegungen zur kanonischen Schriftauslegung," in: Steins/Ballhorn (eds.), *Bibelkanon* (2007), 74–84.

Nicklas, Tobias, "Leitfragen leserorientierte Exegese. Methodische Gedanken zu einer 'biblischen Auslegung'," in: Steins/Ballhorn (eds.), *Bibelkanon* (2007), 45–61.

Niebuhr, Karl-Wilhelm, "Die Gestalt des neutestamentlichen Kanons. Anregungen zur Theologie des Neuen Testaments," in: Steins/Ballhorn (eds.), *Bibelkanon* (2007), 95–109.

Nieuwpoort, Ad van, *Tenach opnieuw: Over het Messiaanse tegoed van het evangelie naar Lukas* (Amsterdam: Van Gennep, 2006).

Nissen, Johannes, "Scripture and Community in Dialogue. Hermeneutical Reflections on the Authority of the Bible," in: Auwers/De Jonge (eds.), *Canons* (2003), 651–658.

Noble, Paul R., *The Canonical Approach. A Critical Reconstruction of the Hermeneutics of Brevard S. Childs* (Leiden: Brill, 1995).

Noort, Ed, "Het Oude Testament en zijn levers: Van toen naar de toekomst," in: Wessel Stoker/Henk C. van der Sar (eds.), *Heroriëntatie in de Theologie* (Kampen: Kok, 2003), 56–63.

Norris, Richard A. Jr., "Confessional and Catechetical Formulas in First- and Early-Second-Century Christian Literature," in: Marsha L. Dutton/Patrick Terrell Gray (eds.), *One Lord, One Faith, One Baptism. Studies in Christian Ecclesiality and Ecumenism in Honor of J. Robert Wright* (Grand Rapids: Eerdmans, 2006), 14–28.

Oeming, Manfred, *Gesamtbiblische Theologien der Gegenwart* (Stuttgart: Kohlhammer, 1985).

Ohme, Heinz, *Kanon ekklesiastikos. Die Bedeutung des altkirchlichen Kanonbegriffs* (Berlin: De Gruyter, 1998).

Ollenburger, Ben C. (ed.), *Old Testament Theology: Flowering and Future* (Winona Lake: Eisenbraun, 2004).

Oost, Roel, *Omstreden bijbeluitleg, aspecten en achtergronden van de hermeneutische discussie rondom de exegese van het Oude Testament in Nederland, een bijdrage tot gesprek* (Kampen: Kok, 1986).

Osiek, Carolyn, "Catholic or Catholic? Biblical Scholarship at the Center," *JBL* 125 (2006), 5–22.

Palache, Juda L., *Het heiligdom in de voorstelling der Semietische volken* (Leiden: Brill, 1920).

Palache, Juda L., *Inleiding in de Talmoed* (Amstelveen: Amphora, 1922).

Palache, Juda L., *De Sabbath-idee buiten het Jodendom* (Amsterdam: Hertzberger, 1925a).

Palache, Juda L., *Het karakter van het oud-testamentische verhaal* (Amsterdam: Hertzberger, 1925b).

Palache, Juda L., *The 'Ebed-Jahveh-enigma in Pseudo-Isaiah: A New Point of View* (Amsterdam: Hertzberger, 1934).

Palache, Juda L., *Over beteekenisverandering der woorden in het Hebreeuws (Semietisch) en andere talen: een vergelijkende studie* (Amsterdam: Hertzinger, 1939).

Palache, Juda L., *Semantic Notes on the Hebrew Lexicon* (Leiden: Brill, 1959a).

Palache, Juda L., *Sinai en Paran: Opera minora* (Leiden: Brill, 1959b).

Pannenberg, Wolfhart/Theodor Schneider (eds.), *Verbindliches Zeugnis I. Kanon-Schrift-Tradition* (Göttingen: Vandenhoeck & Ruprecht, 1992).

Parker, David, *The Living Text of the Gospels* (Cambridge: Cambridge University, 1997).

Pecknold, C.C./David F Ford (eds.), *The Promise of Scriptural Reasoning* (Oxford: Blackwell, 2006).

Pokorný, Peter/Jan Roskovec (eds.), *Philosophical Hermeneutics and Biblical Exegesis* (Tübingen: Mohr Siebeck, 2002).

Pontifical Biblical Commission, *The Interpretation of the Bible in the Church* (Città del Vaticano: Libreria Editrice Vaticana, 1993).

Radner, Ephraim, "The Absence of the Comforter: Scripture and the Divided Church," in: Seitz/Greene-McCreight (eds.), *Exegesis* (1999), 355–394.

Radner, Ephraim/George Summer (eds.), *The Rule of Faith: Scripture, Canon and Creed in a Critical Age* (Harrisburg: Morehouse, 1998).

Räisänen, Heikki, *Beyond New Testament Theology* (Philadelphia: Westminster John Knox, 1990).

Raiser, Konrad, *Wir stehen noch am Anfang: Ökumene in einer veränderten Welt* (Gütersloh: Gütersloher Verlagshaus, 1994).

Ratzinger, Joseph, *Theologische Prinzipienlehre* (München: Wewel, 1982).

Ratzinger, Joseph, "Schriftauslegung im Widerstreit. Zur Frage nach Grundlagen und Weg der Exegese heute," in: Joseph Ratzinger (ed.), *Schriftauslegung im Widerstreit* (Freiburg: Herder, 1989), 15–55.

Reeling Brouwer, Rinse, *Over kerkelijke dogmatiek en marxistische filosofie: Karl Barth vergelijkenderwijs gelezen* (Den Haag: Boekencentrum, 1988).

Reijendam-Beek, Lenie van (ed.), *'Hier blijven half alle ogenblikken': een keuze uit het werk van M.A. Beek* (Baarn: Ten Have, 1988).

Reventlow, Henning Graf, *Hauptprobleme der biblischen Theologie im 20. Jahrhundert* (Darmstadt: Wissenschaftliche Buchgesellschaft, 1983).

Richter, Wolfgang, *Exegese als Literaturwissenschaft. Entwurf einer alttestamentlichen Literaturtheorie und Methodologie* (Göttingen: Vandenhoeck & Ruprecht, 1971).

Ricoeur, Paul, "The 'Sacred' Text and the Community," in: Idem, *Figuring the Sacred, Religion, Narrative and Imagination* (Minneapolis: Fortress, 1995), 68–72.

Ricoeur, Paul, "The Canon between the Text and the Community," in: Pokorný/Roskovec (eds.), *Hermeneutics* (2002), 7–27.

Riesner, Rainer, "Der Papst und die Evangelien-Forschung," in: Thomas Pola/Bert Roebben (eds.), *Die Bibel in ihrer vielseitigen Rezeption* (Münster: LIT, 2010), 35–49.

Ritter, Adolf Martin, "Glaubensbekenntnis(se) V," *TRE* 13 (1984), 399–412.

Robinson, James M., "Foreword," in: Weiss/Carr (eds.) *Gift* (1996), 14–15.

Sanders, James A., *Discoveries in the Judean Desert* 4 (Oxford: Clarendon, 1965).

Sanders, James A., *The Dead Sea Psalms Scroll* (Ithaca: Cornell University, 1967).

Sanders, James A., "Cave 11 Surprises and the Question of Canon," in: D.N. Freedman/J.C. Greenfield (eds.), *New Directions in Biblical Archeology* (New York: Doubleday, 1969a), 101–116.

Sanders, James A., "Dissenting Deities and Philippians 2:1–11," *JBL* 88 (1969b), 279–290.

Sanders, James A., *Torah & Canon* (Philadelphia: Fortress, 1972).

Sanders, James A., "The Ethic of Election in Luke's Great Banquet Parable," in: J.L. Crenshaw/J.T. Willis (eds.), *Essays in Old Testament Ethics* (New York: Ktav, 1974), 245–271.

Sanders, James A., "From Isaiah 61 to Luke 4," in: J. Neusner (ed.), *Christianity, Judaism, and other Greco-Roman Cults 1* (Leiden: Brill, 1975), 75–106.

Sanders, James A., "Adaptable for Life: The Nature and Function of the Canon," in: F.M. Cross/W.E. Lemke/P.D. Miller Jr. (eds.), *Magnalia Dei: The Mighty Acts of God* (New York: Doubleday, 1976), 531–560.

Sanders, James A., "Hermeneutics of True and False Prophecy," in: G.W. Coats/B.O. Long (eds.), *Canon and Authority: Essays in Old Testament and Authority* (Philadelphia: Fortress, 1977a), 21–41.

Sanders, James A., "Torah and Paul," in: W.A. Meeks (ed.), *God's Christ and His People* (Oslo: Universitetsforlaget, 1977b).

Sanders, James A., "The Gospels and the Canonical Process: A Response to Lou H. Silberman," in: W.O. Walker Jr. (ed.), *The Relationships Among the Gospels: An Interdisciplinary Dialogue* (San Antonio: Trinity University, 1978), 219–236.

Sanders, James A., "The Conversion of Paul," in: *A Living Witness of Oikodome* (Claremont: Disciples Seminary Foundation, 1982), 71–93.

Sanders, James A., *Canon and Community: A Guide to Canonical Criticism* (Philadelphia: Fortress, 1984).

Sanders, James A., "A New Testament Hermeneutic Fabric: Psalm 118 in the Entrance Narrative," in: C.A. Evans/W.F. Stinespring (eds.), *Early Jewish and Christian Exegesis* (Atlanta: Scholars, 1987a), 177–190.

Sanders, James A., *From Sacred Story to Sacred Text, Canon as Paradigm* (Philadephia: Fortress, 1987b).

Sanders, James A., "'Nor do I...': A Canonical Reading of the Challenge to Jesus in John 8," in: B.R. Gaventa/R.T. Fortna (eds.), *The Conversation Continues: Studies in Paul and John in Honor of J. Louis Martyn* (Nashville: Abingdon, 1990), 337–347.

Sanders, James A., "Stability and Fluidity in Text and Canon," in: C.J. Norton/S. Pisane (eds.), *Tradition of the Text: Studies Offered to Dominique Barthélemy in Celebration of His 70th Birthday* (Göttingen: Vandenhoeck & Ruprecht, 1991), 203–217.

Sanders, James A., "Paul and Theological History," in: Idem/C.A. Evans (eds.), *Paul and the Scripture of Israel* (Sheffield: JSOT Press, 1993), 98–117.

Sanders, James A., "Ναζωραῖος in Matthew 2.23," in: Craig A. Evans/W. Richard Stegner (eds.), *The Gospels and the Scriptures of Israel* (Sheffield: Sheffield Academic Press, 1994), 116–128.

Sanders, James A., "Scripture as Canon for Post-modern Times," *Biblical Theology Bulletin* 26 (1995), 56–63.

Sanders, James A., "Text and Canon: Concepts and Method," in: Idem, *Story* (1987b), 125–151.

Sanders, James A., "What's up now? Renewal of an Important Investigation," in: Lee M. McDonald/James H. Charlesworth (eds.), *Jewish and Christian Scriptures: The Function of "Canonical" and "Non-Canonical" Religious Texts* (London: T&T Clark, 2010), 1–7.

Sanders, James A./Craig A. Evans, *Luke and Scripture: The Function of Sacred Tradition in Luke-Acts* (Minneapolis: Fortress, 1993).

Sanecki, Artur, *Approccio canonico: tra storia e teologia, alla ricerca di un nnovo paradigm post-critico: l'analisi della metodologia canonical di B.S. Childs dal punti di vista cattolico* (Rome: Pontificia Università Gregoriana, 2004).

Scalise, Charles J., "Canonical Hermeneutics: Childs and Barth," *SJT* 47 (1994a), 61–81.

Scalise, Charles J., *Hermeneutics as Theological Prolegomena. A Canonical Approach* (Macon: Mercer University, 1994b).

Schmithals, Walter, "Der Kanon, die Apostolische Sukzession und die Ökumene," *BThZ* 22 (2005), 266–283.

Schnabel, Eckhard J. "Die Entwürfe von B.S. Childs und H. Gese bezüglich des Kanons. Ein Beitrag zur aktuellen hermeneutischen Fragestellung," in: Maier (ed.), *Kanon*, 102–152.

Scholz, Stefan, "*Kanones* in Theologie, Literaturwissenschaften und Kulturwissenschaften. Einführende Bemerkungen zur Kanonforschung der Neuzeit und Moderne," in Becker/Idem (eds.), *Kanon*, 33–38.

Schröter, Jens, "Überlegungen zum Verhältnis von Historiographie und Hermeneutik in der neutestamentlichen Wissenschaft," in: Pokorný/Roskovec (eds.), *Hermeneutics* (2012), 191–203.

Schröter, Jens, *Von Jesus zum Neuen Testament. Studien zur urchristlichen Theologiegeschichte und zur Entstehung des neutestamentlichen Kanons* (Tübingen: Mohr Siebeck, 2007).

Schuller, Eileen, "The Dead Sea Scrolls and Canon and Canonization," in: Becker/Scholz (eds.), *Kanon* (2012), 293–314.

Schürmann, Heinz, *Das Lukasevangelium* 1 (Freiburg: Herder, 1984).

Scoralick, Ruth, "Kanonische Schriftauslegung," *BiKi* 38 (2009), 645–647.

Seckler, Max, "Über die Problematik des biblischen Kanons und die Bedeutung seiner Wiederentdeckung," *ThQ* 180 (2000), 30–53, 30–31.

Segovia, Fernando F., "Biblical Criticism and Postcolonial Studies: Towards a Postcolonial Optic," in: R.S. Sugirtharajah (ed.), *The Postcolonial Biblical Reader* (Oxford: Blackwell, 2006), 33–44.

Segovia, Fernando F., "Cultural Studies and Contemporary Biblical Criticism. Ideological Criticism as Mode of Discourse," in: Idem (ed.), *Decolonizing Biblical Studies. A view from the Margins* (Orbis: Maryknoll, 2000), 34–52.

Segovia, Fernando F., "My Personal Voice: The Making of a Postcolonial Critic," in: Ingrid Rosa Kitzberger (ed.), *The Personal Voice in Biblical Interpretation* (London: Routledge, 1999), 25–37.

Seitz, Christopher/Kathryn Greene-McCreight (eds.), *Theological Exegesis. Essays in Honor of Brevard S. Childs* (Grand Rapids: Eerdmans, 1999).

Seitz, Christopher R./Kent Harold Richards (eds.), *The Bible as Christian Scripture: The Work of Brevard S. Childs* (Atlanta: Society of Biblical Literature, 2013).

Sheppard, Gerald T., "Canonical Criticism," *ABD* 1 (1992), 861–866.

Siebert-Hommes, J.C., *Let the Daughters Live! The Literary Architecture of Exodus 1–2 as a Key for Interpretation* (Leiden: Brill, 1998).

Siebert-Hommes, J.C., "De 'Amsterdamse School'," in: P.J. Knegtmans/P. van Rooden (eds.), *Theologen in ondertal: Godgeleerdheid, Godsdienstwetenschap, het Athenaeum Illustre en de Universiteit van Amsterdam* (Zoetermeer: Boekencentrum, 2003), 177–196.

Sim, David, "Does the Gospel of Matthew Presuppose a Canon of Scripture?" in: Becker/Scholz (eds.), *Kanon* (2012), 449–468.

Sim, David, "Matthew's Use of Mark: Did Matthew Intend to Supplement or to Replace His Primary Source?" *NTS* 57 (2011), 176–192.

Sinn, Simone, "Hermeneutics and Ecclesiology," in: Gerard Mannion/Lewis S. Mudge (eds.), *Routledge Companion to the Christian Church* (London: Routledge, 2008), 576–593.

Sinn, Simone, *The Church as Participatory Community: On the Interrelationship of Hermeneutics, Ecclesiology and Ethics. Studies in Ecumenism, Reconciliation and Peace* (Dublin: Columba, 2002).

Sinner, Rudolf von, *Reden vom dreieinigen Gott in Brasilien und Indien* HUT 43 (Tübingen: Mohr Siebeck, 2003).

Smelik, K.A.D., *Saul: de voorstelling van Israëls eerste koning in de Masoretische tekst van het Oude Testament* (Amsterdam: P.E.T., 1977).

Smelik, K.A.D., *Hagar en Sara: de verhouding tussen Jodendom en Christendom in de eerste eeuwen* (Baarn: Ten Have, 1979).

Smelik, K.A.D., *Converting the Past: Studies in Ancient Israelite and Moabite Historiography* (Leiden: Brill, 1997).

Smit, Peter-Ben, "Biblische Hermeneutik im Spannungsfeld persönlicher und kirchlicher Identität," *Internationale Kirchliche Zeitschrift* 96 (2006a), 135–151.

Smit, Peter-Ben, "Wegweiser zu einer kontextuellen Exegese? Eine Miszelle zu einem Nebeneffekt der kanonischen Hermeneutik von Brevard S. Childs," *ThZ* 62 (2006b), 17–24.

Smit, Peter-Ben, "The Meaning of 'Life'. An Essay in Ecumenical Hermeneutics," *JEC* 43 (2008), 320–332.

Smit, Peter-Ben, "The Reception of the Truth at Baptism and the Church as Epistemological Principle in the Work of Irenaeus of Lyons," *Ecclesiology* 7 (2011a), 354–373.

Smit, Peter-Ben, *De canon – een oude katholieke kerkstructuur?* (Utrecht: Utrecht University, 2011b).

Smit, Peter-Ben, 'Diversiteit in het onderwijs van het Nieuwe Testament: over het nut van biografische, levensbeschouwelijke en culturele diversiteit,' *Nederlands Theologisch Tijdschrift* 68 (2014), 277–296.

Smit, Peter-Ben, *Old Catholic and Philippine Independent Ecclesiologies in History. The Catholic Church in Every Place* Brill's Series in Church History 52 (Leiden: Brill, 2011c).

Smit, Peter-Ben, *Tradition in Dialogue. The Concept of Tradition in International Anglican Bilateral Dialogues* (Amsterdam: VU University, 2012).

Smith, Dwight Moody, *The Fourth Gospel in Four Dimensions: Judaism and Jesus, the Gospels and Scripture* (Columbia: University of South Carolina, 2008).

Snoek, J.A.M., "Canonization and Decanonization: An Annotated Bibliography," in: Van der Kooij/Van der Toorn (eds.), *Canonization* (1998), 435–506.

Söding, Thomas (ed.), *Das Jesus-Buch des Papstes. Die Antwort der Neutestamentler* (Freiburg: Herder, 2007).

Söding, Thomas, "Der Kanon des alten und neuen Testaments. Zur Frage nach seinem theologischen Anspruch," in: Auwers/De Jonge (eds.), *Canons* (2003), xlvii–lxviii.

Söding, Thomas, "Entwürfe Biblischer Theologie in der Gegenwart," in: Hans Hübner/Bernd Jaspert (eds.), *Biblische Theologie. Entwürfe der Gegenwart* (Neukirchen-Vluyn: Neukirchener Verlag, 1999), 41–103.

Söding, Thomas, *Einheit der Heiligen Schrift. Zur Theologie des biblischen Kanons* (Freiburg: Herder, 2005), 18–55.

Spek, W. van der, "Exegese en Politiek," in: Deurloo/Zuurmond (eds.), *Bijbel*, 108–114.

Stegeman, Janneke, "'Reading Jeremiah Makes Me Angry!' the Role of Jeremiah 32 [39] in Transformation within the 'Jeremianic' Tradition," in: Wido Th. van Peursen/Janet Dyk (eds.), *Tradition and Innovation in Biblical Interpretation* (Leiden: Brill, 2011), 45–67.

Steins, Georg, "Der Bibelkanon als Text und Denkmal. Zu einigen methodologischen Problemen kanonischer Schriftauslegung," in: Auwers/De Jonge (eds.), *Canons* (2003), 177–198.

Steins, Georg, *Die "Binding Isaaks" im Kanon (Gen 22); Grundlagen und Programm einer kanonisch-intertextuellen Lektüre* (Freiburg: Herder, 1999).

Steins, Georg/E. Ballhorn (eds.), *Der Bibelkanon in der Bibelauslegung. Beispielexegesen und Methodenreflexion* (Stuttgart: Kohlhammer, 2007).

Stendahl, Krister, "Biblical Theology, Contemporary," in: G.A. Buttrick (ed.), *The Interpreter's Dictionary of the Biblical* (Nashville: Abingdon, 1962), 1418–1432.

Strecker, Georg, "'Biblische Theologie?' Kritische Bemerkungen zu den Entwürfen von Hartmut Gese und Peter Stuhlmacher," in: Dieter Lührman/Georg Strecker (eds.), *Kirche* (Tübingen: Mohr Siebeck, 1980), 425–445.

Stuckenbruck, Loren T./Stephen C. Barton/Benjamin G. Wold (eds.), *Memory in the Bible and Antiquity* (Tübingen: Mohr Siebeck, 2007).

Stuhlmacher, Peter "Joseph Ratzinger's Jesus-Buch – ein bedeutsamer geistlicher Wegweiser," *Communio* 36 (2007), 399–407.

Stuhlmacher, Peter, "Der Kanon und seine Auslegung," in: Idem (ed.), *Biblische Theologie und Evangelium : gesammelte Aufsätze* (Tübingen: Mohr Siebeck, 2002)

Stuhlmacher, Peter, *Gerechtigkeit Gottes bei Paulus* (Göttingen: Vandenhoeck & Ruprecht, 1965).

Stuhlmacher, Peter, *Das paulinische Evangelium. I. Vorgeschichte* (Göttingen: Vandenhoeck & Ruprecht, 1968).

Stuhlmacher, Peter, *Schriftauslegung auf dem Weg zur biblischen Theologie* (Göttingen, Vandenhoeck & Ruprecht, 1975).

Stuhlmacher, Peter, *Das Evangelium von der Versöhnung in Christus* (Stuttgart: Calwer, 1979a).

Stuhlmacher, Peter, *Vom Verstehen des Neuen Testaments. Eine Hermeneutik* (Göttingen: Vandenhoeck & Ruprecht, 1979b [2nd edition: 1986]).

Stuhlmacher, Peter, *Jesus von Nazareth – Christus des Glaubens* (Stuttgart: Calwer, 1988).

Stuhlmacher, Peter, *Wie treibt man Biblische Theologie?* (Neukirchen-Vluyn: Neukirchener Verlag, 1995). English translation: *How to Do Biblical Theology* (Allison Park: Pickwick, 1995).

Stuhlmacher, Peter, *Was geschah auf Golgatha?* (Stuttgart: Calwer, 1998a).

Stuhlmacher, Peter, *Der Brief an die Römer* (Göttingen: Vandenhoeck & Ruprecht, [15]1998b [1989]).

Stuhlmacher, Peter, *Biblische Theologie und Evangelium. Gesammelte Aufsätze* (Tübingen: Mohr Siebeck, 2002).

Stuhlmacher, Peter, *Die Verkündigung des Christus Jesus* (Wuppertal: Theologische Verlagsgemeinschaft, 2003).

Stuhlmacher, Peter, *Der Brief an Philemon* (Neukirchen-Vluyn: Neukirchener Verlag, [3]2004 [1975]).

Stuhlmacher, Peter, *Biblische Theologie des Neuen Testaments* I–II (Göttingen: Vandenhoeck & Ruprecht, 2005a).

Stuhlmacher, Peter, *Die Geburt des Immanuel. Die Weihnachtsgeschichten aus dem Lukas- und Matthäusevangelium* (Göttingen: Vandenhoeck & Ruprecht, 2005b).

Stuhlmacher, Peter/Helmut Claß (eds.), *Versöhnung, Gesetz und Gerechtigkeit. Aufsätze zur biblischen Theologie* (Göttingen: Vandenhoeck & Ruprecht, 1998).

Stuhlmacher, Peter/Theo Sorg, *Das Wort vom Kreuz. Zur Predigt am Karfreitag* (Stuttgart: Calwer, 1996).

Sundberg, A.C., *The Old Testament Canon of the Early Church* (Cambridge, MA: Harvard University, 1964).

Taschner, Johannes, "Kanonische Bibelauslegung – Spiel ohne Grenzen?" in: Ballhorn/Steins (eds.), *Bibelkanon*, 31–44.

Theißen, Gerd, *Die Religion der ersten Christen. Eine Theorie des Urchristentums* (Gütersloh: Gütersloher Verlagshaus, [3]2003).

Theißen, Gerd, *Die Entstehung des Neuen Testaments als literaturgeschichtliches Problem* (Heidelberg: Winter, [2]2011).

Theron, Daniel J., *Evidence of Tradition* (Grand Rapids: Baker, 1958).

Thomassen, Einar (ed.), *Canons and Canonicity: The Formation and Use of Scripture* (Copenhagen: Museum Tuscalanum, 2010).

Treier, Daniel J., *Introducing Theological Interpretation of Scripture* (Nottingham: Apollos, 2008).

Trobisch, David, *Die Endredaktion des Neuen Testaments* (Göttingen: Vandenhoeck & Ruprecht, 1996).

Trobisch, David, *The First Edition of the New Testament* (Oxford: Oxford University, 2000).

Tromp, Johannes, "M.A. Beek en de historische kritiek," in: R.B. ter Haar Romeny/ Johannes Tromp (eds.), *Quisque suis viribus 1841–1991. 150 jaar theologie in dertien portretten* (Leiden: Collegium Theologicum c.s. "Quisque suis viribus," 1991), 215–243.

Tück, Jan Heiner (ed.), *Annäherungen an "Jesus von Nazareth," Das Buch des Papstes in der Diskussion* (Mainz: Grünewald, 2007).

Ukachukwu Manu, Chris, "Interpretations of the Bible in Africa," in: Auwers/De Jonge (eds.), *Canons* (2003), 659–669.

Vanoni, Gottfried, "Der biblische Kanon. Institutionalisierte Erinnerung," *ThPQ* 151 (2003), 29–36.

VanHoozer, Kevin J., *Is There a Meaning in this Text? The Bible, the Reader, and the Morality of Literary Knowledge* (Grand Rapids: Zondervan, 1998).

VanHoozer, Kevin J., *First Theology: God, Scripture & Hermeneutics* (Westmont: IVP, 2002).

VanHoozer, Kevin J., "Theology and the Condition of Postmodernity: a report on knowledge of God," in: Idem (ed.), *Cambridge Companion to Postmodern Theology* (Cambridge: Cambridge University, 2003), 3–25.

VanHoozer, Kevin J., *The Drama of Doctrine: A Canonical-Linguistic Approach to Christian Theology* (Louisville: Westminster John Knox, 2005).

VanHoozer, Kevin J., *Remythologizing Theology: Divine Action, Passion, and Authorship* (Cambridge: Cambridge University, 2010).

Vassiliadis, Petros, "The Canon of the Bible: Or the Authority of Scripture from an Orthodox Perspective," in: J.M. Poffet (ed.), *L'Autorité de L'Écriture* (Paris: Cerf, 2002), 113–135.

Veerkamp, Ton, *Die Vernichtung des Baal: Auslegung der Königsbücher (1.17–2.11)* (Stuttgart: Alektor, 1983).

Venema, G.J., *Reading Scripture in the Old Testament: Deuteronomy 9–10; 31 – 2 Kings 22–23 – Jeremiah 36 – Nehemiah 8* (Leiden: Brill, 2004).

Verheyden, Joseph, "The Canon Muratori. A Matter of Dispute," in: Auwers/De Jonge (eds.), *Canons*, 487–556.

Vischer, Lukas (ed.), *A Documentary History of the Faith & Order Movement 1927–1963* (St. Louis, MO: Bethany, 1963a, b).

Voss, M. Heerma van/Ph.H.J. Houwink ten Cate/N.A. van Ugchelen, *Travels in the World of the Old Testament* (FS M.A. Beek; Assen: Van Gorcum, 1974).

Wall, Robert W., "Canonical Criticism," in: Stanley E. Porter (ed.), *Handbook to Exegesis of the New Testament* (Leiden: Brill, 2997), 291–312.

Wall, Robert W., "Reading the New Testament in Canonical Context," in: Joel B. Green (ed.), *Hearing the New Testament. Strategies for Interpretation* (Grand Rapids: Eerdmans, [2]2010), 372–396.

Wall, Robert W./Eugen E. Lemcio (eds.), *The New Testament as Canon: Reader in Canonical Criticism* (Sheffield: JSOT, 1992).

Walton, T., *Experimenting with Qohelet: A Text-Linguistic Approach to Reading Qohelet as Discourse* (Maastricht: Shaker, 2006).

Watson, Francis, *Text, Church and World: Biblical Interpretation in Theological Perspective* (Grand Rapids: Eerdmans, 1994).

Watson, Francis, "The Fourfold Gospel," in: Stephen C. Barton (ed.), *The Cambridge Companion to the Gospels* (Cambridge: Cambridge University, 2007), 34–52.

Watson, Francis, *Gospel Writing – A Canonical Perspective* (Grand Rapids: Eerdmans, 2013).

Webster, John, "'A Great and Meritorious Act of the Church?' The Dogmatic Location of the Canon," in: Barton/Wolter (eds.), *Einheit*, 95–126.

Weder, Hans, "Einverständnis. Eine Überlegung zur Peter Stuhlmachers Hermeneutik," in: Ådna/Hafemann/Hofius (eds.), *Evangelium*, 403–418.

Weiss, Richard D./David M. Carr (eds.), *A Gift of God in Due Season* (FS James A. Sanders: Sheffield: Sheffield Academic Press, 1996).

Wengst, Klaus, "Glaubensbekenntnis(se) IV," *TRE* 13 (1984), 392–399.

West, Gerald O., *Biblical Hermeneutics of Liberation. Modes of Reading the Bible in the South African Context* (Pietermaritzburg: Cluster, [2]1995).

Wieringen, A.L.H.M. van, *The Reading-Oriented Unity of the Book of Isaiah* (Maastricht: Shaker, 2006).

Wilckens, Ulrich, *Theologie des Neuen Testaments* I–II (Neukirchen-Vluyn: Neukirchener Verlag, 2002–2009).

Williams, Rowan, "The Unity of the Church and the Unity of the Bible: An Analogy," *IKZ* 91 (2001), 5–21.

Wischmeyer, Oda, *Hermeneutik des Neuen Testaments* (Tübingen: Francke, 2004).

Wit, J.H. de, *'My God', She Said. 'Ships Make Me So Crazy', Reflections on Empirical Hermeneutics, Interculturality and Holy Scripture* (Amsterdam: VU University, 2008).

Wit, J.H. de/Gerald O. West (eds.), *African and European Readers of the Bible in Dialogue. In Quest of a Shared Meaning* (Brill: Leiden, 2008).

Wit, J.H. de/Louis Jonker/Marleen Kook/Daniel S. Schipani (eds.), *Through the Eyes of Another: Intercultural Reading of the Bible* (Amsterdam: VU University, 2004).

Wolter, Michael, "Die Vielfalt der Schrift und die Einheit des Kanons," in: John Barton/Michael Wolter (eds.), *Die Einheit der Schrift und die Vielfalt des Kanons* (Berlin: De Gruyter, 2003), 45–68.

Wolter, Michael, "Probleme und Möglichkeiten einer Theologie des Neuen Testaments," in: Rieuwerd Buitenwerf/Harm W. Hollander/Johannes Tromp (eds.), *Jesus, Paul, and Early Christianity* (Brill: Leiden, 2008), 417–436.

Wünsch, Dietrich, "Evangelienharmonie," *TRE* 10 (1982), 626–636.

Xun, Chen, *Theological Exegesis in the Canonical Context. Brevard Springs Childs' Methodology of Biblical Theology* (Frankfurt: Lang, 2010).

Young, Frances M., *Biblical Exegesis and the Formation of Christian Culture* (Cambridge: Cambridge University, 1997).

Zaman, Luc, *Bible and Canon* (Leiden: Brill, 2008).

Ziegenaus, Anton, *Kanon: Von der Väterzeit bis zur Gegenwart* (Herder: Freiburg, 1990).

Zuurmond, Rochus, "A Man of Letters: Karel Deurloo as a Theologian," in: Janet W. Dyk (ed.), *Unless some one guide me...* (FS Karel Deurloo; Maastricht: Shaker, 2001), 1–8.

Zwiep, Arie W., *Christ, Spirit, Community* (Tübingen: Mohr Siebeck, 2010a).

Zwiep, Arie W., *Tussen tekst en lezer* I (Amsterdam: VU University, 2010b).

Zwiep, Arie W., *Tussen Tekst en Lezer* II (Amsterdam: VU University, 2013).

Index

Names

Abma, Richtsje   86, 89
Abraham, William J.   10
Ådna, Jostein   53, 54
Agouridis, Savas   9
Alexander, Loveday C.   96
Allison, Jr., Dale C.   118
Amsterdam School of Exegesis   8, 18, 86–102, 103–138, 141, 169, 174
Aquinas, Thomas   31
Arnold, Mathew   43
Arx, Urs von   54
Assmann, Aleida   5, 6, 15
Assmann, Jan   5, 6, 15
Athanasius of Alexandria   135, 136
Augustine, Aurelius   43
Auwers, Jean-Marie   2, 3, 13, 22, 50, 109, 115, 117, 134

Bakker, Nico T.   87, 92, 100
Baldermann, Ingo   4, 13
Ballhorn, Egon   8, 13, 112, 181
Barkenings, Hans J.   92
Barr, James   3, 14, 26
Barth, Karl   19, 88, 92, 93, 100, 101, 115, 123, 131, 141, 169
Barthel, Jörg   7, 11–12, 19, 22, 26, 104, 105, 106, 108, 120, 123, 179
Barton, John   13, 14, 22 ,26, 119, 134, 135, 136, 137
Barton, Stephen C.   5, 129
Bauckham, Richard   178
Bauer, Uwe F.W.   86, 88, 89, 90, 92
Beale, Gregory K.   118
Becker, Eve-Marie   4, 5, 19, 42, 104, 111, 118, 119
Beek, Martinus Adrianus   86, 92
Bekker, Ype   87, 92
Benjamin, Walter   43
Berg, Evert van den   87
Berge, Kåre   6
Berndt, Rainer   135
Beuken, W.A.M.   87
Bird, Michael   14
Bockmuehl, Markus   10–11
Boer, Dick   87, 89

Boeve, Lieven   140
Böhler, Dieter   13
Bonino, José Míguez   142
Bori, Pier Cesare   121
Bouhuijs, K.   86
Bovon, François   96, 98, 130
Bowen, Nancy R.   8, 113
Braaten, Carl E.   11
Breck, John   9
Brenneman, James E.   41, 116, 171
Brett, Mark G.   26, 111
Breukelman, Frans H.   87, 141
Bruce, F.F.   14
Bruggen, Jacob van   96
Buitenwerf, Rieuwerd   182
Bultmann, Rudolf   111
Busch, Eberhard   87
Butting, K.   88
Buttrick, G.A.   108

Callaway, Mary C.   13, 41
Calvin, John   131, 169
Campenhausen, Hans Freiherr von   14
Carpzov, J.G.   20
Carr, David M.   8, 44
Carson, D.A.   13
Carstens, Pernille,   6
Cartwright, Michael G.   142
Charlesworth, J.H.   41
Childs, Brevard S.   2, 4, 8, 10, 12, 13, 14, 15, 17, 19–40, 41, 43, 45, 73, 103–138, 140, 141, 168, 169, 173, 178, 180
Coats, G.W.   49
Commission on Faith and Order   113, 142–172, 182
Conzelmann, Hans   97
Crenshaw, J.L.   41
Croatto, J. Severino   109, 117
Cross, F.M.   44
Crossan, John Dominic   31
Cyril of Jerusalem   134

Daalen, A.G. van   87
Davies, Philipp R.   113, 132
Davis, Ellen F.   11

Delp, Alfred 79, 84
Derrida, Jacques 15
Deurloo, Karel A. 86, 87, 88, 89, 95, 100
Dicou, Bert 89
Diebner, Bernd J. 87
Dodd, C.H. 31
Dohmen, Christoph 3, 13
Driver, Daniel R. 19, 20, 23, 25, 26, 111
Dubbink, Joep 88
Dungan, David L. 128, 135
Dunn, James D.G. 5
Dutton, Marsha L. 136
Dyk, Janet 86, 89

Ebner, Martin 13
Eckstein, Hans-Joachim 122
Epiphanius of Salamis 135
Eusebius of Caesarea 134, 136
Evans, Craig A. 5, 41, 96

Farkasfalvy, Denis 14
Farmer, William R. 14
Fiebig, Paul 31
Fiedrowicz 137
Finkelberg, Margalit 5
Fish, E. Stanley 15, 112
Flesseman-Van Leer, Ellen 153
Florovsky, Georges 37
Flusser, David 31
Focant, Camille 50
Ford, David F. 11, 140
Fortna, R.T. 46
Foucault, Michel 112
Fowl, Stephen E. 11
Freedman, D.N. 41
Frey, Jörg 72
Frye, Northrop 43, 123

Gadamer, Hans-Georg 15, 111, 112, 121, 122, 127, 130
Gamble, H.Y. 14
Gassmann, Günther 151
Gaventa, B.R. 46
Gerny, Hans 54
Gestrich, Christoph 113
Gorak, Jan 5, 43
Graf, Daniel 53, 54, 55, 56, 57, 58, 59, 122
Gray, Patrick Terrell 136
Grech, Prosper 112, 118

Green, Joel B. 13
Greene-McCreight, Kathryn 10, 37
Greenfield, J.C. 41
Greer, Rowan 23
Gregory the Great 43, 121
Greschat, Katharina 13
Grube, Christoph 5
Gruber, Judith 179, 180

Haar Romeney, R.B. ter 86
Hafemann, Scott J. 53, 54
Hägglund, Bengt 22
Hahn, Ferdinand 55
Hahn, Scott 11
Halberthal, Moshe 9
Halbwachs, Maurice 6
Haschitka, Martin 115
Haynes, Stephen 13
Hays, Richard B. 11, 117
Heckel, Theo K. 13, 178
Heerma van Voss, M. 86
Helmer, Christine 9, 137
Hengel, Martin 72, 119
Hennecke, Susanne 88
Herodotus 131
Heydebrand, Renate von 5
Hofius, Otfried 53, 54
Hollander, Harm W. 182
Holmén, Tom 110
Hoogewoud, F.J. 87
Horn, Friedrich-Wilhelm 119
Hoskyns, Edwyn 29
Houwink ten Cate, Ph.H.J.
Hübenthal, Sandra 6
Huber, Konrad 115
Hübner, Hans 25

Irenaeus of Lyon 22, 23, 31, 37, 43, 112

Janowski, Bernd 7, 11, 13, 122, 140, 177
Janssen, Claudia 8
Jaspert, Bernd 25
Jeanrond, Werner 115
Jenson, Robert W. 11
Jeremias, Joachim 31
Jonge, Henk Jan de 2, 13, 22, 50, 109, 115, 117, 134
Jonker, Louis 175
Jülicher, Adolf 31

Kafka, Franz   43
Käsemann, Ernst   2, 134
Kermode, Frank   43
Kessler, M.   89
Kinzig, Wolfram   136
Kirk, Alan   6
Kitzberger, Ingrid Rosa   108
Klauck, Hans-Josef   31
Klijn, A.F.J.   86
Klouwen, Wouter   92
Knegtmans, P.J.   95
Kooi, C. van der   111
Kooij, Arie van der   14, 140
Kook, Marleen   175
Krašovec, Jože   112
Krauter, Stefan   19
Kristeva, Julia   42
Kugel, James   23
Kuhn, Peter   72

Landmesser, Christoph   9, 137
Lategan, Bernard   111
Le Donne, Anthony   5
Lehmann, Karl   72
Lemcio, Eugen E.   13
Lemke, W.E.   44
Lieu, Judith M.   180
Lindbeck, George   176
Lips, Hermann von   4, 13, 15, 174
Löhr, Winrich A.   134
Long, B.O.   49
Lossky, Nicholas   142
Ludlow, Morwenna   135, 136
Lührmann, Dieter   132
Luz, Ulrich   54, 55, 105, 111, 119, 140
Lyons, William John   20, 26

MacIntyre, Alisdair   112
Maier, Gerhard   13, 19
Mannion, Gerard   112
Markschies, Christoph   19, 133, 134, 174, 175
Mayordomo, Moises   9, 110, 112, 139
McDonald, Lee M.   12, 13, 14, 41, 130, 134, 136
McKenzie, Steven   13
Meeks, W.A.   41
Melugin, Roy F.   40
Mendels, Doron   5
Menken, Maarten J.J.   117, 118
Meßner, Reinhard   136

Metzger, Bruce M.   14, 135, 136
Midden, Piet van   87, 95
Mihoc, Vasile   9
Miller, Patrick D.   4, 44
Miskotte, K.H.   88, 131, 141
Monshouwer, Dirk   88
Moos-Gründewald, Maria   5
Mudge, Lewis   112
Muis, Jan   88
Müllner, Ilse   8, 113

Neusner, J.   41
Niebuhr, Karl-Wilhelm   13, 18, 130
Nieuwpoort, Ad van   92, 93–102, 114, 141
Nissen, Johannes   117
Noble, Paul R.   24, 26, 111
Noort, Ed   176
Norris, Jr., Richard A.   136
Norton, C.J.   44

Ochtendung, Ute   8
Oeming, Manfred   13, 26
Ohme, Heinz   12, 133, 134, 135, 136
Ollenburger, Ben C.   20
Oost, Roel   89, 90
Origen   81
Osiek, Carolyn   139

Pahl, Michael   14
Palache, Juda L.   86, 92
Pannenberg, Wolfhart   113
Parker, David   128
Pecknold, C.C.   140
Petersen, David L.   26, 40
Pettit, Peter   41
Pisane, S.   44
Pobee, John   142
Poffet, J.M.   9
Pokorný, Peter   2, 110, 111, 118
Pola, Thomas   72
Polybius   131
Pontifical Biblical Commission   14, 72, 73, 111
Porter, Stanley E.   13, 110
Prudky, Martin   89

Radner, Ephraim   11, 37
Räisänen, Heikki   4
Raiser, Konrad   143

Ratzinger, Joseph/Benedict XVI   1,3, 8, 10, 14,
    17, 18, 72–85, 103–138, 141, 168, 169,
    171, 178
Reeling Brouwer, Rinse   88
Reijendam-Beek, Lenie van   86, 92
Rein, Harald   54
Rendtdorff, Rolf   26
Reventlow, Henning Graf   13, 89
Richards, Kent Harold   11, 177
Richter, Wolfgang   3
Ricoeur, Paul   2, 104, 106, 107, 108, 111, 113,
    121, 123, 130
Riesner, Rainer   72
Ritter, Adolf Martin   136
Robinson, James M.   45
Roebben, Bert   72
Rooden, P. van   95
Roos, Johan de   86
Roskovec, Jan   2, 110, 111, 118

Sanders, James A.   8, 10, 14, 15, 17, 20, 24,
    40–53, 73, 103–138, 140, 141, 169, 178, 179
Sanecki, Artur   14
Sar, Henk C. van der   176
Sauter, Gerhard   137
Scalise, Charles J.   19, 37
Scheider, Theodor   113
Schifman, Lawrence H.   121
Schipani, Daniel S.   175
Schippers, Arie   87
Schmithals, Walter   113
Schnabel, Eckhard J.   19, 20
Scholz, Stephan   4, 5, 19, 42, 104, 118, 119
Schottroff, Luise   8
Schreiber, Stephan   13
Schröter, Jens   110
Schuller, Eileen   42
Schürmann, Heinrich   98
Scoralick, Ruth   13
Seckler, Max   2, 4, 6, 13, 75, 104, 124, 128,
    132, 177
Segovia, Fernando F.   108, 109, 110, 139, 175
Seitz, Christopher   10, 37, 177
Sheppard, Gerald T.   13, 20
Siebert-Hommes, J.C.   89, 95
Sim, David   118, 119
Sinn, Simone   112
Sinner, Rudolf von   142, 143
Smelik, Klaas   88, 91

Smit, Peter-Ben   10, 19, 26, 106, 110, 112, 113,
    122, 133, 139, 140, 141, 148, 165, 168,
    169, 171, 175
Smith, Dwight Moody   12, 119
Snoek, J.A.M.   14
Söding, Thomas   2, 4, 6, 7, 13, 25, 72, 104, 116,
    117, 130, 140, 175, 176
Soloviev, Vladimir   81, 84
Sorg, Theo   54
Spek, W. van der   88
Spinoza, Baruch de   43
Stanton, Graham   11
Stegeman, Janneke   179
Stegner, W. Richard   41
Steiger, Lother   87
Steins, Georg   3, 8, 13, 21, 26, 112, 116, 181
Stendhal, Krister   108
Stephens, Peter   2
Stinespring, W.F.   41
Stoker, Wessel   176
Stransky, Tom F.   142
Strecker, Georg   132
Stroumsa, Guy G.   5
Stuckenbruck, Loren T.   5
Stuhlmacher, Peter   8, 17, 53–71, 72, 103–138,
    141, 168, 173, 178
Sugirtharajah, R.S.   108
Summer, George   11
Sundberg, A.C.   12

Talmon, Shemaryahu   41
Taschner, Johannes   112, 116
Thatcher, Tom   6
Theißen, Gerd   12, 13, 107, 133, 135,
    136, 181
Theron, Daniel J.   135
Thiselton, Anthony C.   112
Thomassen, Einar   14
Thucydides   131
Toorn, Karel van der   14, 140
Treier, Daniel   10
Trench, Richard   31
Trobisch, David   121, 128
Tromp, Johannes   86, 182
Tück, Jan Heiner   72
Tucker, Gene M.   26, 40

Ugchelen, N.A. van   86, 89
Ukachukwu Manu, Chris   109

VanHoozer, Kevin   16, 103, 179, 182
Vanoni, Gottfried   5
Vassiliadis, Petros   9
Veen, Wilken   87
Veerkamp, Ton   89
Venema, René   88, 89
Verheyden, Joseph   134
Vinzent, Markus   136
Vischer, Lukas   142, 143, 144, 147, 148

Wainwright, Geoffrey   142
Walker, Jr., W.O.   46
Wall, Robert W.   13
Walton, T.   89
Watson, Francis   11, 104, 115, 123,
   126, 129
Webb, Pauline   142
Webster, John   137
Weder, Hans   31, 54
Wehn, Beate   8
Weiss, Richard D.   8, 45
Wengst, Klaus   136
Wesselius, Jan Willem   87
West, Gerald O.   117, 175
Weyermann, Maja   54
Wieringen, A.L.H.M.   89
Wilckens, Ulrich   55, 139
Williams, Raymond   43
Williams, Rowan   140
Willis, J.T.   41
Wilson, Robert R.   26, 40
Wischmeyer, Oda   110, 111
Wit, J.H. de   175
Wold, Benjamin G.   5
Wolter, Michael   119, 135, 137, 179, 180, 182
Woodbridge, John D.   13
Wünsch, Dietrich   129

Xun, Chen   19

Young, Frances   137

Zacharias, H. Daniel   5
Zaman, Luc   13
Ziegenaus, Anton   135
Zuurmond, Rochus   86, 87, 88
Zwiep, Arie W.   10, 20, 57, 89, 112, 122,
   130, 131, 176

Scriptural References

Genesis 28:12   83
Exodus 20:1–6   58
Exodus 23:1   48
Exodus 23:7   48
Exodus 24:8   65
Exodus 31:18   48
Deuteronomy 6:4–5   58
Deuteronomy 8:3   79
Deuteronomy 9:10   48
Psalm 22   65
Psalm 69   65
Psalm 91:11   77, 83
Psalm 118   30
Psalm 118:22   34
Psalm 139:1–17   58
Proverbs 1:17   58
Proverbs 8:22–36   58
Isaiah 5   30, 32, 33, 35
Isaiah 7:9   58
Isaiah 9:5–6   58
Isaiah 11:2   75
Isaiah 11:6   77
Isaiah 25:1   97
Isaiah 25:6–9   58
Isaiah 43:1–7   58
Isaiah 52:13–53:12   58
Isaiah 53:10–12   65
Isaiah 27:2–9   36
Isaiah 61   27
Isaiah 61:4   76
Jeremiah 7:13   48
Jeremiah 31:31–34   58
Daniel, Book of   31, 50
Daniel 5:24   48
Hosea 11:8–9   58
Zechariah 13:7   65

Wisdom 2:18   78

Matthew, Gospel of   118, 119, 128, 178
Matthew 3:13–4:11   75
Matthew 3:6   77
Matthew 4:1   76
Matthew 4:3   78
Matthew 4:5   80
Matthew 4:8   81

Matthew 4:11   82
Matthew 22:7   63
Matthew 22:33–46   26–39
Matthew 27:40   78
Matthew 28:16–20   81
Mark, Gospel of   28, 62–67, 118, 119, 128, 178
Mark 1:1   64
Mark 1:1–15   63
Mark 1:9–13   75
Mark 1:13   77, 82
Mark 1:16–8:26   63
Mark 2:1–3:6   63
Mark 4:1–34   63
Mark 4:35–6:52   63
Mark 8:27–10:52   63
Mark 10:45   67
Mark 11:1–16:8   63
Mark 12:1–12   30
Mark 12:6   33
Mark 13:1–37   63
Mark 13:14   63
Mark 14:1–16:8   63
Mark 14:22–24   65
Mark 14:22–25   67
Mark 14:61–62   65
Mark 15:39   66
Mark 16:8   66
Luke, Gospel of   28, 93–102, 119, 178
Luke 1:1–4   94–102
Luke 3:10   77
Luke 3:21–4:13   75
Luke 4:3   78
Luke 4:5   81
Luke 4:9   80
Luke 4:18   76
Luke 19:43–44   63
Luke 20:9–18   30
Luke 20:13   33
Luke 24:31   95
Luke 29:28   31
John, Gospel of   28, 50, 52, 53, 119, 120, 178
John 1:1   95
John 1:14   132
John 1:51   83
John 6:33–34   164
John 7   47
John 7:19   47
John 7:24   47

John 7:36   47
John 7:51   47
John 7:53–8:2   46
John 8   49
John 8:1–11   46–50
John 8:13   47
John 8:15   47
John 8:18   47
John 11:25–26   58
John 12:24   79
John 14:6   58
John 20:31   96
John 21:24   96
John 21:25   47
John 21:38   47
John 24:53   47
Acts of the Apostles 4:11   34
Acts of the Apostles 7:51   33
Acts of the Apostles 10:36–43   62, 63, 69
Acts 12:12.25   63, 69
Acts 13:5.13   63
Acts 15:7   64, 95
Acts 15:37.39   63, 69
Acts 18:25   95, 98
Acts 20:24   64, 95
Acts 21:21   95, 98
Acts 21:24   98
Romans 1:1–6   58
Romans 1:16   64
Romans 1:16–17   58
Romans 2:18   98
Romans 3:21–31   58
Romans 5:5–8   62
Romans 8:19   77
Romans 10:9–10   59
Romans 11:16   58
1 Corinthians 13:9–12   156, 170
1 Corinthians 13:13   59
1 Corinthians 14:16   98
2 Corinthians 4:7   155, 156
Galatians 4:9   59
Galatians 6:6   98
Ephesians 3:18–19   152
Colossians 4:10   63, 69
1 Timothy 2:5–6   58
2 Timothy 4:11   63, 69
Philemon, Letter to   115
Philemon 24   63, 69

Hebrews 2:17–18   76
Hebrews 5:15   76
1 Peter 2:7   34
1 Peter 5:13   63, 69
1 John 2:1–2   58
1 John 4:9–10   58
3 John   115, 120
Jude   115, 120

Revelation of John   115, 120
Revelation of John 1:1–3   96

Q   27, 96, 118, 178

Thomas, Gospel of   31, 32
Thomas   65, 30, 35

Printed in the United States
By Bookmasters